King Hussein and the Evolution of Jordan's Perception of a Political Settlement with Israel, 1967–1988

In memory of my parents
Hanna and Eliha Kalmanovich

King Hussein and the Evolution of Jordan's Perception of a Political Settlement with Israel, 1967–1988

JOSEPH NEVO

sussex
ACADEMIC
PRESS
Brighton • Portland • Toronto

2 4 6 8 10 9 7 5 3

First published 2006, reprinted 2012, in Great Britain by
SUSSEX ACADEMIC PRESS
PO Box 139
Eastbourne BN24 9BP

and in the United States of America by
SUSSEX ACADEMIC PRESS
920 NE 58th Ave   Suite 300
Portland, Oregon 97213

and in Canada by
SUSSEX ACADEMIC PRESS (CANADA)
8000 Bathurst Street, Unit 1, PO Box 30010, Vaughan, Ontario L4J 0C6

British Library Cataloguing in Publication Data
A CIP catalogue record for this book is available from the British Library.

Library of Congress Cataloging-in-Publication Data
Nevo, Joseph.
King Hussein and the evolution of Jordan's perception of a
    political settlement with Israel, 1967–1988 / by Joseph
    Nevo.
    p. cm.
Includes bibliographical references and index.
ISBN 1-84519-147-1 (hc : alk. paper)
    1. Jordan—Foreign relations—Israel. 2. Israel—Foreign
relations—Jordan. 3. Jordan—Politics and government—
1952–1999. 4. Hussein, King of Jordan, 1935– . I. Title.
DS154.16.I75N48 2006
956.04′6—dc22

                                                            2005037863

Typeset and designed by Sussex Academic Press, Brighton & Eastbourne.
Printed by TJ International, Padstow, Cornwall.
This book is printed on acid-free paper.

CONTENTS

Acknowledgments   vii

Introduction: The Crystallization of Jordan's Perception   1

PART I   THE HISTORICAL BACKGROUND

1   The Special Relationship between King Abdullah and the
    Zionist Movement   9

2   The Friendly Foe: Hussein and Israel prior to 1967   14

3   Adjusting to the New Reality: From June 1967 to
    Resolution 242   25

4   Political Activities and Initiatives, 1967–1988   36

PART II   JORDANIAN TERRITORIAL AND CONCEPTUAL
            DEMANDS OF ISRAEL

Territorial Demands

5   Withdrawal from the West Bank, East Jerusalem and the
    Gaza Strip   67

6   The Question of Jerusalem   82

7   Settlements and Natural Resources   94

Conceptual Demands

8 Changing Israel's Policy and Ideology: The Hashemite
Viewpoint   99

9 The Palestinian Issue   104

PART III   JORDAN'S OPTIONS AND ITS *QUID PRO QUO*

10 A Military Option?   123

11 The Perception of a Comprehensive Peace   129

12 Frameworks for a Possible Agreement   146

Conclusion: The Change in King Hussein's Political and
Ideological Thinking   166

Notes   171
Bibliography   200
Index   205

ACKNOWLEDGMENTS

I would like to thank Professor Moshe Shemesh of Ben-Gurion University for reading the manuscript and for his useful comments. Professor Avi Shlaim from Oxford and Professor Mohanna Haddad from Amman were pleasant interlocutors for discussing some ideas relating to this book. Dr. Iris Fruchter-Ronen, Ms. Anna Pospik, Ms. Karmit Adler and Mr. Avi Mor assisted me in various stages of the research. Thanks also go to Ms. Gila Haimovic for her skilful editing of the manuscript and to Mr. Ori Kosovsky for preparing the index. Mr Anthony Grahame and his staff at Sussex Academic press have meticulously turned the manuscript into a book. Any mistakes or inaccuracies are my own responsibility.

I am also grateful to the Bertha Von Suttner Foundation and the Jewish–Arab Center at the University of Haifa for their research grant that helped me to begin this project.

Last, many thanks to my wife Nitsa, whose patience, help and encouragement have contributed immensely to this book.

J. N.

INTRODUCTION

THE CRYSTALLIZATION OF JORDAN'S PERCEPTION

No one, no country, no people wants a settlement more than we do. Certainly, no one pays a heavier price for the continuation of the conflict than do we here in Jordan.[1]

On 26 October 1994, the State of Israel and the Hashemite Kingdom of Jordan signed a peace treaty. Formal negotiations began one year earlier, following Israel and the PLO's mutual recognition and the conclusion of a Declaration of Principles between Prime Minister Yitzhak Rabin and Chairman Yassir Arafat on the White House lawn, on 13 September 1993. This peace treaty was not only the result of extensive year-long negotiations. It was preceded by thirty years of secret meetings between King Hussein and Israeli leaders. It was also predated by twenty-odd years of what numerous writers tend to call 'a *de facto* peace'. These ties were cemented in tacit understandings, clandestine arrangements and unwritten agreements from which both countries benefited.

Events in the Middle East after 1967 contributed to the crystallization of Jordan's perception regarding the viability of a political settlement to the Arab–Israeli conflict. This perception was not merely the private, personal conviction of the King and a handful of his advisors. It became public domain (albeit never enjoying either consensus or open support) via overt messages, delivered by King Hussein, Crown Prince Hassan, and their close circle. These texts and discussions prepared the grounds for an eventual peace treaty.

This study examines Jordan's official and public views on the possibility of a political settlement with Israel, as these views and positions evolved between 1967 and 1988; that is, between the loss of the West Bank in the June 1967 war and the decision to give up the claim to regain it. The task ahead is to explore the constant and changing components of these views and attempt to identify their development. To this end we shall not only examine Jordan's attitude towards a political settlement, but also its motivation; i.e., the assessment of what Jordan would get *vis à vis* what it would give in return, the prospects of the viability of a settlement, as well as the prospects of its acceptance by the inter-Arab system and internal public opinion. These tasks are accomplished through textual analysis of the public statements of Jordan's leaders (namely, King Hussein, Crown Prince Hassan and their Prime Ministers) on the subject, throughout the period surveyed.

The study begins in 1967, not only because the June war turned out to be an important landmark in the history of the Middle East but also on the assumption that in the wake of that war, Jordan's attitude towards the feasibility of a political settlement to the conflict with Israel began gradually to take a different course, both from its own pre-1967 views and from the Arab consensus of the time. The study ends with the suspension of Jordan's ties with the West Bank in July 1988. It took several more years until a new era in Jordanian–Israeli relations began: the commencement of overt, bilateral negotiations in late 1993 that yielded the formal peace treaty. Nevertheless, Hussein's decision of July 1988 formally (and to a greater extent, practically) took the West Bank out of the Jordanian–Israeli equation. It thus removed the main bone of contention and the major barrier that had hitherto blocked a bilateral political understanding, and thereafter facilitated achievement of the peace accord.

The intention is to focus on overt and public statements of the King and his very close circle as the key elements of this study. I believe this is the most reliable source material for comprehending Jordan's official views, for the following reasons:

I.   The pattern of a two-track approach in bilateral relations between national entities that emanates not from hypocrisy but from political, ideological or other constraints, is not uncommon in the international system. Relations between Transjordan and the Jewish community in Palestine (and later between the Hashemite Kingdom of Jordan and the State of Israel) are a telling instance of such a dual relationship. They were characterized by hostile public statements on one hand and by correct, even cordial, clandestine ties on the other. Though at the end of the day, decisions are made and deals negotiated and struck in private, public statements still have merit. From statements for public consumption one can still learn a great deal from what was said to whom; and whether different things were said to different audiences; or if positions remained constant in various periods and on various occasions. The frequency with which certain arguments were asserted publicly is also an essential indicator of political intentions.

II.   Though public statements cannot always be taken at face value, they may constitute a message, a test balloon or a commitment. These components also usually exist in secret negotiations but are less conspicuous and sometimes totally missing. Hence, changes that can be traced through overt expressions, on a sensitive issue such as dealing with an enemy, are most important and meaningful. King Hussein maintained a friendly clandestine dialogue with Israel before the June 1967 war, at a time when Jordan's formal attitude implied that Israel had no right to exist. After the war, negotiations continued as before (albeit more intensely), yet the real innovation, as will be shown, was in the sphere of public statements.

III.   Hussein's views, presented to the Israelis in private, were very similar, if not almost identical, in principle, from his public statements. There were, of course, different tunes and different emphases but his basic demands of Israel remained the same in both channels. The differences between the overt and covert Jordanian statements were tactical rather than strategic. Hussein's demands for a complete Israeli withdrawal to the June 1967 line (in return for a political settlement), for example, were made with the same fervour both over and under the table.

IV.   In order to examine Jordan's perception of these issues, this study primarily focuses on Hussein's own statements. The King was the principal decision-maker, particularly in the realm of inter-Arab affairs and foreign policy. He dominated, shaped and determined Jordan's foreign policy, including policy regarding the Palestine question as well as the official and practical attitude towards Israel. Though in the 1950s and the early 1960s the King was not always the exclusive maker and shaker, by 1967 his supreme position was a well-established fact.[2] Hussein utilized public speaking as a means of communicating with his subjects.[3] His speeches, as well as his other public statements, as in the case of other national leaders, constituted an important vehicle for presenting his views and introducing his political credo. However, Crown Prince Hassan's statements as well as his books and articles, and those of certain other Jordanian officials, are also analyzed here. The King consulted them and their opinions contributed to the shaping of the King's position.[4]

The study was not conducted merely by observation of the relevant statements but also by juxtaposing them with similar Jordanian expressions prior to 1967. They were also compared with statements of other Arab heads of state on the same issues and – to some extent – with Hussein's views throughout the secret negotiations with Israel.

The study assumes that prior to 1967 there was a relatively high correlation between Hussein's public views and those of other Arab leaders. One objective of the textual analysis is to examine the validity of this assumption, and also to determine whether Hussein's statements after 1967 became conspicuously different from those of other Arab leaders.

The contents of the statements surveyed (speeches, interviews, books, articles, etc.) were divided into several major categories, each broken down into more specific issues. Jordan's attitude towards the following topics was studied and analyzed:

A. *Jordan's demands of Israel*: withdrawal, a solution to the Palestinian question (both territorial and demographic aspects: Palestinian rights, a Palestinian state, refugees), the status of Jerusalem and the holy places, water rights, the building of settlements.

B. *Jordan's quid pro quo*: non-belligerency, recognition of Israel, a peace agreement, normalization, recognition of Israel's security needs (border modifications, demilitarization).

C. *A framework for a settlement and ways to achieve it*: surveying the options: multilateral agreements (a comprehensive peace) vs. bilateral agreements, partial ones, direct negotiations, third-party mediation, an international umbrella (the role of the UN, the US, Europe, the USSR).

D. *The purpose of peace*: a goal in itself? incentive for Israeli withdrawal? or a means to achieve additional aims (economic welfare, political stability)?

E. *The viability of a military option*: Jordanian, Palestinian, an Arab coalition.

The intention of this study is not to evaluate the *prospects* of an actual settlement at the various stages of the period surveyed. It is obvious that Jordan could not have concluded a separate peace agreement with Israel at an earlier time, even if Israel had agreed to all its demands, due to regional and domestic constraints. Palestinian and local opposition would have objected vehemently to such an eventuality, as would the regimes and the public in other Arab states. I have tried, however, to discern the components of a political settlement as perceived by Jordan, as a model for future agreements (probably multilateral ones). What preconditions would Israel have to accept and what conditions would it have to fulfil? The argument presented is that the actual discussion, by Hussein and his close circle, of the various components and the demands of Israel indicated that Jordan was ready to enter into peace negotiations once the prevailing obstacles were removed; i.e., when some other Arab states had taken steps towards a political settlement, and when some solution to the Palestinian problem was achieved, one way or another. At such a time, it would even be possible to negotiate *quid pro quo*. Eventually, that was the case in 1993. After

Egypt, the most important Arab state, had concluded a peace treaty with Israel and after Israel and the PLO had declared mutual recognition and committed themselves to settling their disputes peacefully, Jordan began an open political dialogue with Rabin's government.

Indeed Jordan's readiness for the political option had to undergo a process of ripening.[5] Jordan's various ideas and proposals for an arrangement were, in a way, a mechanism that created the momentum to keep the political option alive and would lead, at the end of the day, to a settlement.

Compared to the other Arab states, Jordan's position *vis-à-vis* Israel was unique, as was its position regarding the Palestinian question. Jordan enjoyed only a narrow margin in which to manoeuvre between the commitment to Arabism and to the inter-Arab system – which necessitated closing ranks with a more extreme Arab position against Israel – and its own national and dynastical interests which necessitated a pragmatic policy and, hopefully, a political settlement.

This dilemma was not new. Amir (later King) Abdullah, founder of the Hashemite Kingdom of Jordan and King Hussein's grandfather, had faced a similar dilemma in the 1930s. It was definitely reflected in his grandson's views and statements during the period surveyed. How King Hussein negotiated this dilemma is also examined here.

PART I

THE HISTORICAL BACKGROUND

1 THE SPECIAL RELATIONSHIP BETWEEN KING ABDULLAH AND THE ZIONIST MOVEMENT

The origins and course of relations between Amir Abdullah of Transjordan and the Jewish community in mandatory Palestine have been recorded and analyzed in numerous publications.[1] Abdullah's relatively moderate views towards the Jewish *Yishuv* (community), were, from the outset, interwoven with his territorial desiderata. He believed that he could use the Jews of Palestine, directly or indirectly, to promote his ambitions. As early as April 1921, when British Colonial Secretary Winston Churchill suggested that the Hijazi Prince consider the governance of Transjordan (as a face-saving device, to replace his declared intention to confront the French in Syria), Abdullah suggested that whoever ruled Transjordan should also rule Palestine. His main argument to justify such expansion was that it might serve as the best way to ease the tension between Jews and Arabs in Palestine. The Jews would be able to implement the Balfour Declaration in certain parts of the country, while the Arabs' fear of Jewish domination would be soothed, as unification with Transjordan would preserve their territorial and demographic majority. Abdullah took pains to convince both the British and the Zionist leaders of the advisability of such a solution.[2]

Nevertheless, there was more than mere 'territorial ambition' in Abdullah's attitude towards the Jews. The special ties between Palestine and Transjordan pre-dated his arrival in that part of the world, and were a combination of historical reasons, British policy and strategic considerations. Hence Abdullah's relations with the inhabitants of Palestine (and with the Jews in particular) stemmed from a combination of geographic, demographic, economic, political, personal and dynastical considerations. Clinton Bailey summarizes them as follows:

As a materialist he [Abdullah] admired the fabled wealth and imagined connections of World Jewry. As a practical man, he appreciated both their success in obtaining British patronage for their Jewish National Home and their efficiency and energy in developing the Home. As a result, Abdullah saw that the Zionists enjoyed a combination of advantages that would eventually result in the fulfillment of their goals despite any Arab opposition. Therefore, as future neighbors in one political form or another, they were a powerful group, whom it was better to mollify than to antagonize. Being basically a pragmatic as well as a man of easy nature, Abdullah also had little capacity for prejudice. Thus, individual Jews, like others, were able to approach him and some became great friends.[3]

Moreover, Abdullah regarded the Jews as potential allies against the radicalizing nationalism of the Palestinian Arabs, inspired by the charismatic Mufti of Jerusalem al-Hajj Amin al-Husayni. The latter vehemently opposed a Jewish presence in Palestine as well as Abdullah's ambitions to take it over. In the spirit of the concept that 'my enemy's enemy is my friend', the common interests of Abdullah and the Jews (to curb the Mufti's influence and activity) cemented their strategic bonds. Yet these bonds also had an economic aspect. Zionist organizations, as well as private Jewish businessmen, showed interest in Transjordan, particularly in the possibility of settling Jews and/or purchasing land there. Not a few prospective vendors, mainly Bedouin tribal chiefs, who owned large tracks of land, encouraged interested Jews to undertake land transactions. Amir Abdullah himself was willing, in the early 1930s, to lease tens of thousands of dunams of his own property in the eastern Jordan valley to the Jewish Agency.

However, nothing came of these ventures due to British objections as well as opposition both within Transjordan and on part of the Palestinian Arabs. In the course of the Zionist attempt to obtain a foothold in Transjordan, Abdullah began to accept payments from the Jewish Agency. These payments – originally designed by the Jews to 'buy' the Amir's good will and his influence over potential local business associates – gradually grew more or less constant and became an integral part of the amiable ties between the Amir and the Jewish leadership in Palestine. Abdullah himself, always short of funds, occasionally demanded more and more money.[4]

Despite his friendly relations with the Jews, Abdullah perceived their future as a permanent autonomous minority within a unified (Transjordan–Palestine) kingdom under his rule. Jews would enjoy civil rights and would run their own communal affairs, yet they would have to accept Arab-Muslim sovereignty and dominance. In time Abdullah realized that the Jews – who were gradually increasing their demographic, territorial, economic and military potency in Palestine – would not settle for mere autonomy. After the 1937 recommendation by the Peel commission to divide Palestine into a Jewish and an Arab state, and particularly a decade later, after the UN had endorsed the 1947 partition plan, Abdullah was ready, when no other option seemed viable, to acquiesce to the concept of partition and to Jewish control over part of Palestine, providing that the rest of the country, the designated Arab state, would be incorporated into Transjordan and would not constitute an independent Palestinian Arab state. His preferred option, however, remained the annexation of all Palestine with autonomy for the Jews, and until the last minute he attempted to persuade them to accept this.[5]

After the end of World War II, the moment of truth was rapidly approaching. It was clear to all concerned that the future of Palestine would soon be decided. Abdullah estimated that in order for his plan to materialize, he had to secure the compliance, or at least the acquiescence, of the British, the Jews, the Arab states and the Arabs of Palestine. The British were the most important element in his design. Their endorsement was a *sine qua non* for any territorial move in Palestine and, indeed, he obtained it in early 1948. Yet even before approaching the British, he reached an oral understanding with the Jewish Agency, the second most important factor in his scheme. The Jews would not oppose his invasion of Palestine and takeover of those areas designated to be the Arab state. In return, Abdullah undertook not to send his army into the territories allotted to the Jews and not to interfere with the establishment of a Jewish state there.[6]

Abdullah hoped that the Jordanian army (commonly known as The Arab Legion) would be the only Arab force to invade Palestine thus enabling him to act without interruption. He did, however, expect logistic, financial and political support from the Arab League. When the end of the British mandate neared, Abdullah had second thoughts about the advisability of his tactics. On one hand, he feared defeat if he acted alone (despite his understanding with the Jews) and suspected that his fellow Arab leaders would make him the scapegoat in case of military failure. On the other hand, if other Arab states decided to join the invasion of Palestine, Abdullah worried that he might lose his free hand there and that his associates would try to interfere in his designs. He thus concluded that his interests would be best served if there were no invasion. This could be achieved only if the Jews did not declare statehood when the British left. If that were the case, Abdullah thought, he could take over all of Palestine quietly and swiftly. About half of his army was already stationed there in order to secure the British evacuation. The local Palestinian forces were no match for the Arab Legion, which was considered the most efficient and disciplined Arab army. The key factor was the Jewish leadership. In a last minute bid, three days before the end of the mandate, Abdullah met with Golda Meyerson (later Meir), deputy director of the Jewish Agency's political department (with whom he had 'concluded' the unwritten understanding in November 1947). He once again resorted to his favoured option regarding the future of Palestine and advised her that the Jews not declare the establishment of their state. That way, the Arab armies would not invade Palestine and he would take it over. The Jews would enjoy, under his sovereignty, generous autonomy and, would have 50 per cent representation in the executive and legislative bodies of the unified state. Mrs. Meyerson turned down his proposal, and soon after the Arab armies invaded Palestine.

In the first round of battles, Abdullah achieved most of his aims. When the first truce was declared on 11 June 1948, his army controlled most of the Arab territories in Palestine that bordered on Transjordan and which he sought to incorporate into his kingdom. (Though the northern parts of Samaria were occupied by the Iraqi army, as a Hashemite sister state, Iraq allowed Abdullah to exercise his political influence over the territories its army controlled.) The *de facto* annexation of Arab Palestine had begun.

As far as Abdullah was concerned, the first truce could have been the end of the war. The other Arab leaders declined proposals to prolong it, *inter alia*, because they were not happy with Abdullah's achievements. Parallel to the resumption of hostilities (9 July 1948), they tried to foil Transjordan's efforts to annex its newly-occupied areas. As the potential threat to his territorial gains stemmed from both Israel and the Arab states, Abdullah believed that an agreement with Israel might serve as a guarantee to prevent his Arab foes from endangering his spoils of war.

First contacts were made in the summer of 1948. At the end of that year and in early 1949, they turned into direct, clandestine, bilateral political negotiations that promoted and, in practice, formulated the Israeli–Jordanian armistice agreement. The parallel UN-sponsored Israeli–Jordanian talks for that purpose held in Rhodes were actually a façade, while the real decisions were made during negotiations in Shuna, in the Jordan valley, where King Abdullah frequently chaired the Jordanian delegation. (His Israeli counterparts were civilian and military officials.)

After the conclusion of the armistice agreements between Israel and several Arab states, Abdullah, who was preparing the ground for formal annexation of Arab Palestine (henceforth: the West Bank), still feared the Arab reaction to such a move. He was therefore willing to negotiate a peace treaty with Israel, to secure its support in the new territorial reality. Another round of direct talks, in late 1949 early 1950, yielded no agreement as the gap between the parties was too great.[7]

In order to break the stalemate, Abdullah suggested something less pretentious than a peace treaty: A five-year non-belligerency agreement, based on the armistice lines with free passage for people and commodities. Such an agreement was formulated and an initial contract was signed. It was never concluded due to mounting opposition in Jordan and the Arab world. Even Britain, which supported a comprehensive Israeli–Arab peace, was reluctant to give its blessing to a unilateral agreement that might threaten Jordan's precarious position in the Arab world.

The main factor that cooled Abdullah's eagerness for a formal peace with Israel was the fact that he had managed to secure *de facto* Arab recognition of his annexation of the West Bank.[8] Henceforth, a settlement that would provide Israel's recognition of Jordanian control over the West Bank became less essential. Abdullah probably believed that it was in Israel's interest, with or without a peace treaty, to safeguard Jordanian stability and survival against those who challenged the legitimacy of the Hashemite regime or of Jordan as a political entity. He continued to maintain good relations with Israeli officials until his death.[9] Yet the nature of his meetings with Israelis became less operational and political, and more social and courteous.

As noted, Abdullah needed to accommodate his personal and dynastical interests, as well as those of Jordan, as he perceived them, to the image he cultivated of an Arab nationalist. His failure to bridge this wide gap cost him his life. His grandson Hussein internalized this lesson and, as will become evident, his grandfather's experience dictated his attitude towards Israel after the June 1967 war.

The annexation of the West Bank had a decisive impact not only on the future of Jordan and on its socio-political structure but also set in motion a process that Abdullah and his successors could not control: The impact of the Palestinian factor on Jordan's public sphere and on its domestic and foreign policies. The murder of the King on 20 July 1951, on the threshold of Al-Aqsa mosque in Jerusalem, in revenge for his acceptance of partition and for his annexation of parts of Palestine, was only the beginning.

Abdullah's territorial ambitions regarding Palestine, the *fait accompli* that he created and that required certain ties with the Jews, also dictated – after 1967 – King Hussein's attitude towards Israel. He needed Israel's good will in order to retrieve those parts of mandatory Palestine that Abdullah had occupied and annexed, and which he [Hussein] had lost in 1967.

2

THE FRIENDLY FOE: HUSSEIN AND ISRAEL PRIOR TO 1967

When Hussein was proclaimed King on 11 August 1952, he succeeded his father King Talal. In retrospect, however, Hussein was regarded (and probably also considered himself) to be the heir of his grandfather, Abdullah. Disappointed with his sons Talal and Naif, Abdullah pinned his hopes on his favourite, eldest grandson and created the impression that he viewed him as his real successor. The grandfather and grandson developed a special relationship; immense sympathy and esteem together with pride on part of the former, and respect and admiration on the part of the latter. Talal's mental condition probably brought his father and his son very close. Talal's very short term as king and his prompt deposition also contributed to the perception of Hussein as Abdullah's successor.

Hussein indeed regarded the enlarged Kingdom, and the West Bank in particular, as a heritage bequeathed to him by Abdullah. He pursued his grandfather's policy of integrating the Palestinians into the Jordanian society and state in a way that would perpetuate the dominance and hegemony of the East Bankers. Seeing the West Bank as Abdullah's bequest added a personal sentiment and an emotional attachment to Hussein's policy towards this area, years after he lost it in the 1967, and almost up to 1988.

Nevertheless, Hussein's inter-Arab policy diverged from that of his grandfather not only due to differences of age, education, temperament and perspectives, but also because of the political changes in the Middle East in the first half of the 1950s. The most salient of these changes was the emergence of Abd al-Nasser's Egypt as the vanguard of the new pan-Arab nationalism that embraced the Middle East, and the parallel declining influence of Britain in its traditional strongholds and assets in the region. Hussein did not pursue Abdullah's expansionist ambitions, such as his

Greater Syria scheme. Unlike his grandfather, he was aware of his limits. Yet, though he returned Jordan to its actual size and dimensions within the inter-Arab system and focused on domestic issues, his fellow Arabs' suspicions of the Jordanian regime did not entirely disappear. Indeed, though relations between Hussein and Jamal Abd al-Nasser, for example, were usually devoid of the personal animosity that had dominated the attitude of their respective predecessors, King Abdullah and King Faruq, the Egyptian president (and to a certain extent the leaders of republican Syria as well), did not completely trust the weak, moderate, and conspicuously pro-Western Hashemite monarch.

Even Hussein's attitude towards Israel was, in his first years on the throne, similar to the Arab consensus more than to his grandfather's views. Abdullah's contacts with Israel which continued, as noted, almost to his death, were not resumed by Hussein, despite Israeli efforts to induce him to resume them.[1] This position did not emanate from ideological conviction. Hussein, as Uriel Dann claims, had inherited his grandfather's lack of anti-Zionist zeal.[2] He refused to have contacts with Israel only because he wished to close ranks with the rest of the Arab world and not to antagonize his Palestinian subjects. Hussein's Jordan, like the other Arab states, boycotted Israel in the international arena and refused to take part even in UN-sponsored conferences when Israel was invited.[3]

Yet, over the years, Hussein became well aware that, militarily, his army was unable to effectively confront the IDF in cases of border incidents or ensuing hostilities. He correctly assumed, however, that Israeli political thinking regarded Hashemite Jordan as the lesser evil when compared to the agents of radical Arab nationalism, who jeopardized his monarchy no less than they endangered Israel. Hence, Israel would prefer to retain Jordan as its eastern neighbour rather than see the country superseded by Syria or Iraq. In other words, the territorial integrity of Jordan and the preservation of the Hashemite regime were in Israel's interest. This attitude yielded a tacit understanding between the two governments that the frontier should remain as quiet as possible. There was also an unwritten agreement to share the Jordan river basin waters, along the lines of the Johnston proposals of 1953.[4] This policy of practical understandings was implied in Hussein's 1962 autobiography: 'There is an Arab proverb which says that "Peace comes from understanding, not from [formal] agreement." Agreements are more easily broken than made; but understanding never. It is urgent, therefore, and in the interest of peace, that there be better understanding among nations.'[5]

Nevertheless, Jordan's official position towards Israel was within the realm of the general Arab rhetoric; i.e., reluctance to accept its legitimacy and denying it recognition as a sovereign state. Israel's right to exist was rejected by the Arab consensus on the pretext that its establishment inflicted a severe injustice upon the Palestine Arabs and deprived them of personal and national rights in their own homeland.[6] That evil could be corrected only by the abolition of Israel (Abd al-Nasser referred to Israel as an 'evil that should be uprooted') and the establishment of a Palestinian Arab state in its stead. In the first 'Speech from the Throne' after Hussein became King, his Prime Minister declared that 'there is no peace with the Jews'.[7] The vicious verbal Arab attacks on Israel and on Zionism were occasionally tainted by strong anti-Jewish overtones. Jordan was no exception: an anti-Jewish, anti-Zionist and anti-Israeli hate campaign was launched, *inter alia*, in school textbooks, especially in the elementary schools of the West Bank.[8] Such textbooks, in the 1960s, included ample examples of anti-Jewish and anti-Israeli stereotypes and their de-legitimacy. The Zionists were depicted as thieves and usurpers: 'The Zionist thieves hold the most precious part of the Arab and Islamic homeland', 'The Jews have taken over the world press, spread networks of spies and defiled the human race with moral degradation', 'The Jews are fabricating history when they claim to have an historical right to Palestine'.[9]

The Arab preconditions for even a *discussion* of questions regarding the existence of a Jewish state, on the rare occasions that this was mentioned, were Israel's withdrawal to the 1947 UN partition lines and the repatriation of the 1948 Palestinian Arab refugees.[10] No Arab leader (Hussein included) undertook to recognize Israel even if it complied with these draconic conditions. 'Israel was created by violence and oppression of the Palestinians. Justice should be done and Palestinian rights should be retrieved, even if this means that Israel should disappear. Israel is an aggressor and its existence constitutes a threat to other parts of the Arab world.' Such items can be found in official views expressed by Abd al-Nasser, Hussein and other Arab leaders".[11] The only exception was the idea forwarded by Tunisian President Habib Bourguiba. When visiting Jordan in March 1965, he delivered a speech in a refugee camp near Jericho that called for Arab recognition of Israel in return for what were also Abd al-Nasser's preconditions; i.e., withdrawal to the borders of the UN 1947 partition of Palestine plan and repatriation of the 1948 refugees. Bourguiba believed that the only way to prevent Israeli expansion beyond the *de facto* borders gained in 1948, was to return to the 1947 partition borders.[12] It was also claimed that Bourguiba's idea was designed as a piecemeal solution to the question of Palestine: If Israel complied, it would become extremely weak by giving up almost one-third of its territory and admitting hundreds of thousands of refugees; if Israel refused, as Bourguiba himself put it: "The (great) powers would regard Israel's refusal to yield to UN resolutions, a condemnable refusal . . . the separation between Israel and its supporter would shake the basis of the Zionist imperialism."[13]

Even in his autobiography, written in English for European and

American readership, whenever Hussein mentioned the desire to achieve a 'stable peace in the Middle East', or 'a just and honourable solution', he referred to a solution of the Palestine question and not to an Arab–Israeli settlement. Moreover, even though 'a solution to the Palestine tragedy' was the precondition to any 'real peace', the components of this solution were not a prescription for peace with Israel. On the contrary, they indicated peace *without* Israel.[14]

A just solution, according to Hussein, meant 'complete restoration of the rights of the Arab people of Palestine'. His brother Hassan (before becoming Crown Prince) supported this view, stating that the 'Arabs of Palestine can never accept a substitute for their country and homes'. He demanded that 'the people of Palestine are given their right of self deter-mination'.[15]

One has to bear in mind that there was some ambivalence in Jordan's position regarding the Palestine question. On the declarative and ideolog-ical level, Jordan, like the other Arab states, was committed to the Palestinian cause and demanded to right the wrong; i.e., the formation of an Arab state in Palestine. Simultaneously, however, on the practical level, Jordan had formally annexed and was controlling a considerable part of Palestine. Since the West Bank was considered by the Hashemite regime to be an integral part of Jordan – it was even forbidden by law to refer to this area as Palestine in official documents – this implied that only the terri-tory of the State of Israel comprised 'occupied Palestine'. Palestinians' right to self-determination, as well as the restoration of all their other rights (in the spirit of the all-Arab consensus), should be implemented only in those parts of mandatory Palestine which were not annexed to Jordan; i.e., the State of Israel. In other words: Jaffa, Haifa and Nazareth were in Palestine, while Jenin, Nablus and Hebron were in Jordan. That percep-tion was also indicated in Jordanian schoolbooks and in the writings of Crown Prince Hassan. When discussing the refugee problem, Hassan wrote that 'the overwhelming majority of these refugees (726,000 according to his figures) have never returned to Palestine'. Since about 400,000 refugees who resided in the West Bank and an additional 100,000 in the Gaza Strip had actually never left Palestine, the unavoidable conclu-sion is that, according to Hassan, the West Bank and Gaza were not Palestine.[16]

In addressing a Western audience, Hussein tried, on the one hand, to create the impression that a common ground for a political settlement did exist: 'There can be no solution to this [Palestine] problem unless all the parties concerned genuinely desire a solution. There must exist a real wish to find a general area of agreement, from which progress towards just and honourable solution can be made.' On the other hand, however, on the same occasion, the King seriously questioned the viability of that option:

'At the present time, it is difficult for me to perceive such an area of agreement. Without doubt, the State of Israel is doing everything to consolidate its position in a manner as nationalistic as that by which Hitler drove the Jews from Germany.'[17]

In his overt attitude towards Israel, even beyond the immediate question of the Palestinians' rights, Hussein was reluctant to formally admit Israel's existence as a *fait accompli* and criticized those nations who based their Middle Eastern policy upon that fact. Hussein and his brother Hassan adhered to maximalist Arab position that opposed the existence of a Zionist Israel (i.e., denying any Jewish sovereignty there). Not only was Zionism referred to as the most dangerous threat to Arabism, together with communism ('So long as Zionism is the dominating political force in Israel,' Jews and Arabs would not be able to live together as neighbours and friends as they used to 'for centuries'), but the actual physical existence of Israel threatened the Arabs. This was mainly because of the expansionist ambitions attributed to the Jewish state. The establishment of Israel was regarded as a wedge driven into the very heart of the Arab world and an obstacle to its complete unity.[18]

An analysis of the public views, expressed by Hussein towards Israel, reveals a certain resemblance to his grandfather Abdullah's favourite alternative regarding the future of Palestine and its Jewish *Yishuv* during the British mandate. Abdullah regarded the Jews as a sort of a modern version of the Ottoman *Millet* system; i.e., he was ready to recognize them as a religious community, entitled to autonomous status in part of Palestine, within an enlarged Arab state under his own throne. They were to enjoy civil and religious liberties and certain political rights such as representation in the legislative and executive bodies , as long as this did not include Jewish independence and that they recognized Arab sovereignty in Palestine.[19] It seems that Hussein too, who regarded the Israelis, basically as a religious group but not as members of a national entity,[20] was ready in his public statements to acquiesce to Jewish presence in 'occupied Palestine' (i.e., Israel) on a personal basis as individuals, providing that they acknowledged Arab supremacy.

After the late 1950s, Hussein underwent a change in his attitude towards Israel, albeit one not manifested on the declarative level. This change was triggered by the political events of 1958, particularly the union between Egypt and Syria, the United Arab Republic (UAR), the establishment of the Iraqi–Jordanian union that followed (the Arab Federation) and its abrupt and bloody dissolution after the coup d'etat in Baghdad in July. These events proved to the King what he already knew: that the real danger to his regime and his own survival did not emanate from Israel, but loomed from the militant, 'revolutionary', Arab nationalists in Cairo and Damascus.

Following the *coup d'état* in Baghdad in July 1958, when the Iraqi branch of the Hashemite dynasty was butchered, Hussein himself felt threatened and asked for Britain's protection. Jordan was surrounded by hostile neighbours: The UAR, Iraq and Saudi Arabia were reluctant to allow planeloads of British paratroops to cross their air-space en route to Amman. Only Israel agreed that the British air-lift from Cyprus fly over its territory.[21] During the same crisis Jordan was cut off from its major source of oil – Lebanon's refineries – as Syria closed the border with Jordan. The border with newly-republican Iraq was also closed. Jordan immediately suffered a severe shortage of fuel which was exacerbated by a blockade duly imposed by its Arab neighbours. American's attempt to dispatch emergency fuel shipments by air from the Persian Gulf was foiled by the Arab states. Once again it was Israel which enabled the American cargo planes shipping oil from Lebanon to cross its air space and saved the Jordanian economy from total paralysis.[22] These gestures had an impact on Hussein, even though Israel's role – which in practice saved him –also placed him in a sensitive situation. The fact that his economic and military salvation was achieved via Israel's airspace undermined his image as an ardent Arab nationalist.[23] He commented on that Arab criticism in his autobiography: 'so in the end the fuel came from Lebanon, and every gallon had to be flown over the skies of Israel, the mortal enemy of all Arab states. Where an Arab nation refused, an enemy agreed'.[24]

In the same year, the King's 'debt' to Israel grew even larger when its intelligence services obtained information on a conspiracy against his life. The Israeli military attaché in London passed the information on to the Foreign Office which promptly updated Hussein. Israel gained the King's confidence and henceforth occasional messages were delivered between Amman and Jerusalem via the good offices of the chargé d'affaires at the British embassy in Tel Aviv.[25]

After 1959, Jordan's ideological and political opponents in the Arab world, namely the UAR and republican Iraq, touched an extremely sensitive nerve in their struggle against Hussein. They promoted the idea of the 'Palestinian Entity' (*al-Kiyan al-Filastini*) in order to de-legitimize Hussein's claim to representing the Palestinians and to drive a wedge between citizens of the West Bank and the Hashemite regime. Given Jordan's ambivalence on the Palestinian issue, this initiative put Hussein in an extremely awkward position. Fortunately for the King, his government's activities in the West Bank to undermine the idea bore their fruits.[26] Yet the verbal and political encounter with external Arab opponents soon became violent. In August 1960, Jordanian Prime Minister Haza'a al-Majali was murdered by assailants who came from Syria. The King was infuriated by the loss of a personal friend and he contemplated military action against his country's northern neighbour. A senior Jordanian officer then arrived at the Mandelbaum Gate (the crossing point between the Israeli and the Jordanian sectors of Jerusalem) asking to meet General Haim Herzog, Chief of Military Intelligence (and later the sixth President of Israel). The Jordanian explained his government's intentions towards Syria and asked his interlocutor that Israel not take advantage of the situation, as the forces deployed along the border with Israel were thinned in order to reinforce the units along the Syrian border.[27] After this incident, as one scholar suggests, it became clear to Hussein that Israel was one of the only neighbours he had, that had not tried to kill him.[28]

In 1963 Hussein crossed the Rubicon as far as his attitude towards Israel was concerned. Relations with the radical, anti-Western, 'revolutionary' regimes in the neighbouring countries did not improve. Yet their activities had an impact on political public opinion in Jordan, especially on the Palestinians in the West Bank. Hussein was particularly perturbed by the mass demonstrations that broke out in East Jerusalem and other towns in April–May 1963, in support of the proposed Egyptian–Syrian–Iraqi federation. The demonstrators demanded that Jordan join as well.[29] The idea of the triple federation never came about, and Hussein soon regained control. He had made up his mind, however, and agreed to a direct clandestine meeting with an official Israeli representative after having being urged to do so both by the Israelis and by external mediators for quite a long time. In September 1963 – shortly after Ben-Gurion resigned and was succeeded as Prime Minister by Levi Eshkol, King Hussein met in London with Dr. Jacob Herzog, deputy director general of the ministry of foreign affairs. Until the June 1967 war, they met at least three more times. In the autumn of 1965 in Paris, Hussein also met with Golda Meir, Israel's Foreign Minister who, 18 years before, had met with his grandfather, King Abdullah, when together they had decided the future of mandatory Palestine.

In spite of the drastic change in policy that these meetings reflected, neither peace negotiations nor a political settlement were discussed. It seems that Hussein adhered to the spirit of the Arab proverb he quoted in his autobiography, that peace comes from understanding not from agreement. Given his position in the region and the attitude of the Arab world towards Israel, it was obvious that a separate Jordanian agreement with Israel was not feasible. Hussein never forgot the fate of his beloved grandfather, whose assassination was generally construed as a revenge for his consent to partition Palestine and for his negotiations with Israel.

What Hussein did seek in his meetings with the Israelis was their good offices in convincing the Americans to assist Jordan financially and militarily.[30] He particularly wanted to remove Israeli opposition to the sale of advanced American tanks to his army and he formally undertook that they would not be deployed in the West Bank. This partial demilitarization of the West Bank became one of cornerstones of an (American sponsored) Israeli–Jordanian understanding prior to the June 1967 war.[31] Hussein was also concerned about Israel's irrigation project that entailed the transport of water from the Sea of Galilee to the Negev. He was afraid that this would violate the unwritten agreement on sharing the Jordan basin waters. A decrease in the quantity of the waters that his country could use could jeopardize Jordan's own irrigation project in the Jordan Valley (East Ghor). The Israelis failed to allay the King's apprehensions regarding that scheme but an unwritten understanding was ratified at one of the bilateral meetings.[32]

As indicated, the discreet change in Hussein's attitude toward Israel was not reflected in either his or his government's public statements. In that respect, he continued to close ranks with the collective Arab view, until after the June 1967 war. His comments on the ideas of Tunisian President Habib Bourguiba in March 1965 regarding possible recognition of Israel were no exception.[33]

The tough public attitude toward Israel while secret ties with its officials were ongoing probably had Israel's acquiescence, as it served the interests of both parties and was designed to clear Jordan of any suspicion of collaboration with the enemy. It seems that up to 1967 there was at least a partial correlation between Hussein's public views on Israel and his outright reluctance to discuss a political agreement with Israeli officials, even secretly and even in the most rudimentary terms. One has to bear in mind, however, given the Arab views on their conflict with Israel, that public reference to issues such as recognition of Israel or negotiating a settlement were scarce. The standard Arab rhetoric insisted on the impossibility of such eventualities.

In Jordan, more than in any other Arab country, most references to the Arab–Israeli conflict focused on its Palestinian aspects. Controlling parts of Arab Palestine and at least half of its population, the Hashemite regime in Jordan occasionally reiterated its commitment to the Palestinians and emphasized its position as their representative. Such references became more intense in the 1960s when the Palestinian problem more frequently occupied the Arab agenda. Attempts to organize the Palestinians into political frameworks were regarded by Hussein and his government as anti-Jordanian steps and put them on the defensive.

First, between 1959 and 1961, when the issue of the Palestinian Entity was raised (see p. 19), Jordan's statements on the conflict in general and on Palestine in particular were closely linked to its campaign against the entity. Stress was laid on Jordan's stand 'in the forefront' of the struggle to recover Palestine and that 'the Palestinian problem is the No. 1 issue in our thoughts all the time'. Hussein emphasized that 'it is the duty of all to spare no effort in preparing ourselves to the battle to regain our usurped rights'.[34]

However, in his speeches concerning the struggle against the Palestinian Entity, there were almost no direct comments on Israel.

In March 1962 the Egyptians promulgated a constitution for the Gaza Strip.[35] They intended to form a Palestinian National Union there that would represent all Palestinians and thus challenge Jordan's claim and question its authority in the West Bank. In response, a few months later Jordan published a White Paper entitled *Jordan and the Palestine Problem and the Inter-Arab Ties*. It stated that Jordan had a closer and more direct connection with the question of Palestine than the rest of the Arab states. For Jordan, the question was not merely a political issue but a vital and crucial problem. It was a part of the Jordanian reality as most Palestinians had become Jordanian citizens. *Jordan as such was the heir and successor to Palestine* and the only one who had the right to speak on behalf of its population.[36]

While the Egyptian initiative had almost no impact, the Palestinian question returned to the limelight in 1964 when the establishment of the Palestine Liberation Organization (PLO) attracted intense public interest. As in the case of the Palestinian Entity, the idea of a Palestine Liberation Organization also threatened the unity of the two Banks and offered the Palestinians in Jordan an alternative loyalty.

The founding fathers of the PLO were well aware of their dependence on the Arab states and went out of their way not to antagonize them. Article 24 of the Palestinian National Covenant, issued in 1964, stated that 'The organization does not exercise any regional sovereignty over the Western Bank in the Hashemite Kingdom of Jordan, over the Gaza Strip or the Hammah area.[37] Its activities will be on the national popular level in the liberational, organizational, political and financial fields.' By relinquishing their claim to those areas of Palestine that were controlled by Arab states in advance, the PLO strengthened Jordan's perception that Palestinian rights should be exercised only in those parts of Palestine that constituted Israel.

Nevertheless, in spite of the PLO's declaration of intentions in its Covenant, the Organization's activities (and particularly those of its chairman, Ahmad Shuqayri) from 1965 onward indicated that the Organization did covet the West Bank. Not only was that area the 'natural' territorial base for any attempt to create a Palestinian political or national framework, but Jordan was the weakest link among all the states that had any territorial interest in Palestine.

Once again Hussein and his government were on the defensive. They frequently stressed the genuine unity that prevailed between the two Banks and regarded themselves as authentic representatives of the Palestinians in order to undermine the role the PLO was trying to play in the West Bank and to depict it as an entirely unnecessary organ.[38] A few months after the establishment of the PLO, 17 year-old prince Hassan, Hussein's brother and the future Crown Prince, delivered a lecture at his English public school in Harrow, on the Palestine Question. Completely ignoring the PLO, Prince Hassan underscored Jordan's contribution to the Palestinians and particularly its efforts to alleviate the plight of the refugees.[39]

In order to thwart the PLO's demand to become the exclusive representative of the Palestinians, Hussein and his spokespersons also reiterated that the Palestinian issue was an Arab issue and thus the Palestinians, more than any others, should insist that it remain the cause of all Arabs. (Indeed, the White Paper that Jordan had issued in July 1962 was entitled, as already mentioned, *Jordan and the Palestine Problem and the Inter-Arab Ties*.) The efforts to regain the usurped Palestinian rights in their homeland should be within a unified Arab campaign: 'We can not leave it to the Palestinians to tackle. This would mean surrender of whatever remains of Palestine.' Moreover, the unity of the two Banks was the key to wider Arab unity.[40] This line was adhered to until the June 1967 war.

Throughout the two years that preceded the June 1967 war, another source of Jordanian–Palestinian tension was added to the intensifying struggle between the Hashemite regime and the PLO over the loyalty and support of West Bank residents. Terrorist attacks against Israelis by Palestinians infiltrating from Jordan led to harsh public Israeli warnings to Jordan that were, occasionally, followed by retaliation against Jordanian targets. Most of these terrorist activities were carried out by al-Fatah group, which at that time had nothing to do with the PLO but was operating from Damascus, under the aegis of the Syrian regime. Israel's wrath, however, targeted Jordan, either because the terrorists infiltrated from and retreated to Jordan, or because Israel was reluctant to contend with Syria, a country unequivocally supported by the Soviet Union. Jordan, on its part, tried hard to prevent this activity by arresting al-Fatah members. Jordan also asked Israel to show restraint and to avoid reprisals.[41] Shuqayri took pains to turn these events into political gains, especially after the killing of three Israeli soldiers in November 1966 and a massive Israeli retaliation against the village of Samu', south of Hebron. They accused the Jordanian government of having abandoned the Palestinians on the West Bank and demanded that they be armed. A mounting wave of violent demonstrations that called to topple the Hashemite regime caused the split between Shuqayri and Hussein to become unbridgeable. Moreover, Historian Moshe Shemesh claims that the attack on (or, in Jordanian terminology, the invasion of) Samu' constituted a crucial turning point in Hussein's attitude towards both Israel and the West Bank Palestinians and contributed heavily to the King's decision, about seven months later, in June 1967, to join the war against Israel. On one hand, the King was convinced that Israel was determined to take over the West Bank and that the Samu' affair was a prelude to a comprehensive Israeli–Arab war. The violent demonstrations and other reactions of the West Bankers to what they regarded as being relegated by their government to 'the Israeli predator', threatened Jordan's internal stability and jeopardized the Hashemite regime.[42]

In January 1967 Jordan withdrew its recognition of the PLO and closed its offices in Jerusalem. These moves against the PLO evoked hostile reactions in the Arab world. Jordan was the target of all-out criticism and denounced by fellow Arab states. Hussein was accused of having betrayed the Palestinian cause. In the first half of 1967, Jordanian relations with several Arab states, Egypt and Syria in particular, deteriorated and soon Jordan was isolated by 'progressive' Arab regimes. In May 1967, a car bomb originating in Syria exploded near the Syrian–Jordanian border and claimed the lives of several Jordanians. When Egyptian troops entered the Sinai desert in mid-May (a move that three weeks later led to the outbreak of the June war), the Jordanian media mocked Abd al-Nasser for hiding behind the UN observers (along the Egyptian Israeli border) and provoked him into demanding UN withdrawal and closing the Gulf of Aqaba to Israeli navigation. Only when war seemed inevitable did King Hussein realize which way the wind was blowing, and he took action to extract Jordan from its position as an outcast. On 30 May 1967 he flew to Cairo, as if going to Canossa, concluded a defence agreement with Jamal Abd al-Nasser and flew back to Amman with Ahmad Shuqayri, whom he was forced to appease, on board.

3 ADJUSTING TO THE NEW REALITY: FROM JUNE 1967 TO RESOLUTION 242

There is more than one explanation for why Jordan entered the June war. Domestic constraints and external pressures, Egyptian insinuations and deceit, and inter-Arab euphoria are the most common.[1] All these factors combined to manipulate King Hussein into a war that he did not want and could not win. In view of Jordan's position within the inter-Arab system throughout the first half of 1967, it was clear that Hussein had little choice if he wished rehabilitation and re-admittance into the lap of the Arab world. As he himself explained almost twenty years later, 'We took part in the 1967 war not because we believed, even slightly, that it was possible to win, but because we believed that the Arab nation should face aggression and dangers with one hand and one heart.'[2] He took into account the possibility that the price for joining the war might be the loss of the West Bank. Yet the price for *not* joining might be higher: he could lose the entire Kingdom and even his life. On the eve of his trip to Cairo in late May, Hussein soberly analysed his situation: If the Jews did not attack Abd al-Nasser (following the redeployment and re-enforcement of the Egyptian army in the Sinai and the closing of the Straits of Tiran to Israeli navigation), he would become so strong that he could (and would) remove Hussein from his throne. If the Jews attacked the Egyptians and Hussein sat idly by, his position would be severely shaken and he would be branded a traitor, like his late grandfather. On the other hand, if the Jews defeated Abd al-Nasser and Hussein joined in, he might lose the West Bank.[3]

The King seems to have been guided by this analysis. He had considered the risk of losing the West Bank since the raid on Samu' seven months earlier. Though this was one of his greatest fears, it was the lesser of two evils. Hussein probably expected to receive more military assistance from

Egypt and Syria; it seems that he miscalculated the totality of their military fiasco. He may also have toyed with the idea of turning a military defeat into a political victory. Yet at the end of the day, he decided that he would rather lose territory than lose his kingdom. His prediction proved accurate: he joined the war and lost the West Bank.

The West Bank housed about half of Jordan's population and some of the country's most valuable economic assets, including about 90 per cent of its income in foreign currency. Because about 40 per cent of the population of the East Bank were Palestinians, the loss of the West Bank could have a negative impact on their attitude to the Hashemite regime. However, it was the emotional dimension and the sense of personal failure that played a decisive role in Hussein's determination to retrieve the lost territory. He regarded the West Bank as a bequest from Abdullah, who had taken pains to incorporate it into his kingdom. Losing it, Hussein was convinced, meant betrayal of his beloved grandfather's heritage.

The results of the June war were a tremendous blow to the Arabs. Three of their armies were defeated and the IDF, in six days, took over an area more than three times larger than the entire State of Israel. Pre-war Arab rhetoric gave way to more elaborate propaganda, that claimed that the demand for an Israeli withdrawal to the 1949 armistice lines 'need not prejudice the long term solution of the "Palestine problem" (i.e., the elimination of the state of Israel)'. The 'two-stage' concept now evolved: In the first stage the results of the recent war would be erased; in the second, the 'Palestine problem' would be dealt with.[4]

In Syria and Egypt, the crisis was manageable. After the initial shock, both regimes estimated that they would survive the defeat even without the prompt retrieval of the Golan Heights or the Sinai peninsula. They hoped to regain their lost territories eventually (or, as Abd al-Nasser phrased it as early as June 9th: 'eliminate the traces of aggression' - *'Izalat Aathair al-'Udwan*),[5] without changing their attitude towards Israel, without meeting its demands and without making any political concessions in return. This could be achieved by eliciting international pressure on Israel to withdraw from the occupied territories, or by revitalizing the military option and mobilizing the support and the resources of the entire Arab world to the cause.

For Jordan, however, the territorial and material losses were far greater than those of Egypt and Syria. Given its ethno-demographic structure and the nature of the regime, it was obvious why the King was afraid that both his reign and country were doomed, unless the West Bank were soon retrieved. 'While other countries could be compensated for their losses [through material aid],' Hussein said, 'the loss of the West Bank endangered Jordan's very existence as a state.'[6] Moreover, time was also an essential factor. Jordan radio advised the Arabs to temporarily set aside the wider aspects of the Palestine problem and to focus on the demand for an immediate Israeli withdrawal from the occupied territories.[7]

It is worth noting that about one week after the end of the war, the Israeli government decided that Israel was ready to withdraw to the international borders with Egypt and Syria in return for bilateral peace treaties that would include, *inter alia*, the demilitarization of the Sinai peninsula and the Golan Heights, and freedom of navigation for Israeli vessels in the Suez canal and the Straits of Tiran.[8] No such arrangement with Jordan was broached. On the contrary, the government decided that East Jerusalem would be incorporated into Israel and the rest of the West Bank would remain under military government. In the long run, efforts would be made – possibly through negotiations with King Hussein – to create a Palestinian autonomy and to achieve an Israeli–Jordanian economic union.[9]

These resolutions, according to Dan Bavly,[10] were not only kept secret from the public, but were not disclosed to the IDF's general staff or to Israel's intelligence community. The content of the resolutions was delivered only to the Americans who were to pass them on to the Arabs. A week later US officials reported to Israel that, on the basis of their inquiries, the Israeli conditions were unacceptable to the Arabs. Bavly claims that the Americans, because of their own global considerations, never passed on Israel's proposals to the Arab leaders. Taking the American report at face value, Israel did not seek other channels through which to contact the Arabs and soon determined that direct negotiations were the precondition to reaching secure borders. The Israeli cabinet also decided that East Jerusalem was non-negotiable.[11]

King Hussein knew nothing of these Israeli resolutions; neither of the 'generous' offers to Egypt and Syria, nor of Israel's reluctance to withdraw from the West Bank. Nevertheless, because of Jordan's particular plight, and thanks to his acute political sense and sober disillusionment, he was the first Middle Eastern leader to understand that the June war had created a new reality (just as, twenty years later, he was the first to grasp the full meaning of the outbreak of the *intifada*) and that he needed to adapt to the changing conditions as soon as possible. In view of the vital importance of the West Bank for Jordan, the King was determined to explore all possible avenues for regaining it. These included the inter-Arab system, international involvement (particularly the United States), or direct secret negotiations with Israel.

Moreover, unlike other Arab rulers, almost from the outset Hussein was ready for a *quid pro quo* in return for the West Bank. He became the first Arab head of state to abandon his previously-held public position and to admit that the pre-1967 views were obsolete, even though his peers still adhered to them. Abd al-Nasser's public interpretation of his own slogan to 'eliminate traces of aggression' was that 'what was taken by force will be retrieved by force'. Egyptian and other Arab spokespersons committed themselves to continuing the struggle against the very existence of the State of Israel. 'Our battle for the liquidation of Israel will continue whether she withdraws from the territories she has occupied or not.'[12] Hussein, on his part, realized that adopting the political option, by mobilizing world public opinion and suggesting a give-and-take attitude, was by far the better policy. He even implied that if the Arab states would not consider the political option and unless a summit conference was convened to determine a joint strategy, he would consider acting independently to regain his lost territories.[13]

Between June and November 1967, Hussein took extensive tours abroad, visiting twenty countries (some of them several times) in order to elicit support in his efforts to achieve an Israeli withdrawal and in order to shape a Jordanian foreign policy that would take into account the new post-war situation. During these tours, he realized that eventually he would have to negotiate with Israel. The outcome of his consultations was, therefore, the formulation of the principles that not only became the foundation for Jordan's foreign policy, but also played an important role in the final phrasing of UN Security Council resolution 242 on 22 November 1967 (see below).[14]

On 28 June, while visiting the US, Hussein told President Johnson that Jordan was ready to demilitarize the West Bank in return for an Israeli retreat to the pre-war borders.[15] As noted, partial demilitarization of the West Bank was the basis for the Jordanian–Israeli–American understanding prior to 1967, an understanding that was not honoured by the Jordanians in the June war when American-made tanks *were* deployed in the West Bank. Yet, offering this as the first concession to achieve an Israeli withdrawal was probably designed to introduce it as merely the elaboration of an existing understanding and not as a violation of the Arab consensus. In fact, the King did not even rule out minor border modifications, in return for a complete Israeli withdrawal.

One of the lessons that Hussein had learned from his political isolation prior to the June war (and probably also from his grandfather's fate) was, if possible, to avoid unilateral steps and to seek prior coordination with, or at least the acquiescence of, other Arab states. For this reason, a few days after the war, Hussein called for an Arab summit meeting and when he failed, he discussed the issues with Abd al-Nasser. The Egyptian President agreed that Hussein could officially end the state of belligerency as long as he did not recognize Israel or negotiate with the state directly. The King publicly declared that he would take no unilateral action. When it became clear that it would be impossible to obtain an Israeli withdrawal from the West Bank in return for demilitarization, Hussein and Abd al-Nasser agreed, according to Hussein, that further concessions could be made. Abd al-Nasser gave the King his full support to use every diplomatic channel open to him to win the West Bank back.[16]

In the first weeks after the war, Hussein wanted to wait and see whether the Arab and the international tracks would yield any fruit before resorting to direct negotiations. He made no secret of the line to which he adhered. When asked by the Israelis whether he was prepared to move forward towards a peace treaty, the King replied, 'Give us time, we must advance together with the Arab camp'. In spite of this, Hussein could not ignore the advantages of a direct channel with the Israelis. On 2 July 1967, only a few weeks after the war (and four days after President Johnson reportedly advised him to enter into direct negotiations with Israel), the King met his old acquaintance, Dr. Jacob Herzog, in London. According to Herzog, who was then director general of the Prime Minister's office, Hussein presented no demands and set no conditions. He did not even ask for an Israeli withdrawal, but preferred to discuss the mistakes that had led to his involvement in the war. It seems that the King regarded this meeting not as an *ad hoc* discussion of a specific issue, but as the renewal of a line of communication whose greatest importance at that stage was the channel itself, rather than the specific message conveyed.[17]

The authorized guidelines of the 'Arab camp' regarding the post-war situation were announced at the summit conference convened in Khartoum between 29 August and 1 September 1967 to discuss 'eliminating the traces of aggression'. The debate indeed focused on 'the first stage' and not, as PLO chairman Ahmad Shuqayri demanded, on the wider solution to the Palestine problem; i.e., the liquidation of Israel (or: 'the second stage'). Hussein was one of the persistent advocates of the moderate course. The summit resolution emphasized the political option. Article 3 stated that 'The Arab heads of state have agreed to unite their *political* efforts and the international and diplomatic level to eliminate the effects of the aggression and to ensure the withdrawal of aggressive Israeli forces from the Arab lands which have been occupied since the aggression of 5 June. This will be done within the framework of the main principles by which the Arab states abide, namely no peace with Israel, no recognition of Israel, no negotiation with her and insistence on the rights of the Palestinian people in their own country.'[18] The resolution, however, aimed to clarify that Arab readiness for a political solution per se was such a major concession that Israel should reciprocate with a complete withdrawal for which the Arabs would not render any additional payment.

While Israeli spokespersons analyzing the Khartoum resolution underscored the three 'no's' which they construed as an indication of total rejection of any compromise (in other words: Israel was asked to resort unconditionally to *status quo ante* and gain nothing in return), their Arab counterparts emphasized the political means that had been chosen to

29

pursue Arab goals. Conspicuous among these were King Hussein, his brother Crown Prince Hassan, and other Jordanian officials. They depicted the resolution as a major turning point and as proof of Arab moderation. The King called it 'a great step forward' and said that the Arab position had become 'reasonable and moderate and acceptable to the world'.[19] By expressing this attitude, King Hussein was clearly the best choice of harbinger of Arab moderation. In October and November he travelled, *inter alia*, to Spain, France, West Germany, Britain and the US to present his interpretation of the Khartoum resolutions to policy-makers and the general public.

The King insisted that a total and immediate Israeli withdrawal from all Arab lands occupied in June 1967 was a precondition to any discussion of a political solution of 'the Middle Eastern problem'. To this he added the demand for a satisfactory solution of the refugee problem as well as an acceptable settlement concerning Jerusalem. He indicated, however, that if these conditions were met, this might help to solve some of the other questions such as freedom of passage for Israeli ships through the Suez canal and the Straits of Tiran.[20] In other words, in order to gain a few Arab concessions (far from a peace agreement or recognition), Israel was required not only to relinquish all territorial gains of June 1967, but also to compromise on issues concerning the 1948 war (refugees).

Aware of the concern of American public opinion for the welfare and security of Israel, King Hussein's most far-reaching statements were made in the United States. He repeatedly spoke of the quest for a lasting peace and even stated that 'if the right formula was found' the Arabs were ready to issue a declaration recognizing the right of all to live in peace and security in the Middle East. *All*, he explained, would mean *all states* (i.e., including Israel). In the printed text of his speech at Georgetown University in Washington on 6 November, Hussein said that even though Israel was 'a present fact of life' Jordan might choose not to recognize it, 'just as Jordan did not recognize Communist China'. (This passage was eliminated when the King actually spoke.) He avoided a direct answer to the question of Arab recognition of Israel saying, 'which Israel? Israel within the 1947 UN resolution borders? Israel of 1948? or present-day Israel which speaks about her natural boundaries?'.[21]

Hussein also hinted at the evil Israel created (as a pretext for not recognizing the state), saying that the cause of the 'present crisis' originated in the establishment of the State of Israel at the expense of the Arabs. In the same address at Georgetown University, Hussein said that Israel should "de-Zionise", and the Jewish inhabitants should estrange themselves from the Zionist movement. The Jews of Israel should choose between living peacefully with the Arabs or remaining an isolated alien outpost in the Arab world. The call that 'the Jews in Palestine should be "de-Zionised"' was made by the Tunisian leader Habib Bourguiba as early as 1946, but the same idea (save for using the term) was put forward by Hussein's grandfather Abdullah when he was still Amir of Transjordan in the 1920s and the 1930s. He meant – as probably did Bourguiba and Hussein – that the Jews should give up their claim to statehood and sovereignty in Palestine and settle for civil rights as a religious community under Arab rule and protection. Hussein 'admitted' however that 'Israel is a nation whether we like it or not'.[22] These views imply that even if Hussein had not changed his basic attitude towards Israel, because the reality had changed, there was a need to adapt to it *nolens volens.*

Hussein also rejected Israel's demand for direct negotiations as a matter of principle: the Arabs denied the right of the enemy to dictate its conditions and therefore refused to talk 'in the current situation' with 'those who were occupying their lands'. The Arab states, the King said, 'cannot give up any more than what they have already done'. Direct negotiations, therefore, were out of the question 'for the present'. Hussein expressed his hope, while in Washington, that 'just as we have modified our position towards accepting a political settlement, [the Israelis] will modify their view on insisting on direct negotiations'.[23] Even though Hussein repeatedly indicated throughout the tour that his views were shared by Abd al-Nasser, the King of Jordan definitely seems to have interpreted the Khartoum resolutions more freely than the Egyptian President. There were conspicuous discrepancies regarding certain issues such as freedom of navigation for Israeli vessels through the Suez canal. While Hussein implied that this might be possible in return for Israel's meeting Arab demands, Abd al-Nasser stated on 23 November (following the UN Security Council's adoption of resolution 242) that 'we shall never allow Israel, whatever the cost, to pass through the Suez canal'.[24]

Hussein's views as manifested in his October–November tour were even less acceptable to other Arab states, especially Syria, which had boycotted the Khartoum conference. The Syrians resented the King's statement in Washington that he was speaking for 'the whole Arab nation' (as his great grandfather, Sharif Hussein of Mecca, claimed when he began his correspondence with the British in 1915). The Syrians declared that Syria had 'authorized no one to speak on her behalf'.[25]

In spite of the implied criticism of the way he presented Arab views to the West, Hussein took pains to mobilize a wide Arab consensus around the peace plan which he envisaged. He also hoped to persuade the United States, the Soviet Union and the UN to adopt it as the basis for the solution not only to the situation created by the 'June 1967 aggression', but also to the generation-long Palestine problem and the Arab–Israeli conflict. This twofold effort shed light on Hussein's crystallizing perception of how to regain his lost territories. First, the endorsement, or at least the acquiescence, of the inter-Arab system, or of parts of it, was a precondition to any form of negotiation. Second, the UN was the most suitable framework to pursue such negotiations, a framework that the Arabs could live with, as it bypassed Israel's constant demand for direct negotiations. This dual point of departure then needed to be filled with content. After the Khartoum conference, Hussein formulated his ideas in a five-point plan, based on the views he had expressed during his foreign tours and, probably, on the responses he elicited during these tours:

1. Recognition of the right of every country in the Middle East, Israel included, to live in peace and security.
2. Agreement on the end of belligerency and on putting an end to war.
3. The opening of international waterways, including the Suez canal, to vessels of all countries.
4. An Israeli withdrawal from Arab lands occupied in the June war.
5. A final solution to the problem of the Palestinian refugees and recognition of their right of repatriation.[26]

These ideas seem rather daring and far-fetched, and well ahead of their time. It is worth noting that Hussein emphasized freedom of navigation for Israel in international waterways as a major Arab concession, in view of the fact that one of the reasons for the outbreak of the June war was the blocking of the Gulf of Aqaba (Eilat) to Israeli navigation by Jamal Abd al-Nasser.

Hussein hoped that his ideas would constitute a common ground to accommodate the demands of both the Arabs and the Israelis. His proposals were formulated in such a way as not to infringe on the Khartoum resolutions. On one hand, they called for a total withdrawal, yet on the other hand, Israel could gain a state of non-belligerency, a *de facto* recognition of its right to exist in peace and security, and freedom of navigation in the Suez canal and the Gulf of Aqaba. He believed that the Arabs could live with the proposed concessions which they could construe as no negotiations with Israel, no recognition and no peace with the Jewish state.

Hussein discussed these ideas with Abd al-Nasser, but did not make them public as a comprehensive plan. Abd al-Nasser, as already indicated, was not happy with all the elements of Hussein's initiative. However, he probably gave the King the go ahead to promote a UN resolution toward a political settlement. The UN, on its part, discussed the situation after the June war at an emergency session of the General Assembly (that began a few days after a cease-fire was achieved), in a Security Council debate, and at the 22nd regular session of the General Assembly in September 1967. As all three forums yielded no agreed-upon resolution, the matter was returned to the Security Council which endeavoured to draft such a resolution. On 22 November 1967, after debating several draft proposals, the Security Council unanimously adopted the proposed British resolution that emphasized the 'inadmissibility of the acquisition of territory by war and the need to work for a just and lasting peace in which every state in the area can live in security'. This should be achieved by the following means:

I. Withdrawal of Israeli armed forces from territories occupied in the recent conflict;
II. Termination of all claims or states of belligerency and respect for and acknowledgement of the sovereignty, territorial integrity and political independence of every State in the area and their right to live in peace within secure and recognized boundaries free from threats or acts of force.

The resolution also affirmed the necessity for:

A. Guaranteeing freedom of navigation through international waterways in the area;
B. Achieving a just settlement of the refugee problem;
C. Guaranteeing the territorial inviolability and political independence of every State in the area, through measures including the establishment of demilitarized zones.

The Security Council also asked that the Secretary General send a special representative to the Middle East to 'establish and maintain contacts with the States concerned in order to promote agreement and assist efforts to achieve a peaceful and accepted settlement'.[27]

In view of the similarity between resolution 242 and the points made earlier by Hussein, both during his foreign tour and in the provisions of his 'peace plan', the King was considered as one of the driving forces behind the resolution. When he began his trip, a Jordanian newspaper reported that the primary objective of Hussein's tour was to convince the Soviet Union (which the King visited for the first time earlier that month) and the US to support a joint Security Council resolution 'guaranteeing the withdrawal of the aggressor forces from Arab territory'. King Hussein later claimed that he 'was one of the Arab negotiators who participated with representatives of the United States Government in formulating the interpretation of resolution 242'. There is no doubt that he played a vitally important role in drafting the resolution.[28]

Indeed, Jordan's official attitude to the adoption of resolution 242 was more favourable than that of the other Arab states, of Israel and of the

Palestinian organizations.[29] It was obvious that of all the parties concerned, Hussein was most satisfied with the resolution, whose acceptance was a personal triumph for him. First of all, on the face of it, resolution 242 seemed workable. It seemed a balanced and even-handed document, not a unilateral attempt to impose a solution on one of the concerned parties. Even if the gap between the parties still seemed wide and they might ask for amendments, it could serve as a basis for negotiations towards a peace settlement. Moreover, if implemented, the resolution could restore the West Bank to Jordan without his having to make any concession that he was not willing to make, providing that other Arab states agreed. Finally, resolution 242 referred only to the *states* of the Middle East and not to other frameworks. Hence, the re-emerging Palestinian question was only indirectly mentioned, in context of the solution to the refugee problem. Mentioning the Palestinians only in the humanitarian context removed (or, as it turned out, postponed), Jordan's fear of a PLO challenge to its sovereignty in the West Bank. Jordan had faced this challenge before the June war but it now seemed more threatening because of rising Palestinian nationalism and due to the absence of Jordanian authority in the West Bank.

Adhering to this resolution, King Hussein could publicly insist on Israeli withdrawal from the territories occupied in June 1967.[30] On the face of it, resolution 242 simplified Hussein's efforts to gain a settlement. It set the framework and the final goals, and determined, within the principle of reciprocity and mutual concessions, each party's *quid pro quo*. He could offer Israel an end to the state of belligerency and vague recognition, and he could insist on UN mediation. Indeed Jordanian spokespersons, from King Hussein and his brother, to Prime Ministers and Ministers, reiterated time and again that resolution 242 was the best available remedy to the Middle East conflict and the most suitable basis for any future political settlement. It was designed to simultaneously allay Israel's apprehensions and to satisfy Arab demands. Jordan consistently adhered to its principles, particularly in calling for a just and lasting peace between the Arabs and Israel.[31]

In practice, however, this did not come to pass. Resolution 242 did not live up to King Hussein's expectations. Even though the resolution reflected Jordan's concept of a settlement, its comprehensive perception was gradually consolidated through local and regional, political and other developments during the quarter of a century that followed the 1967 war. The reluctance of all the parties to accept it at face value, the failure of the UN mediator to persuade them to move towards common ground, the unpredicted centrality of the Palestinian issue and the political and military troubles in the Middle East after 1967 – all these changed the parties' views towards a political settlement. Jordan was no exception. Jordan's demands of Israel, the *quid pro quo* it was willing to give, the final objectives of the settlement and the ways to achieve them, were all dynamic components that reflected and were influenced by the events mentioned above. The changes in the Jordanian position, their background, context, scope and meaning, will be discussed and analysed in the following chapters. Yet, in order to grasp the full meaning of what occurred, an overview of the course of the major developments following the adoption of the resolution is required.

4 POLITICAL ACTIVITIES AND INITIATIVES, 1967–1988

The notion of a possible political arrangement with Israel began to take shape among policy-makers in Jordan shortly after the June war. King Hussein was the first Arab leader to publicly abandon the traditional, pre-1967 attitude towards the Arab–Israeli conflict, implying that such an attitude had become anachronistic. He advocated seeking a political solution, and admitted that it had to be based on mutual concessions. Jordan was the first Arab state ready for a *quid pro quo* in return for its demands being met. While the most far-reaching gesture that other Arab states were willing to make was to utter vague statements on a solution in the spirit of the UN resolutions, Jordan agreed to discuss substantial issues regarding the nature of the future peace, the framework through which it was to be achieved and even to refer to Israel's rights.

On 23 November, one day after the UN Security Council adopted resolution 242 and in accordance with article 3 of the resolution, Secretary General U Thant commissioned Gunnar Jarring, the Swedish ambassador to Moscow, as his Special Representative to the Middle East. Jarring was to contact the concerned governments and to promote efforts to achieve a peaceful settlement to the Arab–Israeli conflict, along the lines suggested by resolution 242. In December Jarring arrived in the Middle East and from his headquarters in Nicosia launched short and frequent visits to Cairo, Jerusalem, Amman, Beirut and New York. (He did not visit Damascus as the Syrians recognized neither resolution 242 nor his mission.) Jarring's intensive shuttle diplomacy, which continued throughout 1968 and 1969, bore little fruit. His attempts to discuss the implementation of resolution 242 were futile. The root of the failure, as Ra'ad al-Kadiri suggested, could be traced directly to the ambiguity inherent in the text of resolution 242, which enabled each government concerned to interpret the conditions for a political settlement of the conflict in its own narrow way.[1] Israel insisted on direct negotiations with the Arabs, while the latter, and primarily Jordan, before committing to any negotiations, demanded that Israel accept the principle of complete withdrawal.

In December 1969 US Secretary of State William Rogers endeavoured to overcome the stalemate in the peace talks and to revitalize the Jarring mission by bringing forth a new initiative. It was formulated and detailed in a ten-point plan that focused on an attempt to reach a settlement between Israel and Egypt as well as between Israel and Jordan. The proposed mechanism was like that of the 1949 Israeli–Arab Rhodes talks under UN auspices; i.e., it required no direct negotiations. Israel, according to this initiative, was to retreat to the international border-line with Egypt (exclusive of Gaza), save for minor border modifications. Egypt was to recognize the Straits of Tiran as an international waterway and Israel would enjoy freedom of navigation therein and in the Suez canal. The Jordanian part of the plan also called for Israeli withdrawal to the 1967 borders, again with minor modifications. Jerusalem and the refugee problem were to be discussed by the two parties, who would mutually recognize the sovereignty of the other and the right to live in peace. The final agreement would be effective only after an Egyptian–Israeli peace had been achieved. Jordan would also join Egypt and Israel, under Jarring's sponsorship, in discussing the final status of the Gaza Strip.[2]

This plan was designed to encourage the Arabs to accept the idea of a permanent peace and to encourage Israel to return the occupied territories. Abd al-Nasser (as well as the government of Israel) rejected these concepts. Jordan basically favoured any political initiative that would eventually yield a complete Israeli withdrawal. Nevertheless, when Egypt rejected the plan in early 1970, Jordan could not – out of solidarity as well as political and economic dependency – publicly defy Abd al-Nasser and continue to support the plan.

In the summer of 1970 Rogers resumed his initiative, this time in order to reach a cease fire in the Israeli–Egyptian war of attrition along the Suez canal. The US feared that escalation of this war would deepen Soviet involvement in Egypt and would implicate the US in a direct confrontation with the USSR in the Middle East. Rogers also asked Israel, Jordan and Egypt to subscribe to Jarring's plan, outlined in his recent report to the UN Secretary General, and indicate their acceptance of resolution 242 and their readiness to implement all its components. He also asked them to announce their willingness to resume discussions, under Jarring's good offices, in order to reach a peace agreement, based on mutual recognition of the sovereignty and territorial integrity of all countries and on [Israeli] withdrawal from territories occupied in 1967. The parties were also asked to observe a three-month cease fire.[3] Of the three parties concerned, Jordan was the most willing to accept this plan; Israel and Egypt were reluctant. Only a month later, in late July, Jordan followed Egypt in accepting the cease-fire and in August Jamal Abd al-Nasser and King Hussein accepted the other provisions of the 'Rogers Plan'; i.e., to enter negotiations with Israel on the basis of resolution 242 through Jarring's mediation.

Jordan espoused the Rogers initiative for the same reasons it supported the Jarring mission. Yet the clashes between the Jordanian army and the Palestinian organizations (see below) on the one hand, and the demise of Abd al-Nasser on the other (both in September 1970), diverted regional and global attention from the proposed course of negotiations. The political process – as well as Jordan's prospect of regaining the West Bank – moved from the limelight to backstage. The cease-fire along the Suez Canal was indeed observed (until Egypt advanced SAM missiles to the West Bank of the canal), but no other progress was achieved in implementing resolution 242. Jarring and the US initiated resumption of negotiations including direct ones, which Jordan declined, out of solidarity with Egypt. The second phase of his mission, however, seemed no more than sheer inertia with hardly any substance. Jarring duly submitted his resignation in early 1972.

Uncompromising, doctrinaire, ardent pan-Arabist Egyptian president Jamal Abd al-Nasser was succeeded by pragmatic, less dogmatic and less charismatic Anwar al-Sadat. His proposal for a partial Israeli withdrawal along the Suez canal (in order to reopen it to international navigation) brought forth an American effort to achieve an Israeli–Egyptian interim agreement as a first stage towards a permanent settlement. Once again, these efforts proved futile due to the wide gap between the positions of the parties.

Parallel to US and UN efforts to forge a settlement, King Hussein, as noted, did not hesitate to approach Israel directly. He hoped that face to face meetings with Israel's official representatives would facilitate the return of the West Bank to Jordan, a goal which external mediation, so far, had failed to achieve. Between the June 1967 and the October 1973 wars, contacts were constantly maintained between the King and his senior associates on the one hand, and an Israeli Prime Minister, cabinet ministers and army officers on the other. These yielded a better understanding of the other party's views, forged warm personal ties, and even resulted in practical arrangements concerning various civil and military issues.[4] Nevertheless, the contacts did not 'deliver the goods' that Hussein desired, because the King insisted on a complete Israeli withdrawal and refused to accept the concept of territorial compromise in the West Bank, to which Israel adhered. He rejected the 1968 Allon Plan under which he would regain about 70 per cent of the West Bank and almost full authority over its population.[5] The derivatives of this plan, such as the 'Jericho enclave', the 'Jordanian option' or the concept of any territorial compromise whatsoever, were also unacceptable to Hussein as they failed to meet his preconditions. The gap between Israel's proposed maximal concessions and Hussein's minimal demands was still far too wide to be bridged.

Simultaneous to the efforts to cope with the impact of the June war and repair the military, economic and political damage resulting from it, Jordan took pains to maintain its influence in the West Bank (parallel to insisting on its return). The war and its consequences did not altogether alleviate the tension between the Amman regime and the Palestinians. They may have postponed the showdown, but also contributed to the intensification of the bilateral confrontation. The post-1967 war years witnessed the growing importance of the Palestinian factor as an increasingly crucial element, militarily and politically, with which all the states involved in the Middle East conflict had to reckon. The major Palestinian challenge came from al-Fatah and the other *fida'i* organizations who continued to resist Israel in the occupied territories and attacked from their bases in neighbouring countries, mainly from Jordan. These actions won them the praise and acclamation of Arab public opinion. The *fida'i* groups attributed the escalation that led to the June war to their military activity. The failure of the regular armies compared to their own constant defiance of Israel was construed as proof that their tactic of popular armed struggle was the best, if not the only, method of combating Israel. Their popularity, in Jordan and elsewhere, reached a zenith after the Israeli raid on al-Fatah's strongholds in Karama, in the eastern Jordan valley, in March 1968, when Palestinian *fida'iyun* and the Jordanian army inflicted heavy casualties upon the attackers. In 1968 the *fida'iyun* had expanded their struggle against Israel beyond the Middle East. An El-Al airliner hijacked to Algiers and a plane attacked at Athens airport were the first Israeli targets of Palestinian terrorism abroad.

Palestinian political activity also assumed a new direction, when, in 1968, the *fida'i* organizations joined the passive and impotent PLO and forced the revision of the Palestinian National Covenant, making it a more extreme and uncompromising document. Early the next year, at the fifth meeting of the Palestinian National Council (PNC) in Cairo, representatives of the *fida'i* groups outmanoeuvred the old politicians who had hitherto controlled the organization with the support of the Arab League. These politicians were identified with the Arab regimes and thus with the June 1967 defeat. Yassir Arafat, al-Fatah chief, became the new PLO chairman.

In Jordan the *fida'iyun* constituted a serious problem. Jordan hosted most of their bases and personnel, after Israeli security forces had uncovered and destroyed most of their clandestine infrastructure in the West

Bank. Unable to remain in the Jordan valley, along the border, due to constant Israeli raids on their outposts, they gradually moved eastward to the Jordanian highlands and pitched their camps in and around major towns. Most of them spent time in Amman, where they were welcomed, mainly in the refugee camps and other Palestinian residential quarters. The camps became hotbeds of their activity and turned into military strong-holds where they stored their munitions and supplies, accommodated their warriors and housed their headquarters. Some of these areas became exclusive, 'extra territorial' Palestinian zones, off-limits to Jordanian civilian and military officials. The organizations took advantage of their mounting popularity and gradually turned their residency in Jordan into a state within a state. They defied the authorities' attempts to impose the state's jurisdiction upon them. Throughout 1968–70, occasional clashes broke out between Jordanian security forces and Palestinian *fida'iyun*. The regime could not acquiesce to the Palestinian challenge to its authority, and *fida'iyun* activity exposed Jordan to massive Israeli retaliation that inflicted severe damage on the country's economic infrastructure. The attitude towards the *fida'iyun* presence and activity in Jordan became yet another bone of contention between the regime and the public. It became the topic of an ongoing public debate that crossed the traditional line dividing Jordanians and Palestinians. Not a few Jordanians (East Bankers) supported the *fida'iyun* while some Palestinians questioned their activity. Due to the overwhelming public support they enjoyed, King Hussein was reluctant to confront the organizations militarily, as he genuinely feared a bloody civil war, particularly in view of the fact that almost half of Jordan's (East Bank) population was Palestinian. Hence, each time he decided to contain their activity, he backed off at the last moment. In September 1970 a showdown became inevitable after the Popular Democratic Front for the Liberation of Palestine (PDFLP) made an attempt on King Hussein's life and after the Popular Front for the Liberation of Palestine (PFLP) hijacked three airliners, forced them to land near Zarqa, north-east of Amman, and held their passengers hostage. Under pressure of his senior military officers, the King decided to drive the *fida'iyun* out of Jordanian towns by force. On 16 September 1970 a military government was formed and the next day an all-out military operation against the organizations' presence in Amman and elsewhere began.

Throughout ten days of fierce fighting which claimed the lives of several thousand people, mostly Palestinians, the Jordanian army managed to break their resistance. During the clashes, a Syrian armoured brigade invaded northern Jordan to assist the Palestinians but was quickly repelled by the Jordanian army after suffering heavy casualties. The Syrian retreat was also precipitated by US and Israeli threats to intervene. These events were known as 'Black September'. The *fida'iyun* were eventually saved by joint Arab pressure that forced Jordan – despite its clear military superiority – on 27 September, to sign the Cairo agreement that recognized the *fida'iyun*'s right to remain in Jordan and to continue their struggle against Israel. In an additional agreement, on 13 October, Jordan was compelled to acknowledge that 'the Palestinian people alone, represented by the Palestinian revolution, are the ones who have the right to determine their future'.[6]

Despite these agreements, a new Jordanian government under Wasfi al-Tall, formed on 28 October 1970, continued to put pressure on the Palestinian organizations. The military eroded their power and gradually ousted them from all Jordanian cities and towns. Using the combined tactics of diplomacy and coercion, the government isolated them from the civilian population. In July 1971 Wasfi al-Tall managed to put an end to the *fida'i* military and political presence in Jordan. To achieve this end, Prime Minister Tall pursued a general policy of 'Jordanization'; i.e., an endeavour to radically diminish the political influence of the Palestinians in Jordan by sharply decreasing their number in government departments and public institutions. Simultaneously, he fostered and promoted the Transjordanian component of the population.[7] His achievements in the war against the *fida'iyun* and his anti-Palestinian reputation cost Wasfi al-Tall his life (he was assassinated in November 1971 in Cairo by Palestinian *fida'iyun*) and cost Jordan its position in the Arab world. It also created a temporary rift between the Hashemite establishment and the Palestinians on both banks of the Jordan river. The policy of all Jordanian governments after Tall was chiefly aimed at healing the wounds of 'Black September' and promoting national unity among the rival sectors of the Jordanian population.[8]

In March 1972 King Hussein offered his Palestinian subjects an olive branch. He issued a plan for the redefinition of East Bank–West Bank relations along federal lines, designed to appease the Palestinians and to turn over a new leaf in inter-communal relations. Hussein realized that growing Palestinian national awareness and the enhancement of the PLO's leadership role would make it impossible to turn the wheel back to pre-1967 Jordanian–Palestinian relations. The timing of the release of the federal scheme was not only the aftermath of the confrontation with the *fida'iyun*. It was also a response to Israel's announcement that it intended to hold municipal elections in the West Bank. Jordan feared that Israel either intended to annex the occupied territories or to establish a Palestinian entity there, entirely detached from Amman. The government was afraid that the West Bankers, in revenge for 'Black September', would vote for anti-Jordanian candidates.[9] Another incentive for promoting this plan was Hussein's isolation in the Arab world following the removal of the *fida'iyun* from Jordan as well as the endeavour to achieve an

Egyptian–Israeli interim agreement. Hussein was afraid to be left alone – without Egyptian and Arab backing – facing Israel on the one hand, and the Palestinians on the other.

According to the federal plan, the Hashemite Kingdom of Jordan was to be renamed the *United Arab Kingdom* consisting of two regions (sing. *qutur*), Palestine and Jordan, under the joint crown of King Hussein. Palestine was to include the West Bank and 'any other liberated Palestinian territories' whose inhabitants wished to join (i.e., the Gaza Strip). Jerusalem was to be its regional capital. The other district was to include the East Bank. Amman would be both the regional and the federal capital. Each region would have its own executive, legislative and judicial bodies and would enjoy local autonomy. Yet there would also be federal authorities in which the two regions were equally represented. The federal government would be responsible for foreign and defence matters, and would have one unified army.

On the face of it, this plan offered an improved model for Jordanian–Palestinian relations to substitute for the 1950 annexation (or 'incorporation', in Jordanian terminology) of the West Bank and the *fait accompli* it created. It implied that the concept of integration of Palestinians into the kingdom, which had been Jordan's guideline in the past, was giving way to the concept of separatism, of Palestinian autonomy in a specific territory which was to extend beyond the West Bank.[10]

Even though the scheme emphasized that its implementation should take place only <u>after</u> an Israeli withdrawal, West Bank Palestinians rejected it as a Jordanian plot to come to terms with Israel and to make territorial and other concessions in order to facilitate Jordan's return to the West bank. The plan was also criticized and rejected by all concerned parties: the PLO, the Arab states and Israel, but obviously not for the same reasons.

Simultaneously, the coming to power of Anwar al-Sadat in Egypt following Abd al-Nasser's death generated a new approach to the Arab–Israeli conflict. Sadat was markedly different from his predecessor, not committed to his vehement rhetoric and radical pan-Arabism. Sadat realized that if he was really determined to try to solve Egypt's economic and social problems he should, on one hand, adopt a Western, pro-American orientation and, on the other hand, cut Egypt off from the conflict with Israel which consumed enormous human and material resources. The latter could be achieved, Sadat believed, only after the retrieval of the Sinai peninsula, lost to Israel in the June 1967 war.

Sadat then perceived what King Hussein had realized more than three years before; i.e., he had to make political concessions if he wished to regain the lost territories. In February 1971, a few months after he came to power, Sadat proposed a partial Israeli withdrawal in the Sinai that would enable the clearing and reopening of the Suez canal (blocked since June 1967).

This withdrawal was to be linked with a timetable (to be arranged by UN envoy Gunnar Jarring) for a full Israeli retreat to the international border, according to UN resolution 242, which implied a peaceful, political solution and recognition of Israel. When Israel failed to meet his terms, Sadat resorted to the military option. In July 1972 he sent home 20,000 Soviet experts, advisors, instructors and other military personnel who had assisted, trained and maintained his army, in order to mend fences with the US. In April 1973 Egypt and Syria began planning what would eventually be known as the Yom Kippur war of October 1973.

On the face of it, the shift in Egypt's orientation should have led to closer relations with Jordan, as a pro-Western country willing to reach a political settlement with Israel. Yet Sadat did not at that time consider Jordan and its political views as serving Egypt's interests. Though he was focused on the retrieval of the Sinai peninsula, Sadat realized that as the leading Arab state, Egypt could not afford a separate peace with Israel that would ignore the Palestinians. He therefore supported the PLO's claim to being the legitimate representative of the Palestinians, as well as its right to control the West Bank if and when Israel withdrew. When Hussein issued his federal plan, Egypt severed diplomatic relations with Jordan, more to please the PLO than to punish Hussein.

By late 1973, Jordan's efforts to improve its relations with the Arab world bore fruit. In September 1973, both Egypt and Syria resumed diplomatic ties with Amman. In the same month, Hussein visited Cairo and met with Presidents Sadat and Assad. Though the two presidents probably did not reveal the details of their forthcoming offensive, planned for the following month, the King was aware of the large-scale military operation being planned against Israel.[11] In a last-minute bid to prevent the war, Hussein warned Golda Meir, Israel's Prime Minister, that the continuation of a political stalemate might precipitate a war and urged her to make a political gesture towards the Arabs in order to prevent it.[12] When the war broke out on 6 October, Jordan was not involved and thus took no part in the initial Egyptian and Syrian victories. Only towards the end of the hostilities, when the Arab position on the battlefield was less positive, was a Jordanian armoured division sent to the Syrian front to demonstrate solidarity with the Arab cause (not, however, before asking US Secretary of State Henry Kissinger to obtain Israeli assurance that Jordan's involvement in the fighting would not be used as a pretext for an Israeli attack on the East Bank). One Jordanian brigade engaged in heavy fighting and lost 27 men and 14 tanks.[13]

UN Security Council resolution 338 of 22 October called for an immediate cease fire. All concerned parties were also called on to promptly begin the implementation 'of all the components' of resolution 242 (of November 1967) and to begin negotiations 'under appropriate auspices' in order to establish a just and durable peace in the Middle East. Hostilities, however, continued until 24 October and therefore two additional resolutions were adopted. Resolution 339 of 23 October called on the belligerent forces to retreat to the positions they held when the cease-fire was declared. Resolution 340 of 25 October called, *inter alia*, for the dispatch of new UN emergency forces to the Middle East.

Resolution 338 not only gave new impetus to its six year-old predecessor 242, but also, for the first time, endorsed a process of direct negotiations, a mechanism on which Israel had always insisted. The new resolutions yielded the convening, in December 1973, of a two-day Middle Eastern peace conference in Geneva, by the US and the USSR, which, together with the UN, provided the 'appropriate auspices'. The conference was a mere ceremonial gathering attended by Jordan, Egypt and Israel and boycotted by Syria. Yet it provided an international umbrella under which US Secretary of State Kissinger carried out his 'shuttle diplomacy'. Intensive flights between Cairo, Jerusalem, Damascus and Amman yielded two interim agreements for partial withdrawal and disengagement of forces between Israel and Egypt (January 1974 and September 1975) and a similar agreement between Israel and Syria in May 1974. UN peace-keeping forces were deployed in the Sinai peninsula and in the Golan heights.

Jordan was also eager to conclude such an agreement, once the idea was put forward by Kissinger. It would, hopefully, bring a partial Israeli withdrawal from the West Bank and allow Jordan to regain a territorial foothold there. Hussein proposed that the IDF withdraw to 10 kilometres west of the Jordan river, while his own army would reciprocate with a similar retreat on the East Bank. On its part, Israel, interested in maintaining Jordan's influence in the West Bank, offered Jordan, in the spirit of the Allon plan, a corridor to Nablus and Ramallah via Jericho. Hussein declined and demanded a concrete Israeli withdrawal in the Jordan valley. When Yitzhak Rabin succeeded Golda Meir as a Prime Minister, the Israeli government still refused (due to domestic policy constraints) to consider a retreat along the Jordan Valley. Hussein (for his own reasons) would not settle for the 'Jericho corridor'. Despite the King's intensive meetings in 1974–75 with Israeli leaders, no breakthrough was achieved. The gap between Israel's and Jordan's perception of what disengagement of forces meant was too wide. The King perceived a partial Israeli withdrawal as an interim stage and a prelude to a complete withdrawal. Israel regarded a partial withdrawal as its ultimate concession and insisted on 'territorial compromise', an idea that King Hussein utterly refused to consider. To Jordan's chagrin, no agreement was reached. This failure frustrated Hussein and increased his disappointment with the Israeli leaders. He was particularly infuriated that Egypt and Syria had managed to obtain agreements that entailed Israeli withdrawals. The King could not avoid the impression that while Sadat and Assad were rewarded for their aggression with territorial concessions, he was punished for his moderation. Years later, Hussein still regarded this episode as a sort of missed opportunity for which Israel was to be blamed.[14]

Jordan's frustration was also exacerbated by the growing regional and international prestige of the PLO, its contender for Palestinian represen-tation and control of the West Bank (if and when Israel withdrew). Though the PLO took no part in the October war, the war generated processes that enhanced the organization's position with both 'radical' and 'moderate' Arab states seeking to benefit from publicly supporting the PLO.[15] Shortly after the Yom Kippur war, in November 1973, an Arab summit meeting in Algiers acknowledged – despite Jordan's reservations – the PLO as the sole representative of the Palestinian people. In July 1974, President Sadat and King Hussein issued a joint declaration stating that the PLO was the legitimate representative of the Palestinians, save for those Palestinians who lived in the Hashemite Kingdom of Jordan. As the declaration did not specify whether or not the West Bank was part of Jordan, Jordan could live with it, yet this declaration was severely criticized in the Arab world. One week later, Sadat maintained that the West Bank was only temporarily 'on deposit' with Jordan until its population decided on its own future.[16] Jordan rejected this interpretation while the PLO, on its part, refused to let Jordan represent the inhabitants of the West Bank, even temporarily. In September 1974, the foreign ministers of Egypt and Syria, Isma'il Fahmi and Abd al-Halim Khaddam, and the head of the PLO political section Faruq Qaddumi jointly declared that the PLO was the sole legitimate representative of the Palestinians.[17] This statement was unanimously reaf-firmed by the Arab summit meeting in Rabat in late October of the same year, which also acknowledged the PLO's right to form an 'independent national authority' in any 'liberated' Palestinian lands. A month later the PLO gained world-wide recognition when Arafat addressed the UN general assembly which subsequently endorsed the Rabat resolution. The PLO was allowed to send an observer delegation to UN Security Council meetings whenever issues relating to Palestine were discussed.

The way was thus paved not only for the PLO's international recogni-tion (which implied its right to take part in any future Middle Eastern peace process) but also for growing awareness of the Palestinian issue on the global agenda. This awareness was achieved, *inter alia*, due to the exten-sive Palestinian use of terrorism against Israeli, Jewish and international targets throughout the world. These developments increased the PLO's popularity in the West Bank and jeopardized Jordan's efforts to maintain its influence over the population there, in order to guarantee the re-impo-sition of its sovereignty in the event of Israeli withdrawal. Hussein even claimed that because Israel had rejected his proposals regarding disengagement in the Jordan Valley, it was responsible for the Rabat summit conference that denied his right to represent the Palestinians.

Jordan still maintained economic and administrative ties with the West Bank and still exercised a certain political influence there, with Israel's acquiescence and even tacit encouragement. The bridges over the Jordan river (the border between Jordan and the Israeli occupied West Bank) remained open, allowing relatively free movement of people and goods in both directions. West Bankers retained their Jordanian passports and deposited their money in Jordanian banks. Jordan maintained the dependence of the West Bankers via government agencies such as the Ministry of Occupied Territories Affairs and The Supreme Committee for West Bank Affairs. The Jordanian government paid the salaries and pensions of civil servants in the West Bank, subsidized the religious establishment and charitable associations, and issued various licenses and permits. Jordan's financial support of the West Bank, amounting to about $40m per annum, also explains the conspicuous victory of pro-Jordanian candidates in the 1972 municipal elections there.

Nevertheless, ever since al-Fatah and other *fida'i* organizations took over the PLO leadership in early 1969, the PLO vied with King Hussein and his government, as noted, not only over the representation of the Palestinian people, but also over the right to control the West Bank in case of an Israeli withdrawal. Both claimed to be the legitimate, lawful owner of the West Bank. The confrontation between Jordan and the Palestinian organizations in September 1970 and its aftermath took its toll on the regime's popularity in the West Bank. Between July 1971 and early 1972 Jordan suspended regular payments to individuals and institutes in the West Bank, following public criticism in the West Bank of its treatment of the Palestinians during the September 1970 showdown. However, general public opinion in the West Bank was still, in early 1972, inclined to side with Jordan due to the economic dependence on Amman. It took a few more years – during which the Rabat Arab summit resolutions were embraced and the PLO's international position consolidated – to shift West Bankers' comprehensive support from Hussein to Arafat. The most salient manifestation of this change was evident in the 1976 municipal elections in which, more than in 1972, pro-PLO candidates gained the upper hand.

King Hussein was infuriated by the 1974 Rabat resolution, particularly by the recognition of the PLO as the *sole* legitimate representative of the Palestinians, even though more than one million Palestinians lived in the East Bank and constituted an integral part of Jordan's civil society. Despite his reservations, the King had to accept the resolution mainly in order to stay in line with the general Arab consensus, and to publicly support the

Palestinians' right to self-determination. In practice, however, Hussein adopted a series of measures to prove that the PLO alone was incapable of recovering the West Bank and that any viable solution to the 'Palestine problem' should include Jordan.

Less than a month after the Rabat meeting, the 60–seat Jordanian Chamber of Deputies (half of whom were West Bank Palestinians) was dissolved. The Cabinet also resigned, to be replaced by one in which Palestinians were very poorly represented. Jordan also abolished the Ministry for Occupied Territories Affairs that was responsible for ties with the West Bank.[18] These and other moves, all reflecting 'Jordanization' of the kingdom, were, according to official spokespersons, in compliance with the Rabat resolution that deprived Hussein of any representation of the Palestinians and crowned the PLO as their sole and legitimate representative. The dissolution of the Chamber of Deputies, for example, was explained by noting that since the Palestinians in Jordan were already represented by the PLO, they could no longer be represented in the Chamber. As far as the West Bank was concerned, Jordan did not adhere to the Rabat resolution, albeit with the acquiescence of the PLO. The resolution required, if taken at face value, the abolition of the 1950 unification of the East and West Banks and the suspension of various payments and money transfers to civil servants and municipalities in the West Bank, etc. Nevertheless, it was clear that Israel would not let the PLO fill the vacuum created by Jordan's departure and the result would be that not only Jordan but also the PLO and the Arab world in general would lose the West Bank. Jordan's policy, therefore, was not to detach itself from the West Bank but to signal to the Arab world that the Rabat resolution was unrealistic and that the PLO alone could not carry the burden of being the 'sole legitimate representative' of the Palestinians. Only Jordan together with the PLO could fulfil this mission.

Hussein's point was taken. The Arab states gradually internalized the fact that, in practice, the Rabat resolution had strengthened Jordan by proving that there was no viable Arab alternative to its position in the West Bank. Arab conferences that convened in October 1976 in Cairo and Riyadh acknowledged Jordan's special relationship to the Palestinian question. Later that year, President Sadat called for the establishment of a Palestinian state in the West Bank that would be federally affiliated to Jordan. President Assad also acquiesced. Renewed legitimacy for Jordan's involvement in the Palestine problem, despite the Rabat resolution, was formally endorsed at the ninth Arab summit in Baghdad in November 1978. Among others, the meeting called for forming a joint PLO–Jordanian committee to enhance the 'stand-fastness' (*sumud*) of West Bankers and their opposition to the Camp David autonomy plan for the Palestinians (see below).

Jordan's formal acceptance of the Rabat resolution granted inter-Arab rehabilitation and paved the way for improved bilateral relations with most Arab states. In the mid-1970s relations with Syria dramatically improved. Jordan was the first Arab regime to recognize the 1976 Syrian invasion of Lebanon and practically the only one to defend this step. Talks on a Jordanian–Syrian political and military union were on their way, but in the second half of the 1970s, relations deteriorated as quickly as they had improved a few years before. Iraq soon superseded Syria as Jordan's closest friend and ally.

At the same time, the election of Jimmy Carter as President of the United States, in November 1976, also tipped the Jordanian–Palestinian scale in favour of the latter. Less than two months after his new administration took over, Carter publicly (at a town hall meeting in Clinton, Massachusetts) called for establishing a homeland for the Palestinians. In the course of the year, his aides outlined a plan for a political solution to the conflict based on the principle of Palestinian self-determination. Carter also wished to revitalize the Geneva conference of late 1973 and wasted no time in attempting to bring about a comprehensive peace settlement. Carter even sought the cooperation of the Soviet Union in pursuing such a policy, and on 1 October 1977, US Secretary of State Cyrus Vance and Soviet Foreign Minister Andrei Gromyko issued a joint statement in their capacity as co-chairs of the Geneva peace conference. They called for a comprehensive Israeli–Arab peace based on total Israeli withdrawal, on guaranteeing of the legitimate rights of the Palestinian people, on the termination of the state of war and the establishment of normal, peaceful relations (among the countries in the region) based on mutual recognition of the principles of sovereignty, territorial integrity and political independence. The two powers did not rule out demilitarized zones along Israel's borders to be maintained by UN troops or observers. The best framework to negotiate these issues was the Geneva peace conference. They hoped to reconvene it no later than at the end of 1977. The PLO was not mentioned as it had failed to meet President Carter's preconditions for obtaining US recognition.[19]

Seven weeks later, on 19 November 1977, a few months after the coming to power in Israel of the right-wing Likud under Menachem Begin, the Arab–Israeli conflict (and the entire region) experienced an unprecedented tremor that created a new reality in the Middle East. Anwar al-Sadat, President of the most important Arab state, made a dramatic visit to Israel and commenced direct and separate negotiations with the Jewish state. Those negotiations were designed to put an end to the bilateral conflict and, on the face of it at least, to solve the 'Palestine question'. The first goal was achieved in March 1979 with the signing of an Egyptian–Israeli peace treaty. The second one – failed.

Sadat had initiated the October 1973 war in order to break the Arab–Israeli deadlock. He wanted to regain the Sinai peninsula and to take Egypt out of the conflict that prevented him from paying more attention to his country's domestic problems. Yet Sadat also wanted to improve relations with the US, and to preserve Egypt's leading position in the Arab world. In order to achieve this last goal, he could not ignore the Palestinian issue. Sadat strove to take advantage of the outcome of the October 1973 war, which he construed as an Egyptian victory, as leverage to substitute a political option to solve the conflict for the military one. Indeed the war was followed by direct talks with the Israelis (meetings at kilometre 101), disengagement of forces and interim agreements. The highlight of this process was Sadat's impressive act of flying to Israel (not before Israeli and Egyptian emissaries had met, under the auspices of King Hassan of Morocco, to discuss a bilateral political settlement). Indeed, Sadat's visit broke a psychological barrier in Israeli thought and constituted a genuine breakthrough. It was followed by Israeli–Egyptian discussions that were designed to find practical solutions to the political and territorial bones of contention between Israel and the Arabs.

King Hussein probably hoped to benefit from the process that Sadat initiated. That is why he adopted a cautious and somewhat neutral attitude towards the controversial Egyptian move – a move that antagonized most of the Arab world. Hussein hoped that the process would lead to the aboli-tion of the Rabat summit resolution that crowned the PLO as the sole legitimate representative of the Palestinians. He maintained, in almost so many words, that if the resolution was retracted, he might follow in Sadat's footsteps. Moreover, US president Carter tried to persuade the King to join the negotiations.[20] Yet Hussein soon realized that the *raison d'être* for Sadat's initiative was the retrieval of the Sinai peninsula. The reference to West Bank autonomy was merely a fig leaf – lip service to alleviate Arab and Palestinian suspicions and not a move that would return the West Bank to Jordan. Nevertheless, Hussein tried to keep all options open and did not rule out future participation in the process.

The intensive bilateral Israeli–Egyptian discussions in the following months somewhat narrowed the gap between the parties' positions, but not enough to sign an agreement. For that, American mediation was neces-sary. In September 1978, US President Jimmy Carter summoned President Sadat and Prime Minister Begin to Camp David in Maryland for intensive negotiations. After thirteen days of marathon discussions in the secluded and isolated atmosphere, agreements were reached both on the Egyptian–Israeli conflict and the Palestinian track. In the spirit of UN resolution 242, the two parties undertook to reach a comprehensive, just and lasting peace in the Middle East via peace treaties. Israel pledged to withdraw from the entire Sinai peninsula within three years in return for an Egyptian commitment to sign a peace treaty with Israel and to normalize their future bilateral relations. Both sides recognized the legitimate rights of the Palestinian people and they agreed on a procedure that would grant them 'full autonomy'. Jordan and the Palestinians in the West Bank and Gaza (with no reference whatsoever to the PLO) were also to take part in the negotiations to decide on the question of self-rule for the Palestinians. The agreement, when reached, would be followed by a five-year transitional period and after three years, negotiations on the final status of the West Bank and the Gaza strip would be resumed.

King Hussein was eager to participate in the Camp David talks. Sadat was reluctant, fearing that no agreement could be reached with the King present, due to expected conflicting interests between Jordan and the Palestinians. Sadat, as the Camp David resolutions showed, supported the latter. When the resolutions were made public, Hussein viewed them as a personal insult and a severe blow to his aspirations for the reinstatement of Jordanian sovereignty over the West Bank.

After the conclusion of the Camp David accords, Egypt and Israel gave priority to their bilateral affairs and Palestinian autonomy became a secondary issue. Only after the signing of the peace treaty on 26 March 1979, did the autonomy talks return to the limelight. The renewed discussions were futile. Menachem Begin hoped, in the spirit of the English version of the UN resolution 242 ('withdrawal from territories occupied in June 1967', and not 'from *the* territories'), that his consent to withdraw from all of the Sinai (representing almost 90 per cent of the territories occupied in 1967), would exempt him from the need to make further concessions in the West Bank. Egypt was reluctant to confront Israel over this issue before the latter had completed its withdrawal from the Sinai (due to occur, according to the peace treaty, in April 1982). King Hussein also had no incentive to push forward autonomy talks that would bring about Palestinian (e.g., PLO) control over the West Bank. Even the PLO and the other Arab states were not enthusiastic about the autonomy discussions, as they were a product of the separate agreement that Egypt signed with Israel, an act that reaped all-out Arab condemnation. Israel's foot-dragging regarding the autonomy talks did not, therefore, raise much criticism, and in May 1980 the talks were permanently suspended.

Arab opposition to Sadat's unilateral step was immediate. A handful of Arab-league member states (Syria, Libya, Algeria, and South Yemen) attended an emergency summit meeting in December 1977 at which they decided to freeze diplomatic relations with Egypt and formed, together with Iraq and the PLO, the 'rejection front'. This opposition was institutionalized at two conferences held in Baghdad in November 1978 and in March 1979 (after the Camp David accords and after the Israeli–Egyptian peace treaty, respectively). All Arab states (with the exception of Oman) severed diplomatic relations with Egypt. Egypt's membership in the Arab League, as well as all Arab financial or material support, were suspended. Jordan too joined the front after the conclusion of the Egypt–Israel peace treaty of March 1979.

Regional preoccupation with the bilateral Israeli–Egyptian agreements drove Jordan to seek an alternative to this process for the implementation of resolution 242. King Hussein was well aware of the fact that the Arabs could not simply reject the Camp David accords without offering an alternative. Hence the King and his Prime Minister called for 'a new approach' in order to obtain a peaceful settlement. They proposed to return the Middle East question either to the Security Council or to resume the short-lived Middle East peace conference of December 1973 with the participation of all interested Arab parties, the US, the USSR, and representatives of the European Community. This forum was to explore ways to carry out UN resolutions, particularly 242 and 338. In his quest for such an alternative, Hussein took pains to harness the European Economic Community (EEC) to the mission, urging its member-states to launch an initiative to amend resolution 242.[21] Hussein was afraid that once Israel had completed its withdrawal from the Sinai peninsula, the Camp David process would be terminated, hence he believed that a new political initiative was imperative.

The fact that both Jordan and the PLO considered themselves the major victims of Sadat's initiative, created common interests that paved the way for their slow and cautious rapprochement. Bilateral connections were soon resumed, only to deteriorate once again in the early 1980s. The PLO suspected that Jordan intended to be more actively involved in the West Bank. Jordan, on its part, was angered by PLO attempts to resume violent anti-Israeli activity from its territory. Though Jordan officially adhered to the Rabat resolution and recognized the PLO as the Palestinians' sole legitimate representative, it took advantage of the *de facto* Arab recognition of its own involvement in the quest for a solution to the Palestine question. Jordan therefore did not support the notion of an independent Palestinian state, underscored its own rights and interests in the West Bank, and insisted that the West Bank was still an integral part of Jordan. The government revived Hussein's federal plan of 1972 and introduced it as its favoured solution, since it would allow Jordan a foothold in the West Bank. Jordan's official position supported the idea of a referendum to be held after Israel's withdrawal in which the inhabitants of the occupied territories would decide their own future.

Jordan became more deeply involved in West Bank affairs, simultaneous to the dwindling momentum of the Camp David process and of the autonomy talks. The government continued to pay the civil servants' salaries there and financed various development projects. The new

Jordanian government of August 1980 included, once again, a Minister for Occupied Territories Affairs, a position that had been abolished soon after the Rabat summit.

After being ousted from Jordan in 1971, most PLO personnel moved to Lebanon, where the organization managed to rebuild its military infrastructure. In 1980 they numbered over 20,000 armed men, concentrated in Beirut, in refugee camps and along the border with Israel. Their nationwide deployment and interference in Lebanon's internal affairs resembled their earlier sojourn in Jordan. Yet, unlike the Jordanian case, the Lebanese government failed to check their consolidation in the southern part of the country or to prevent their subversive activity against Israel. The Syrian invasion of Lebanon in 1976 introduced a new dimension into Lebanese–Palestinian relations and also influenced the latter's activities against Israel. In early 1978, following a Palestinian terrorist attack on an Israeli bus along the costal road north of Tel Aviv (designated to foil the nascent Israeli–Egyptian peace process), Israel invaded south Lebanon. This invasion (operation 'Litani') aimed at liquidating the Palestinian military presence along its northern border. Under international pressure, Israel withdrew, not before establishing a 'security zone' controlled by the South Lebanon Army, an Israeli-backed local militia. Another major confrontation between the Palestinian *fida'iyun* and the IDF in 1981 was followed by UN and US mediation that resulted in an unwritten cease-fire agreement between Israel and the PLO. The former undertook not to attack Palestinian targets in Lebanon and the latter undertook not to shoot across Israel's border. This agreement was honoured for almost a year and also strengthened the PLO's international recognition, as party to an agreement with Israel.

In June 1982 Israel invaded Lebanon (operation 'Peace for the Galilee') after the Israeli ambassador in London was critically wounded by Palestinian gunmen. Israeli forces took over south Lebanon, fighting PLO and Syrian forces. They reach Beirut and besieged its western neighbourhoods where Palestinian headquarters and thousands of *fida'iyun* as well as many Syrian soldiers resided. Under American pressure, in late August Israel allowed the retreat of the Syrians from the Lebanese capital and the evacuation of PLO personnel. About 8,000 Palestinians left Lebanon; half went to Syria and the rest to Tunisia (where the organization's new HQ was established), Algeria, Iraq, Sudan and Jordan. An additional 2,000 Palestinians remained in Lebanon, in Tripoli and in the Baqa' valley, under full Syrian control. The PLO was, once again, unable to function as a unified political unit. Its dependence on Arab host countries increased and its constant demand for an 'independent Palestinian entity' was further from being met than ever before.

Jordan turned out to be one of the major beneficiaries of the outcome of the war in Lebanon and the removal of the PLO from Beirut. The (political) balance of power between the two underwent a complete change and the dependence of the Palestinians on Jordan considerably increased. Jordan allowed the return of only a few hundred Palestine Liberation Army (PLA) fighters who were usually stationed there but had been dispatched to Lebanon to fight the Israelis. Otherwise, only Palestinians with Jordanian passports were allowed to enter, providing they arrived as ordinary civilians on an individual basis (i.e., with no uniforms or weapons, and not as part of an organized Palestinian group).

Despite these advantages, Jordan was convinced that operation 'Peace for the Galilee', together with the intensive building of settlements in the West Bank, was part of an Israeli plot to transfer the Palestinian refugees from Lebanon to Jordan on the one hand, and to encourage, if not to force, migration of Palestinians from the West Bank to the East Bank, on the other. This twofold action, the Jordanians believed, was designed to turn Jordan into a substitute homeland (*al-watan al-badil*) for the Palestinians, i.e., a Palestinian state, in order to facilitate Israel's eventual annexation of the West Bank. These Jordanian apprehensions were nourished by occasional statements by some right-wing Israeli politicians who asserted, as of the late 1970s, that 'Jordan is Palestine' and that the Palestinian aspiration for statehood should be exercised – if at all – in the East Bank, at the expense of the Hashemite throne and the indigenous Jordanian population. Most conspicuous among these were Yitzhak Shamir and Ariel Sharon, Foreign and Defence Ministers, respectively, in Begin's second government of 1981. Such statements from top-level officials were taken at face value in Jordan. They were construed not as rhetoric but as a practical political program and thus as a real threat to the regime.[22] Hence, King Hussein endeavoured to persuade the US administration that the new reality created following the war in Lebanon constituted fertile soil for promoting plans and ideas for a comprehensive solution of the Arab–Israeli conflict.

Either because of Jordan's appeal, or from other considerations, in September 1982, following the evacuation of the PLO from Beirut, US President Ronald Reagan issued his Middle Eastern peace plan, which was somewhat advantageous to Jordan. The Reagan plan included elements from UN resolution 242, as well as from the Camp David accords. It called for Arab recognition of Israel and of its right to exist within secure and defensible boundaries to be negotiated by the parties. In return, Israel would withdraw from the territories occupied in 1967, freeze the construction of settlements and recognize the Palestinians' legitimate rights. The plan also proposed a five-year transitional period. Elections in a self-ruled Palestinian entity would be held at the beginning of that period and during that period the Palestinian population of the West Bank and the Gaza Strip would enjoy full autonomy. The plan called for greater involvement of Jordan and the Palestinians in the peace process, yet failed to mention the PLO as the Palestinian representative. It also opposed an independent Palestinian state and settled for a self-ruled 'entity' in the West Bank with affinity to Jordan.

The Reagan plan was welcomed in Jordan, as it improved Jordan's position *vis-à-vis* the PLO. King Hussein openly commended and praised it. He regarded the plan as an incentive to reintroduce his own 1972 federal scheme. The Arab states were less enthusiastic; they preferred to embrace the resolutions adopted by the summit meeting held in Fez, Morocco, a week later. The Fez resolutions re-endorsed the Arab demands for a complete Israeli withdrawal and for a PLO-led independent Palestinian state with Jerusalem as its capital. The resolutions did not mention recognition of Israel, save for a vague and indirect reference that could be construed either way: 'The UN Security Council,' the resolutions stated, 'would guarantee the peace that would be reached among all the states in this region, including the independent Palestinian state.'

The Arab *quid pro quo* proposed by the Fez resolutions was smaller and less obligatory than even the problematic (from Israel's point of view) plan announced by Saudi Crown Prince Fahd in August 1981, which undertook, in return for the same demands as those of the Fez resolutions, to recognize the right of all the states in the Middle East to live in peace.

Despite the change in the positions of Jordan and the PLO due to the war in Lebanon, the mounting dependence of the PLO on Jordan was not entirely unilateral. The war enhanced the symbiotic nature of the ties between the two parties. Jordan needed the PLO's legitimacy in order to enter into political negotiations that would discuss, *inter alia*, the Palestinians' future and rights. On its part, the PLO needed the auspices and good offices of Jordan in order not to be left out of the emerging peace process. Even though the weakness of the PLO was very tempting, Jordan was aware that it could not replace the PLO as the sole legitimate representative of the Palestinians. Not only was the organization recognized as such by the inter-Arab and international systems, it was also in the interest of too many factors within and outside of the Arab world that the current state of affairs remain intact. Hence Jordan was ready to settle for partnership with the PLO in the forthcoming discussions on the Palestinians' future. Even the position of a partner would be considered an upgrade, after the 1974 Rabat resolution had denied Jordan any standing whatsoever on the Palestine question.

Jordan was indeed committed, officially and publicly, to the collective Arab demand for 'a PLO-led independent Palestinian state within the Palestinian territories'. Yet, practically speaking, it preferred a less binding and more flexible interpretation of the 'Palestinians' right to self determination', in the spirit of King Hussein's 1972 federal scheme. Jordan also sought a referendum, to be held in both Banks (after Israel's retreat) in which the population would decide whether to accept or reject Jordan's ideas regarding future relations between the two peoples.

In October 1982 Yassir Arafat arrived in Jordan at King Hussein's invitation. Bilateral negotiations commenced to discuss the parties' participation in the envisaged political process. The dialogue which continued until April 1983, also included the idea of forming a joint Jordanian–Palestinian delegation to take part in peace talks with Israel, in the spirit of the Reagan plan. The question of PLO participation in such a delegation constituted a delicate issue and deserved special attention, since neither the US nor Israel recognized the organization at that point and refused to consider it a partner for negotiations.

Arafat agreed to the concept of a special relationship between Jordan and a future independent Palestinian state in the West Bank, yet he stipulated that the bilateral ties be confederal and not federal.[23] The 16th Palestinian National Council (PNC) that convened in Algiers in February 1983 endorsed these principles but rejected the Reagan plan since it required recognition of Israel. Arafat avoided committing himself, even though the PNC enabled him to do so and despite Jordan's having undertaken to enter negotiations with Israel only under conditions acceptable to him. Jordan regarded the time factor as critical, fearing that without a political arrangement the whole region might deteriorate into major instability and that extremist elements could gain the upper hand. King Hussein was also concerned about the intensive construction of Israeli settlements in the occupied territories and was afraid of an irreversible change of the territorial reality and the demographic balance.

Only after Jordan threatened to enter peace talks (via a Jordanian-crafted joint Jordanian–Palestinian delegation) without PLO participation, did Arafat acquiesce. In early April the chairman of the PLO and the King of Jordan issued a draft of a joint Declaration of Intents. It endorsed the future confederal tie and expressed agreement in principle to join in negotiations for a political settlement (providing, as the PLO insisted, that this would result in a complete Israeli withdrawal and recognition of the Palestinians' legitimate rights). Arafat, however, refused to sign the document, even after Hussein agreed to amend the text in the spirit of his demands. Arafat claimed that the PLO governing bodies should first ratify the agreement. At the end of the day, they too rejected the Reagan plan. Their precondition, that the PLO take part in the negotiations, was considered unacceptable by Hussein. Jordan officially announced the failure of the talks but made it clear that it intended neither to enter into negotiations separately, nor to serve as a substitute for the Palestinians. Even under these circumstances, both parties realized that it was in their interest to continue their bilateral connections. Despite the heightened tension, they decided to keep channels of communications open and to continue their dialogue.

King Hussein did not cease his efforts to keep the peace process alive. His evaluation that time did not work to Jordan's benefit led him to seek creative ideas in order to break the stalemate, by bringing the PLO to recognize Israel's right to exist and by bringing Israel to recognize the Palestinians' territorial and humanitarian rights. In order to bypass Palestinian (and Arab) opposition to the Camp David accords and to the Reagan plan, the King proposed a framework for an international conference (not mentioned in the Reagan plan) with the US and the USSR as co-chairs and with the participation of the permanent members of the UN Security Council and of all the concerned Middle Eastern parties, including the PLO. Under this framework, direct talks between Israeli and Arab representatives (including a Palestinian–Jordanian delegation) would take place. The concept of an international 'umbrella' provided a new formula designed to enable all the parties to participate, despite their adherence to their traditional views. Israel's demand for direct negotiations with no mediation by a third party could be met through direct talks between the delegations. Its reluctance to recognize the PLO did not exclude the possibility of talks with a joint Jordanian–Palestinian body. Such a body was a convenient solution for the PLO as well, as the organization was not required to recognize Israel or to negotiate directly with its representatives. In the first stage of its efforts, Jordan endeavoured to attain PLO recognition of UN resolution 242. Acceptance of this resolution and its implied recognition of Israel was, as noted, the minimal US pre-condition for recognizing the PLO and allowing its participation in political negotiations.

In the course of 1983, PLO dependence on Jordan increased, particularly in light of deteriorating relations between Syrian president Hafiz al-Assad and Yassir Arafat. The latter was declared *persona non grata* in Damascus due to his reserved willingness to join the political process. Simultaneously, the Syrians supported and generously assisted al-Fatah rebels in northern Lebanon who violently challenged Arafat's authority. In addition, in December, Arafat's loyal forces were expelled from Tripoli causing him to become as weak as he had been in September 1982 when he was forced to evacuate Beirut. Having lost his prestige and territorial foothold in all Arab countries bordering on Israel, Jordan remained the only outlet he could use to save himself and his organization. He hoped to resume political coordination with the Hashemite regime as leverage for consolidating his influence in the West Bank. Jordan, on its part, supported Arafat against Syrian-backed al-Fatah rebels and continued to regard him as a partner in representing the Palestinians.

In January 1984 King Hussein summoned the Jordanian Chamber of Deputies (that had been suspended for a decade) to a special meeting to amend the article in the constitution that prohibited holding general elections without the participation of the West Bank constituency. The amended article permitted the *nomination* of Palestinians to the Chamber, to replace, for example, deceased deputies. This measure served *inter alia* as indirect pressure on Arafat to meet Jordan half way. Indeed, Arafat arrived in Amman in February to resume the dialogue that had been suspended in April 1983, and sought renewed coordination with the Jordanian authorities. Nevertheless, this visit, like several others that followed, yielded no agreement.

In November 1984 Jordan hosted the PNC's 17th meeting.[24] As another token of good will, Jordan allowed the PLO to increase its political presence in Amman, hoping that these gestures would cause Arafat to become more flexible regarding a political solution to the regional conflict. The maximal concession that the PLO was ready to make was to accept the principle of 'peace for territories' (which constituted one of the founding stones of UN resolution 242). Jordan took pains to market this 'achievement' as if the PLO had accepted the resolution, but apparently with little success. Jordanian pressure, however, took its toll and the PLO was eventually willing to show some flexibility in other spheres, not less important to Jordan. On 11 February 1985 the PLO and the Jordanian government signed an agreement in which they undertook to 'march together' towards a peaceful and just settlement of the 'Middle Eastern problem' and to put an end to the Israeli occupation of Arab lands. The agreement was to be based on the following principles:

1. Peace, in return for (occupied) territories, as implied by UN resolutions, including Security Council resolutions.
2. Recognition of the Palestinian's right to self-determination that should be exercised within a confederal Arab union between the two states, Jordan and Palestine.
3. A solution to the problem of the Palestinian refugees according to UN resolutions.
4. A solution to all the aspects of the Palestine question.
5. Peace negotiations to be conducted within the framework of an international conference with the participation of the five permanent members of the UN Security Council and the other parties to the conflict, including the PLO, the sole legitimate representative of the Palestinian people, as a part of a joint [Jordanian–Palestinian] delegation.

The February agreement was well received by many West Bankers who viewed with favour the cooperation between the two contesting bodies over the representation of the Palestinians. It was also welcomed by the Arab summit conference, convened in Casablanca in August. Syria, however categorically rejected the agreement, and, within the PLO's domestic sphere, the PFLP and the PDFLP failed to support it. Hussein tried to convince Israel to enter negotiations in the spirit of the February agreement. He took advantage of the fact that the political tie in the Israeli elections in 1984 had yielded a national coalition government (after two consecutive right-wing Likud governments). Its Prime Minister (in rotation) for the first two years was Shimon Peres of the Labour party. Hussein and Peres tried hard, through several meetings in 1985, to bridge the gap between the positions of Israel and the PLO, and to find a formula to make negotiations between Israel and a joint Jordanian–Palestinian delegation viable.[25] Peres was ready to acquiesce to the concept of an international conference as a framework for direct negotiations, yet most of his cabinet opposed the idea. In April 1987 Peres[26] met in London with King Hussein and they formulated a detailed draft of an agenda for an international conference. The Israeli cabinet rejected 'the London Agreement' as the government suspected the involvement of the UN and the Soviet Union, and feared that the conference would turn into an instrument to exert collective political pressure on Israel.

Though the Hussein–Arafat agreement can be construed in different ways, the absence of any *specific* reference to UN resolution 242 was conspicuous and salient; i.e., the US precondition for admitting the PLO into the peace process had not been met. The PLO, as noted, vehemently and persistently opposed direct negotiations as well as recognition of Israel's right to exist. The organization was willing to accept resolution 242 in return for US recognition of the Palestinians' right to self-determination in a state of their own within a Jordanian–Palestinian confederation, but only if the organization's seat at the planned international conference was ensured.[27]

King Hussein therefore faced the double challenge of bridging the gap between Israel and the PLO and also between the PLO and the US. He shared the American view that only unequivocal and unreserved PLO recognition of resolution 242 would yield a breakthrough in the peace process. Hussein was disappointed in Arafat's recalcitrance and his unwillingness (or inability) to make crucial decisions. The King considered Arafat's attitude as ingratitude, after he had taken pains to make the US change its mind regarding the PLO and regarding the idea of an international conference. Hussein felt that Arafat did not sufficiently appreciate this achievement. Early in 1986 Hussein made one last attempt to persuade the PLO to accept resolution 242 but to no avail. After a year of intensive deliberations, Arafat remained adamant. On 19 February 1986 King

Hussein gave in and publicly announced the suspension of political coordination with the PLO. He expressed his deep disappointment with Arafat's attitude and put the blame on him – not on the US – for the failure of the efforts to admit the PLO into the political process. Despite Hussein's attempt to create the impression that he had not left a single stone unturned in his effort to persuade the PLO to embrace the political option, it seems that Jordan did not actually go out of its way in order to obtain US recognition of the Palestinians' right to self-determination and to an independent state. Jordan preferred to discuss these issues with the PLO, within the future confederal state, *after* an Israeli withdrawal, which was its immediate and prime target.

The suspension of coordination put Jordan–PLO relations back by ten years and they were once again characterized by mutual suspicion, accusations and animosity. The PLO liaison office in Jordan was closed down in April 1986 and soon all al-Fatah offices in the country met a similar fate. Many of the organization's officials and military personnel were driven out and joint political meetings became scarce.

Following Hussein's announcement of 19 February, he also reiterated that his government would neither negotiate separately with Israel nor replace the PLO in any political process. Jordan, however, was willing to include representatives from the West Bank in the joint Jordanian–Palestinian delegation scheduled for the expected international peace conference. As long as the PLO persisted in rejecting UN resolution 242, Hussein believed, the Palestinians in the occupied territories should be given an opportunity to speak their own minds. Hence the developments in Jordan's relations with the PLO gave new impetus to the Jordanian ambition to be involved in the decision-making over the future of the West Bank. The first significant result was revitalization of the 1972 federal plan and simultaneous reiteration of Jordan's commitment to the Palestinians' right to self-determination, and the assurance that future ties between the two banks would be decided in a referendum, after Israel's withdrawal, by the two communities. Renewed Jordanian interest in the occupied territories was also highlighted in the announcement of a five-year economic plan (1986–90), designed to invest $1.3 billion in the territories, which included the Gaza Strip as well.[28]

Despite Jordan's considerable investment of material resources and political energy in the West Bank, the support of its population for the PLO did not markedly decline. Even the few achievements that Jordan managed to score there faded away with the outbreak of the *intifada* in late 1987. Jordan, like Israel and even the PLO, was taken by surprise when demonstrations and disturbances erupted in the Gaza Strip and the West Bank. King Hussein was the first national leader to read the map correctly and to grasp the real meaning of the emerging *intifada*: this was a Palestinian national uprising that served no Jordanian purposes. As a matter of fact it proved to Hussein that his grip in the West Bank was practically non-existent.[29] Moreover, it increased the danger of tension and unrest permeating the East Bank. Hussein reached the conclusion that the political stability of his realm required Jordan's retreat from its forty-year claim to the West Bank.

According to Hussein's close adviser, a Jordanian of Palestinian origin, Adnan Abu Odeh (who, by his own testimony, wrote the King's disengagement speech of late July 1988), the King had considered announcing that Jordan would give up claims to the West Bank as early as March 1988. He was, nevertheless, afraid that such a move might damage Jordan's regional position, impede Jordanian–Palestinian relations in the East Bank and could be construed by Israel as a green light to annex the West Bank.[30] Hussein therefore preferred to wait and to explore other possibilities that would 'keep Jordan in the picture' before making his final decision.

In January 1988 US Secretary of State George Shultz tried to rekindle the idea of an international conference in order to save the Middle Eastern political process from the continuing impasse. His plan was based on the rejected April 1987 'London Agreement' between King Hussein and Shimon Peres,[31] which the King still supported. Jordan's response to the Shultz initiative hinted at the King's crystallizing intentions: Jordan would take part in an international conference in order to negotiate *Jordanian* (i.e., East Bank), not Palestinian, territories. The Jordanians even referred to specific areas in Naharayim and the Dead Sea region which constituted bones of contention with Israel.[32]

Hussein's final bid to obtain recognition of his country's special status regarding the Palestine question took place at the Arab summit conference in Algiers in June 1988. The King tried to bring about a new resolution that would revise the Rabat one, but to no avail. The participants reaffirmed the Palestinians' right to an independent state under PLO leadership, with no reference whatsoever to Jordan. On 28 July 1988 Jordan abolished its pretentious five-year plan for the development of the West Bank and Gaza. On the 30th of July the Jordanian Chamber of Deputies was dissolved and the next day the King announced that Jordan was severing its legal and administrative ties with the West Bank. Henceforward Jordan regarded the PLO as the only the address for any issue concerning the occupied territories, as well as its future sovereign, if and when Israel withdrew. As of early August, frequent new regulations and decrees were issued to cope with problems created by the disengagement decision. Soon the new reality became a *fait accompli*.

In the thirty-odd months that elapsed after the suspension of political coordination with the PLO (February 1986), Jordan's West Bank policy underwent a radical change. Shortly after the suspension, Jordan initiated an unprecedented campaign to deepen and intensify its influence over the Israel-occupied Arab territories west of the Jordan river. Two and a half years later, Jordan deserted its policy of the previous forty years. Though the West Bank was regarded as an integral part of Jordan and its rule there was a part of the Hashemite legitimacy, it seems that Jordan had no choice. The prospect of regaining even a toehold in the West Bank, if Israel withdrew, was practically nil. Giving up the historical claim to the West Bank as well as any responsibility for it was a *de jure* endorsement of a *de facto* reality and the only way to preserve the stability of (East Bank) Jordan and the integrity of its delicate socio-demographic balance.

Part II

Jordanian Territorial and Conceptual Demands of Israel

Chapters 5, 6 and 7

Territorial Demands

Chapters 8 and 9

Conceptual Demands

INTRODUCTION
TO PART II

Throughout the period surveyed, Jordan basically introduced two ultimate sets of demands of Israel. First, those that in addition to political decisions, required practical and concrete measures and entailed actual field-activity. These were, by and large, the territorial demands. The most salient among them was total withdrawal to the pre-June 1967 lines, including Arab East Jerusalem (that had been formally annexed by Israel shortly after the June 1967 war). This was an explicit and consistent demand, presented throughout the entire period with slight changes and with differences only in emphasis, dictated by political developments.[1] Demands to put an end to Israeli settlement, and for measures to contain the 'Judaisation' of the West Bank as well as ending Israel's control of the water resources there, can also be included in this category.

The second set was conceptual. These demands, too, necessitated political decisions, yet they were of a more principled and declarative nature. The primary demand was a solution to various aspects of the Palestine problem. Given its somewhat amorphous nature as well as its comprehensive and declarative title, this demand was complex and had many ramifications. As will be shown, Israel was not asked to negotiate *all* aspects of this problem. Some of them required decision-making or actions on the part of the Palestinians themselves, of Jordan, or of other Arab states. What Israel was *actually* asked to agree to in this context was the repatriation of the 1948 and 1967 refugees to Israel and to the West Bank, respectively; recognition of the Palestinians' legitimate rights, including their right to self-determination; recognition of the PLO as the sole legitimate representative of the Palestinians; and, eventually, to negotiate a political settlement with this organization or, alternately, to acquiesce to its participation in Arab–Israeli peace negotiations. Clearly Jordan was not consistent regarding these demands throughout the entire period. Emphasis on each of them derived from the changing course of political developments. Israel, for example, was not asked to recognize the PLO as long as Jordan was reluctant to do so. This could occur either simultaneously with the Israeli withdrawal or even afterwards. The same also applied to some less frequently-made demands of Israel, such as recognition of Jordan's central role in the Middle East conflict, or the 'de-Zionisation' of Israel. Hence, this set of demands also included some that, rather than being actual demands, indicated Jordan's attitude towards Israel's political ideology and political conduct and its wishful thinking regarding their modification.

On the face of it, the demand for total withdrawal, if met, would make Jordan's other 'territorial demands' irrelevant. Such a withdrawal *ipso facto* would eliminate the problems of the Jewish settlements, of land confiscation and of the 'Judaisation' of Jerusalem and the West Bank. Nevertheless, these demands were made on their own merits. Israel was required to comply with them *before* or *until* it began to withdraw. Moreover, they reflected the apprehension that Israel had no intention of giving up the occupied territories (at least not in full and certainly not in the near future). In the interim, the settlements and land confiscation might reach the point of no return and create an irreversible situation of Judaisation of the West Bank, that could lead to *de facto* annexation. Hence Jordan's territorial demands were designed to freeze the situation and the status quo, until some kind of breakthrough or solution was eventually reached, in order to cut Jordan's political and territorial losses to the minimum. Beyond these considerations, the demands were also a kind of protest against Israel's injustice and wrongdoings *per se*, irrespective of the future of the West Bank and the Palestinians.

5 WITHDRAWAL FROM THE WEST BANK, EAST JERUSALEM AND THE GAZA STRIP

TERRITORIAL DEMANDS

The demand for an Israeli withdrawal from *all* Arab territories occupied in the June war was the most common and frequent demand. Though Jordan paid lip service to the other Arab states that had lost territory to Israel, and called for a retreat from the Sinai peninsula and the Golan Heights as well, it naturally emphasized the importance of withdrawal from the West Bank and East Jerusalem, as well as from the Gaza Strip. Jordan was seriously concerned about the voices in Israel that advocated regarding these territories differently from those taken from Syria and Egypt.

The West Bank was an integral part of the biblical and historical land of Israel (Judea and Samaria), as well as of mandatory Palestine, to which Israel considered itself the lawful successor. Moreover, some Israelis challenged Jordan's right to regain control there on the pretext that it had used aggressive force against Palestine in May 1948 to secure its presence there and that the ensuing Jordanian union with the West Bank in April 1950 was therefore invalid.[2] Afraid that such arguments would serve as an excuse for Israel to continue its control over these areas, Jordanian officials, first and foremost Crown Prince Hassan, took pains to show the legal and political differences between Israel's occupation of the West Bank in 1967 and the Jordanian occupation in 1948. Israel (in 1967) was 'no more than a belligerent occupant. That was certainly not the case between Jordan and the West Bank from 1950 to 1967'.[3] Israel, went the Jordanian argument, maintained no territorial or sovereign rights over these areas and thus it was required to promptly retreat to the pre-June 1967 borders.

This demand was reiterated throughout the entire period surveyed in almost every public statement of a political nature – and occasionally even in non-political statements – made by either the King, the Crown Prince, the Prime Minister or cabinet ministers. It became almost a ritual, resembling Cato the Elder's *Ceterum censeo Carthaginem esse delendam*.[4] As already indicated, there were other demands that emanated from or were connected to the withdrawal request and to the fact that Israel was reluctant to comply. If Israel withdrew, the insistence on putting an end to the settlements in the occupied territories, for example, would become obsolete and irrelevant. Even demands for a solution of the refugee problem or of the Palestinian problem in general would assume a different meaning in the event of an Israeli withdrawal, than in a situation when Israel still controlled the territories.

This basic demand was introduced in the same manner to all kinds of audiences: Jordanian, Palestinian, Arab, Muslim or Western. It carried the same message whether in a public speech, a media interview, a magazine article or a meeting with policy-makers abroad. It was even delivered, with equal passion, to Israeli interlocutors at secret meetings.[5] Unlike other demands, the demand for total withdrawal was constant and was for the most part unaffected by developments in the Arab–Israeli conflict since 1967. Other questions, such as what would happen *after* the withdrawal and who would then control the territories, were definitely influenced by on-going events.

It is possible, therefore, to trace certain characteristics and several different points of emphasis in the introduction of this demand, caused by the impact of the course of events or in view of contemporary political realities. These specific emphases reflected either Jordan's reaction to, or adaptation to, the relevant developments.

1. Jordanian spokespersons – in the first years after the war – construed their own demand for total withdrawal as a return to the *status quo*, namely, that the IDF should retreat to the pre-June 1967 lines on all three fronts. Egypt would regain the Sinai peninsula and the Gaza Strip; Syria would get the Golan Heights; and Jordan would return to the West Bank and East Jerusalem. This last point was particularly emphasized, both since Israel regarded them differently than the Sinai and the Golan, and probably because Jordan suspected that its claim to being the rightful owner of the West Bank might be questioned. Pains were therefore taken to justify this claim through a variety of ideological and practical arguments, Jordanian as well as Arab.

As early as 19 June 1967, Hussein told a local audience that 'The West

Bank is an important part of Jordan. It is part of our soil and country and part of the Arab homeland. The question is not whether Jordan can live without the West Bank but what is right. As far as we are concerned, the two banks of the Jordan form one homeland and will continue to do so.' On another occasion, the King pointed out that 'the life of one million *Jordanians* in the West Bank are controlled by Israel'.[6] The official attitude continued to refer to the West Bank as a territory upon which Jordan sovereignty should be reinstated, even after the reawakening of Palestinian nationalism and the PLO's demands to take over the West Bank if and when Israel withdrew. Jordan's position, as will be shown, was that first of all Israel had to withdraw and the West Bank be handed back to Jordan. Only then could its Palestinian inhabitants decide their own future, whether they wished an independent state in the West Bank, a federation with Jordan or to resort to pre-1967 ties.

Nevertheless, whenever Jordanian spokespersons demanded Israel's withdrawal, they referred to 'occupied Arab lands' or 'Arab lands occupied in the June war'.[7] Though they demanded the 'return of the occupied Arab lands in Jordan, Egypt and Syria', or reminded their audiences that Israel 'still occupies the lands of three independent states' and that 'the Jordanian people insists on the liberation of its land and its holy places', they almost never referred to the West Bank explicitly as 'occupied Jordanian land'.[8] This was probably in order not to draw a line between the West Bank, the Sinai peninsula and the Golan Heights as far as the demand for their return was concerned. Obviously, they did not refer to the West Bank as 'occupied Palestinian land'. Its description as 'occupied Arab land' best served Jordan's interests.

In February 1969, the Fatah organization led by Yassir Arafat managed to take over the PLO. Its nature was promptly transformed from a political institution dominated by Arab states through some pre-1948 Palestinian politicians, into a general framework for the *fida'iyun* organizations, which simultaneously intensified their violent activity against Israel in the occupied territories and elsewhere. These developments awakened Arab (and international) public interest in the Palestinian cause. The PLO and the Palestinian people also gained the support of the Arab League's Defense Council which met in Cairo in November 1969 and of the Arab summit conference in Rabat the following month. The Arab states undertook to provide the PLO and 'the Palestinian revolution' with moral as well as material, political and military assistance.[9] Under these circumstances, Jordan, too, had to acknowledge the *rights* of the Palestinian people,[10] though it had hitherto only referred to the Palestine *problem* in vague, general and non-committing terms.[11]

Jordan not only publicly recognized the various legitimate rights of the Palestinian people but also insisted on their fulfilment as yet another precondition to any political settlement. Public statements in this respect intensified after 1970. This did not mean, however, that Jordan agreed to give up its claim to the West Bank and Jerusalem. Jordan tended to detach the question of Palestinian rights from the territorial aspect. The former, including the right to self-determination, was depicted as a humanitarian issue that concerned only the repatriation of the Palestinian refugees of 1948 and 1967. Thus, it did not necessarily require Palestinian political sovereignty over territories which Jordan believed should be returned to its own authority. As Jordanian leaders pointed out, 'the liberation of Palestine is not the mere liberation of the land but the liberation of the Arab person' and 'the West Bank is an inseparable part of Jordan, and its inhabitants are Jordanian citizens'.[12] Hence, when King Hussein stated that 'the only solution that we accept is the one which will bring back all our usurped lands and will save *our* Palestinian people',[13] this implied that the return of the West Bank to Jordan would advance the solution to the Palestinian question. Even when the King stated, on the eve of the major encounter between Jordan and the *fida'iyun* in the late summer of 1970, that the solution to the Middle East crisis necessitated the establishment of a Palestinian state in the West Bank, or when Jordanian spokespersons admitted that the Palestinian right to self-determination included the right to establish an independent state, they insisted that such eventualities might take place only *after* the Israelis completely withdrew and after the West Bank and Arab Jerusalem were returned to Jordan. When Hussein responded to the Israeli announcement on the intention to hold municipal elections in the West Bank, he maintained that such a move was a severe threat to Jordan's sovereignty there.[14]

King Hussein's federal scheme of March 1972 suggested that the West Bank would constitute a Palestinian district (*qutr*) within a United Arab Kingdom, and Jerusalem would be the district's capital. Yet this scheme, too, was designed to be carried out only after Israel withdrew and after the West Bank was again in Jordanian hands. 'Jordan will not give up . . . a single grain of Palestine', said Prime Minister Ahmad al-Lawzi, and King Hussein reiterated that Israel should hand over these territories to Jordan, which claimed sovereignty there.[15] This approach did not immediately change even after the Arab summit conference in Rabat in October–November 1974. The resolutions of this conference recognized, *inter alia*, the PLO as the sole legitimate representative of the Palestinian people and acknowledged its right to establish a national authority (*sulta wataniyya*) in any liberated part of Palestine. Jordan still would not settle for anything less than complete Israeli withdrawal and, despite the summit resolutions, continued to insist on the return of the West Bank to its sovereignty and control.

Jordanian officials continued to demand Israeli withdrawal from the occupied *lands* as a precondition for a political settlement, but these territories were thenceforth referred to as 'Palestinian *and* Arab *lands*'. In early 1975, Prime Minister Zayd al-Rifa'i stated (quoting King Hussein) that 'Jordan adheres to the necessity to return the Palestinian land to the Palestinian people'.[16] Henceforth, the demand for total withdrawal was usually made in conjunction with the demand for the fulfilment of Palestinian rights. Jordan regarded the implementation of these rights as a *sine qua non* to any settlement of the conflict, and rights also included territory: 'The return of the legitimate rights of the Palestinian people over its land and country.'[17]

Even though the King and his officials no longer called the residents of the West Bank and Jerusalem 'Jordanians' as frequently as they had in the past, they made no secret of their lack of enthusiasm, to put it mildly, about the Rabat resolutions. They still insisted on Jordan's special ties with the West Bank and on the unique position it enjoyed there. It seems that Jordan counted on Israel's reluctance to negotiate with the PLO, and certainly to hand the West Bank over to it, when pointing out that only Jordan could negotiate some sort of Israeli withdrawal. Therefore, the Hashemite kingdom should not be excluded from the decision-making process on the future of the West Bank. In late 1977 Hussein was asked about this hypothesis, if Israel were willing to return the West Bank to Jordan. 'With the prospect of total peace,' the King answered, 'which would have to mean the complete recovery of the territories conquered in 1967, including sovereignty over Arab Jerusalem, Jordan would find it impossible to refuse the liberation of Arab land. But we would have to stipulate that only the Palestinians themselves could decide their future. They would have to be able to exercise self-determination after their liberation under conditions of total freedom from any form of pressure, including Jordanian pressure.'[18]

After the conclusion of the Camp David accords of September 1978 and the ensuing Egyptian–Israeli peace treaty of March 1979, Jordan's persistent demand for a *complete* Israeli withdrawal from *all* occupied lands took on an additional dimension: criticism of Egypt's willingness to acquiesce to a partial withdrawal (from the Sinai peninsula only) and to conclude a separate peace with Israel. The publication of the Camp David accords elicited frequent and intensive comments, mainly by King Hussein, that underlined Jordan's demand for a total retreat from *all* the occupied territories.[19] After the Egyptian–Israeli peace treaty and the Israeli evacuation of the Sinai peninsula, Jordanian demands for an Israeli withdrawal also predominantly referred to *Palestinian* lands. Yet occasional demands for retreat from the Golan Heights were also made.[20]

The selection of different adjectives by Jordanian spokespersons to define the territories from which Israel should withdraw (Jordanian,

Palestinian, Arab), reflected Jordan's view of the question of the owner-ship of these lands. But it also indicated how Jordan adapted to changing reality, as it showed Jordan's attitude to the political, rather than the legal, aspects of this question. Moreover, the connection between the demand for withdrawal and the Palestinian problem tightened after the early 1970s when Jordanian demands for Israeli withdrawal were almost always made together with the demand for recognition of the Palestinians' rights – legit-imate, national or the right to self-determination.

2. The demand for a total and unconditional Israeli withdrawal was not justified only by moral and judicial arguments (for the sake of justice; because the territories were occupied by force; the 'traces of Israeli aggres-sion' should be eliminated, etc.). From the outset, Jordanian public statements indirectly implied that withdrawal could promote a political settlement. This implication was voiced, however, without any formal commitment, as the official Arab position rejected such a stipulation and leading states such as Syria and Iraq still opposed the political option.[21] Yet when Jordanian officials stated that 'a settlement with Israel is impossible before it withdraws from the Arab lands', or that 'peace is not possible until an Israeli retreat',[22] one can assume that the implication was that if or when Israel withdrew, negotiations for peace and settlement would become feasible. The same holds for King Hussein's statements, such as his speech at Georgetown University in November 1967. He said that 'the proof which the Arabs look for that Israel wants peace is the returning of the occupied lands in Egypt, Jordan and Syria'.[23]

After resolution 242 was issued and accepted by Jordan, the connection between withdrawal and the possibility of a political settlement became more explicit. It seemed clearer that in return for territorial retreat, the Arabs would have to reciprocate with a kind of political process. 'Israel should withdraw from all Arab lands she occupied. Only this withdrawal will bring a peaceful solution.'[24] These statements eventually resulted in a new formula. In the summer of 1970, Jordan, together with Egypt, accepted the US initiative (the Rogers Plan) for Arab–Israeli negotiations on the basis of resolution 242 under the auspices of the UN and through the offices of Gunnar Jarring.

Probably in view of this occasion, the King wished to publicly signal to Israel what he expected the future round of negotiations to yield. In an interview to *Le Figaro*, he stated that 'Israel should make up her mind whether she coveted peace or the occupied territories. Israel could not have them both'.[25] This equation would became Hussein's favourite phrase and he repeated it frequently with only slight modifications. It was occasion-ally attached to the invariable demand for withdrawal, as a convincing explanation for why Israel should withdraw.[26] Yet though the conditioning indicated a connection between territories and peace, there was no formal undertaking whatsoever to make peace if and when Israel withdrew. Moreover, this implied connection was not shared by non-Jordanian Arab spokespersons; on the contrary: The Khartoum summit resolutions, for example, that constituted the most far-reaching statement that the Arab leaders were ready to accept, insisted on total Israeli withdrawal yet stated explicitly that no peace with Israel, recognition, or negotiations would follow.

3. UN Security Council resolution 242 called, *inter alia*, for Israeli withdrawal from *territories* (*all the territories*, according to another version; see chapter 3) occupied in June 1967. As King Hussein was among those who had contributed to the wording of the resolution, Jordan not only promptly accepted it but also made it a cornerstone of its regional policy. After the resolution was adopted in November 1967, public demands for Israeli withdrawal were frequently supplemented with the words: 'in accordance with the UN resolution which calls for the retreat from all occupied territories'.[27] Security Council resolution 338 of 22 October, 1973, which endeavoured to end the Yom Kippur war, also reiterated resolution 242 and called for its implementation. After 1973, Jordanian spokespersons occasionally mentioned this resolution as well, together with its predecessor 242, as an additional reference to UN resolutions in order to enhance the demand for complete Israeli withdrawal and to make it more forceful.[28]

By the 1970s, Jordan had gradually realized that Israel was in no hurry to leave the occupied territories and that no effective international pressure to do so seemed likely. It looked as if Jordan had abandoned all hope of an Israeli retreat, and the ritual *demand* for its withdrawal, according to the Security Council's resolutions, was sometimes substituted with *condemnation* of Israel for defying the international community and for violating UN resolutions by its refusal to withdraw.

Following the Israel–Egyptian peace treaty of 1979 and the subsequent withdrawal from the Sinai peninsula, Israeli officials, including Prime Minister Menachem Begin, claimed that in so doing, Israel had fulfilled its obligation according to resolution 242. As the Sinai peninsula constituted nearly 90 per cent of the territories Israel had captured in the June 1967 war, its evacuation complied with the requirement to withdraw from '*territories* occupied during the recent conflict'. The Arabs, as indicated, rejected this interpretation and insisted on withdrawal from '*the territories*, occupied during the recent conflict'. King Hussein suspected that under this pretext Israel would not withdraw from the West Bank and Gaza and would only agree to Palestinian autonomy as outlined in the Camp David accords. Addressing the UN General Assembly in September 1979, King

Hussein maintained that the occupied territories are indivisible . . . . The West Bank and Gaza are no different from the Sinai or the Golan Heights. They are occupied territories and their occupation must end. The West Bank and Gaza are the heart of Palestine and the homeland of the Palestinians. The West Bank is not subject to bargaining. There can be no meaning to any international settlement if it leaves the future of the West Bank and Gaza vague or applies to it a status at variance from that which applies to the other occupied territories . . . The only true equation for a just settlement is one of complete withdrawal from all the occupied territories . . . in accordance with the resolutions of the United Nations.[29]

While considering 242 as the best international leverage to force Israel to withdraw, Jordan had several reservations regarding the resolution. It was criticized as being too vague and too general regarding both the Palestinian demands and Israel's security. Hence Jordan insisted that the terms 'recognized and secure borders' and 'the refugee problem' needed to 'be radically supplemented to help the peacemakers address the real issues'.[30]

After the mid-1970s the resolution seemed, at least to the Arabs, to be insufficient because it failed to mention Palestinian rights. Formally Jordan adhered to this notion for several years. Prime Minister Mudir Badran declared, for example, that his country supported the amendment of 242 in a manner that would refer to the Palestinians as a people (and not merely as refugees, as the original resolution reads) with the right to self-determination on their national soil.[31] Publicly, Hussein not only supported the idea but even asked the EEC to launch an initiative to amend resolution 242 to the effect of recognizing the Palestinian right to self-determination.[32] In practice, however, the King had some reservations, suspecting that a new resolution might further deprive him of responsibility for the West Bank, as did the Rabat resolution in 1974. He therefore proposed that the Arabs wait with the demand to amend resolution 242 until they had prepared it themselves and were ready to introduce a unified Arab view.[33]

Following the bilateral Egyptian–Israeli agreements, Jordan sought an alternative to Camp David for implementing 242. Hussein stated that this was the appropriate time to clarify and redefine the resolution. Crown Prince Hassan also affirmed the need to return to the 'spirit and letter' of resolution 242.[34] What they probably had in mind was not so much recognition of Palestinian rights, but a clearer and more specific formulation of the clauses referring to the Israeli withdrawal, or re-interpretation of the resolution by the UN for the same purpose.

4. As Jordan persistently insisted on total withdrawal, it clearly resented the notion of a 'territorial compromise' forwarded and promoted in certain quarters of the Israeli government and public. Jordanian officials insisted

that Jordan had never accepted this principle.[35] A territorial compromise implied not only a partial agreement but also a separate bilateral one, to which Jordan was categorically opposed (see chapter 11). Jordan rejected all of Israel's overtures to reach a settlement based only on partial withdrawal. These began with the Allon Plan that Jordan utterly rejected and continued with the 'Jordanian Option'. The latter was an Israeli idea to conclude a deal over the future of the West Bank based on a partial Israeli withdrawal and handing over the Israeli-evacuated territories to Jordan, not the Palestinians. King Hussein declared time and again that 'there is no Jordanian option' and his Foreign Minister called this idea a 'sugar-coated version of the Allon Plan'.[36]

Jordan also insisted on 'a general solution, not a piecemeal one' and that the withdrawal should be carried out 'in accordance with a clear timetable'.[37] There was, however, an exception, not to the required scope of the withdrawal but to the manner in which it should be executed. After the October 1973 war, disengagement-of-forces agreements were signed between Israel and Egypt, and between Israel and Syria. They yielded partial Israeli withdrawals in the Sinai peninsula and the Golan Heights. The architect of these agreements was US Secretary of State Henry Kissinger who obtained them after intensive shuttle diplomacy. Jordan was also interested in benefiting from the momentum of interim agreements and submitted a proposal to Kissinger for the disengagement of forces along the Jordan river. Hussein was even ready to agree to a mutual withdrawal to several kilometres from both banks of the river Jordan.[38] The issue was also discussed during secret meetings between Israel and Jordan. Israeli Prime Minister Golda Meir offered Hussein a 'corridor' between Jordan and the West Bank near Jericho that would give Jordan free access to the Palestinian population there and even responsibility for the civil administration of the area. Hussein turned down the idea as it did not include actual Israeli withdrawal (saying he refused to crawl into the West Bank via a corridor). His counter-proposal was that the IDF retreat from the Jordan river, in the spirit of the offer he made to Kissinger and which Israel refused to accept.[39]

Jordanian spokespersons made no secret of their readiness to discuss a piecemeal withdrawal but insisted that it should be considered as the first stage of a trajectory that would end in full withdrawal from the West Bank and Jerusalem. They also insisted that before entering into any negotiations on a stage-by-stage retreat, Israel should officially commit herself to the principle of complete withdrawal. The same message was also delivered to the Israelis in private. During secret negotiations with Hussein and his officials in January 1974, Israel Defence Minister Moshe Dayan asked Prime Minister Zayd al Rifa'i, 'What is the final border you have in mind'? Rifa'i answered, 'The 1967 line, but we are ready to reach this line step by step'.[40]

The prospect of even a partial Israeli withdrawal which meant regaining a foothold in the West Bank was so appealing to Hussein that he stated that an Israeli–Jordanian disengagement of forces should be a 'precondition to any permanent settlement in the region'. At a reception for President Nixon during his Middle Eastern tour in June 1974, the King implied that unless such an agreement was reached, Jordan would not be able to pursue its peace-making efforts.[41] Nevertheless, the principle of gradual Israeli evacuation, providing this would eventually lead to the regaining of all occupied territories, was the only territorial concession Jordan was ever ready to make (save for minor and mutual border modifications) either overtly or covertly. This flexibility, however, referred only to the method of withdrawal, not to the actual land that had to be returned.

In order to strengthen Jordan's insistence on total Israeli withdrawal and to underline that it refused even a minimal compromise in the matter, Jordanian spokespersons reiterated that their government would not, under any circumstances, give up even a foot (*shibr*) of ground or a single grain of soil of the occupied lands. This sort of rhetoric resulted both from Israel's interpretation of resolution 242 and from its idea of territorial compromise. Those phrases were frequently used throughout the whole period under survey to signal time and again, Jordan's rejection of anything less than a full retreat.[42]

5. When it became obvious that Israel had no intention of a swift departure from the occupied territories, another argument was added to Jordan's demand for complete withdrawal: Israel should immediately retreat or peace and stability would never prevail in the Middle East. Withdrawal was also depicted as the only way to prevent the recurring unrest in the region and the frequent hostile actions, such as the Israeli invasion of Karama in March 1968 and IDF clashes with the Jordanian army and Palestinian organizations. Moreover, Israel's reluctance to withdraw, the Jordanian argument went, would inflict catastrophe (*karitha*), calamity and destruction on the entire region. Such claims were most often made in the aftermath of the October 1973 war and sometimes in reference to it.[43] A similar statement by Hussein shortly before the outbreak of the war is of special interest. On 30 September 1973 the King declared, 'Israel's insistence on remaining in the occupied territories may yield a disaster . . . if the Israelis stay in these territories I can not see how it is possible to avoid a new catastrophe.'[44] This was not the only statement made just before the October 1973 war. A few days earlier, on 25 September, the King as noted met Israeli Prime Minister Golda Meir, at his request, to warn her about the planned Egyptian–Syrian attack, and urged her to break the political stalemate to prevent it.[45] In light of this meeting and Mrs. Meir's reluctance to relate to his warning, Hussein's statement of 30 September seems

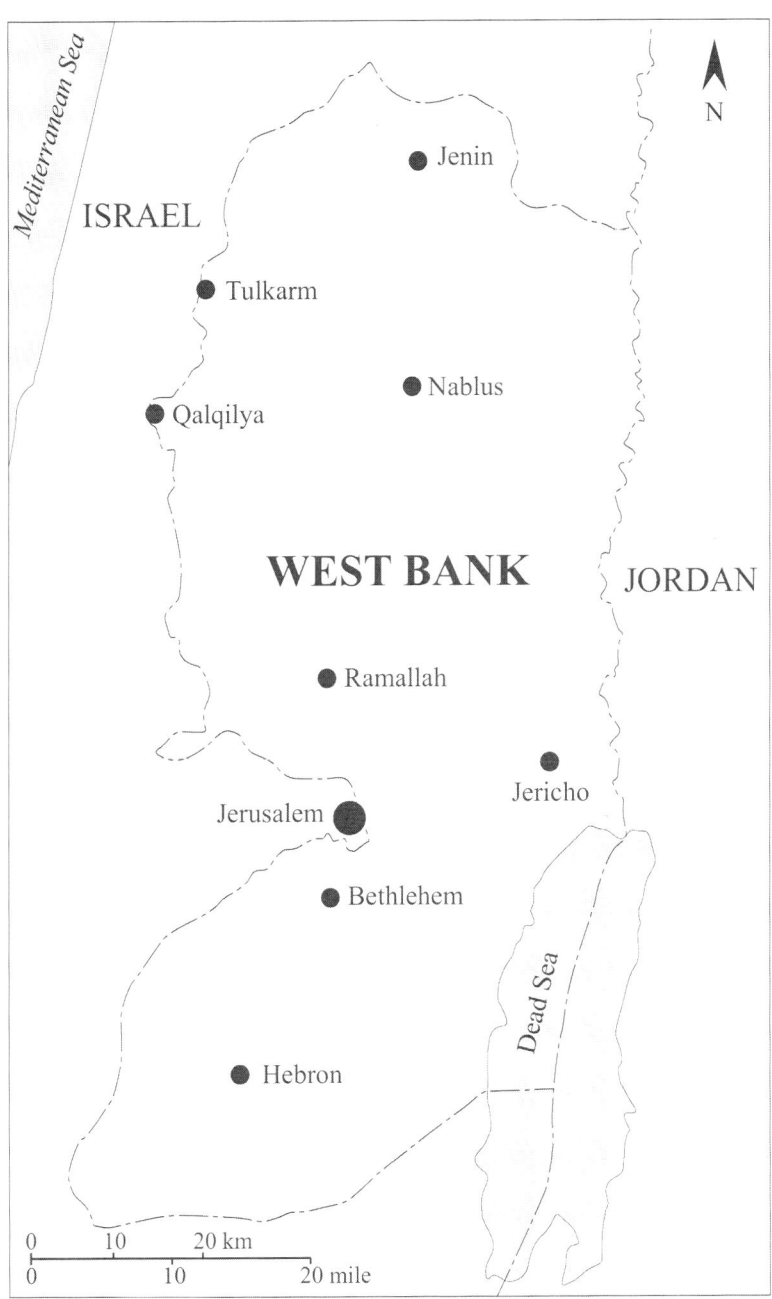

The West Bank

like a last-minute bid to prevent war. Years later, the King still attributed the outbreak of the war to failure to implement UN resolution 242 and to achieve an Israeli withdrawal.[46]

The connection between the on-going occupation and dangers to the region's security and stability were also mentioned in statements during the 1980s, but not as frequently as before and with less fervour.[47] The outbreak of the December 1987 *intifada* in the West bank and Gaza was mobilized by the Jordanians to invigorate the argument of the physical danger that loomed as a result of Israel's reluctance to withdraw. The uprising was construed as emphasizing the need for a prompt Israeli withdrawal: 'The developments created by the *intifada* can be negotiated only by the termination of Israel's occupation.'[48]

6. As of the early 1980s, after Israel had annexed east Jerusalem (1967); applied its judicial system to the Golan Heights and – on the other hand – returned the entire Sinai peninsula to Egypt; the demand for total withdrawal took on a new dimension. The new line adopted by Jordan held that following these measures, Israel was about to annex the West Bank and the Gaza Strip, the last remaining occupied territories. Occasionally, speakers said that the 'creeping annexation' had already begun. The only way to prevent such an eventuality was an immediate and complete withdrawal.[49]

During that period, Jordan's demands in this respect were consolidated, frequently expressed and took on a uniform mode. There was no doubt now that the evacuated territories would be handed over to the Palestinians, under the leadership of the PLO. Israel had been asked to comply with the formula 'land for peace' which, according to the Jordanian interpretation, was the essence of resolutions 242 and 338. Implementation of the latter resolution was increasingly demanded together with the former.[50] Israel was also asked to choose between peace and territories. Jordanian spokespersons reiterated that Israel could not have both. A choice had to be made. The lack of progress in the peace process stemmed from Israel's reluctance to withdraw from the occupied territories. Jordan, on its part, was determined not to give up even an inch of those territories (even though they would be given to the PLO and not to the Hashemite kingdom).[51]

Though Israel's acquiescence to the principle of total withdrawal as a precondition to a political settlement had been stipulated by Jordanian spokespersons, it was generally understood that the actual withdrawal should be discussed and would constitute part of the political negotiations. Yet in February 1988, Jordanian Prime Minister Zayd al-Rifa'i made an exceptional statement, one which, if frequently repeated, might imply a change in the pattern of Jordan demands of Israel. In an interview to the

Times, he insisted that Israel had to agree to total withdrawal, including Jerusalem, *before* Jordan would agree to negotiate a settlement, 'as the soil is non negotiable'.[52] This explicit demand was probably made against the background of the *intifada* and the expectation to convene an international Middle Eastern peace conference. The conference, which Jordan relentlessly worked to convene in 1987–8 (see chapter 12), was to put an end to the Israeli occupation by bringing about a total withdrawal. Jordan believed that such a conference was the best (if not the only) means to regain the occupied territories.[53] Nevertheless, such sentiments were rarely expressed later, both because Jordan gave up its claim to the West Bank and because the idea of an international conference gradually faded away.

The Gaza Strip

As indicated, immediately after the June war, Jordan perceived the Gaza Strip as occupied Egyptian territory, just as the West Bank was occupied Jordanian land, even though the pre-1967 status of the two areas was conspicuously different. The West Bank had been formally incorporated into Jordan and its population, refugees included, became Jordanian citizens at will, equal to East Bankers in civil and political rights. The Gaza Strip was never annexed to Egypt. It remained an occupied territory under military administration. Its inhabitants' carried only local Palestinian IDs and faced difficulties whenever they wished to travel to Egypt or elsewhere, to work or to study, as they needed Egyptians' special permits (laissez passer). Nonetheless, according to Jordan's perception, it was to be returned to Egypt.[54]

Since the Gaza Strip was within the international boundaries of mandatory Palestine, the Israeli government, on its part, viewed it differently from the Sinai peninsula or the Golan Heights. The latter, according to the Israeli government's decision of 19 June 1967, were negotiable and Israel undertook to return them to Egypt and Syria in exchange for peace. Gaza was to remain under Israeli control, though due to the hundreds of thousands of refugees residing there, Israel was reluctant to formally annex it. It seems that it was this Israeli position that gave the Gaza Strip the same status as the West Bank in contrast to the other occupied territories.

The course of events that caused Jordan to change its declared attitude towards the West Bank also had an impact on its views regarding the future of the Gaza Strip, though the latter was a much more problematic issue. From the outset, the Egyptians were not unequivocal in their attitude towards Gaza. There were indications after the June war that they would not insist on its return to their rule.[55] They admitted that in a political settlement, the future of the Strip would be open to bargaining. Though Jordan had not laid claim to the Gaza Strip,[56] others suggested that Jordanian control there was a less antagonizing solution than Israeli control. Egyptian officials proposed handing over the Gaza Strip to King Hussein so that he could negotiate its future while discussing the future of the West Bank with Israel. Alternately, they considered the possibility of its internationalization, but opposed its annexation to Israel.[57] An alleged US proposal after the June 1967 war also envisaged the annexation of the Gaza Strip to Jordan.[58] At about the same time (late 1968) Israel toyed with the idea of handing over the city of Gaza and its nearby refugee camps to Jordan within a comprehensive peace agreement based on the Allon plan. Such a move would relieve Israel of the need to negotiate on the Gaza refugees and would also give Jordan an outlet to the Mediterranean. It seems that King Hussein was ready to consider the idea, providing he received at least part of the Gaza Strip and not only Gaza City and its refugees. Israel, however, was reluctant to meet the King's demand.[59] Hussein and his officials continued to insist on Israeli withdrawal from Gaza in the same way they demanded a retreat from the West Bank and the other occupied Arab lands. Egypt's position, however, posed a problem. Jordan, as indicated, publicly acknowledged Palestinian rights but, until the 1974 Rabat resolution, still claimed sovereignty over the West Bank, if or when 'liberated'. Jamal Abd al-Nasser, on the other hand, had changed Egypt's previous position and maintained, in early 1969 (at the 5th meeting of the PNC in Cairo), that in the wake of Israeli withdrawal, Palestinian rule would be established in the West Bank and the Gaza Strip. He and his officials regarded the Strip as an integral part of the Palestinian territories; its fate should be decided by the Palestinians themselves and it should be part of a future Palestinian state.[60] Jordan therefore had to be very cautious in its public statements on this issue.

Shortly after the war King Hussein was reported to have outlined a peace plan in which – in return for an Israeli withdrawal – the [Jordanian] West Bank and the [Egyptian] Gaza Strip would be demilitarized and a passage between these two areas would be provided. It is not clear whether the King actually submitted such a plan; in any event, the idea was rarely repeated.[61]

King Hussein's federal scheme of March 1972 did not rule out the possible inclusion of the Gaza Strip. This plan, as noted, called for making the Hashemite Kingdom of Jordan into a United Arab Kingdom formed from a Jordanian district (*qutr*) and a Palestinian district. The latter was to consist of the 'West Bank and any other Palestinian territories that would be liberated and whose inhabitants wished to join'. This clearly referred, first and foremost, to the Gaza Strip. Later, with the exception of frequent demands for Israeli withdrawal, the Gaza Strip was referred to only in general contexts where Jordan's support for the Palestinian cause was expressed. Yet whenever the Strip was mentioned, it was explicitly stated that Jordan did not distinguish between the West Bank and Gaza, just as Jordan did not distinguish between the West Bank and the East Bank. In the summer of 1972, a few months after the publication of the federal scheme, King Hussein addressed a delegation from Gaza and stated that 'The Gaza Strip is considered the same as Jerusalem, Nablus and Amman . . . we share the same destiny'. On another occasion, during a TV interview in the US, the King stated that 'Jordan is the home of the Jordanians and the Palestinians, including the brothers in the Gaza Strip'.[62]

Only after the Rabat resolutions did Jordan join the Egyptian perception that regarded both the West Bank and Gaza as Palestinian lands, and that the Palestinian population there should decide their future.[63] In the late 1970s and early 1980s, when Hussein revitalized his federal scheme, the Gaza Strip was mentioned as part of the Palestinian homeland that, hopefully, would enter into federal, or confederal ties with Jordan.[64] It was probably in this context that the King occasionally mentioned his familial ties with Gaza, ties that had pre-Islamic roots. An ancestral member of his family, Hashim, had visited Gaza and was buried there.

6 THE QUESTION OF JERUSALEM

Aside from its sanctity to Islam, Christianity and Judaism, the city of Jerusalem had a special role in Hashemite history, politics and legitimacy. Given the unique place of Jerusalem in the hearts and minds of Israelis, clearly this question constituted one of the most complex bones of contention between the two states. Jerusalem's status, nevertheless, had the potential for confrontation and rivalry not only between Israel and Jordan or between Jews and Arabs, but also between Jordan and the Palestinians.

In view of the unbridgeable conflicting religious and political claims to Jerusalem, the 1947 UN Palestine partition plan excluded the city from the sovereignty of both the Jewish and the Arab state. Jerusalem was designated as a *corpus separatum*, under international control and to be administered by the UN. In the end, however, Jerusalem became a divided city. Both Jordan and Israel resented the idea of internationalization and thus *de facto* divided Jerusalem between themselves in 1948–9. The UN, *post factum*, acknowledged the new reality in the Israeli–Jordanian Armistice Agreement of 3 April 1949.

The Jordanian part of the city (East Jerusalem or Arab Jerusalem) included the Jewish quarter of the Old City and the Wailing Wall, the holiest site in Jewish tradition.[1] East Jerusalem is also the site of most important Christian and Muslim shrines, such as the Church of the Holy Sepulchre, the Dome of the Rock and the al-Aqsa mosques. As a place of worship and pilgrimage for believers of the three monotheistic religions, Jerusalem attracted international political attention, as well as spiritual interest.

Jerusalem and its Temple Mount mosques are considered the third most sacred shrine of Islam, after the Grand Mosque in Mecca and the Prophet's mosque and tomb in Medina.[2] The latter had special meaning for the Hashemites, who had ruled the cities and lost them to Abd al-Aziz 'Ibn Saud', the Wahhabi king of Najd, in the 1920s. Following this defeat, they were expelled from their homeland, the Hijaz, and were deprived of their position as *Custodians of the Holy Places*. Henceforth the Hashemites – who claimed to be descendants of the Prophet Muhammad – focused on Jerusalem, which they regarded as a fallback sanctuary, to enhance their religious legitimacy. The head of the family, Hussein ibn Ali, the deposed King of Hijaz (King Hussein's great grandfather), spent the rest of his life in exile and was buried on the Temple Mount. His son Abdullah, a native of Mecca who became Amir and later King of Transjordan, had yearned for Palestine, and Jerusalem in particular, ever since he pitched his tent in Amman in 1921. During the 1948 war, after his army invaded Palestine, Abdullah took pains to gain control over Arab Jerusalem which he considered the jewel in the crown of his territorial ambitions in Palestine.

Abdullah met his death in July 1951 on the threshold of al-Aqsa mosque, shot by a Palestinian assassin. His 16 year-old grandson, Hussein, was standing at his side, a fact that Hussein later mentioned in some of his public speeches.[3] For King Hussein, therefore, the loss of Jerusalem in June 1967 was also associated with his own private trauma and thus was the most painful experience of the war. If he viewed the loss of the West Bank as a betrayal of his grandfather's heritage, then losing Jerusalem would be regarded as a personal failure in exercising his historical responsibility. He therefore believed that it was his *personal* duty, in addition to his national one, to do what he could to retrieve it. King Hussein's eagerness to regain East Jerusalem was manifested in the secret negotiations he conducted with Israel after the June war. Particularly after the Israelis insisted that Jerusalem was non-negotiable, Hussein was explicit in his position that he could not compromise on this issue and demanded an Israeli withdrawal from Eastern Jerusalem. His determination and persistence led some of his Israeli interlocutors to wrongly believe that if Jordan's demands over Jerusalem were met, the Jordanians would be willing to make concessions regarding other aspects, and that a peace treaty could be achieved 'tomorrow'.[4]

In view of these considerations and historical developments, the question of Jerusalem was somewhat different from that of the rest of the West Bank, particularly in its legal issues. Indeed Jordan wished an immediate and complete Israeli withdrawal from both Jerusalem and the West Bank. The arguments for the return of Jerusalem, however, and the repercussions perceived if Israel did not comply, were not necessarily identical to those applied to the West Bank in general. Jerusalem was considered by the Jordanians a more urgent matter than the other occupied territories since the physical changes and the legislation enacted by Israel created a far more intensive *fait accompli* there than in the rest of the West Bank or Gaza.[5]

Israel's attitude towards Jerusalem was different from its stand on the West Bank. While the rest of the occupied territories were viewed – at least in the immediate wake of the June war and by the majority of the Israel's cabinet ministers – as bargaining cards to be negotiated for peace and recognition, from the outset Jerusalem was considered an inseparable part of the State of Israel, lost in 1948 and retrieved 19 years later. Hence, Jerusalem enjoyed public consensus in Israel as a non-negotiable issue.

This attitude was reflected in deeds as well as in words. On 27 June 1967 the Israeli Knesset enacted three laws that were to prepare the ground for what was called in Israel the 'reunification of Jerusalem' (and 'the annexation of East Jerusalem' elsewhere). The first was the 'Protection of the Holy Places' law, designed to safeguard the holy places of all religions and to guarantee free passage to them, probably to underscore the fact that Jordan had not honoured a similar commitment it undertook in the framework of the Jordanian–Israeli General Armistice agreement in April 1949.[6] The second, the 'Law and Administration Ordinance', enabled the government to apply Israeli law, jurisdiction and administration to areas 'formerly part of mandatory Palestine'. The third, the 'Municipal Corporation Ordinance', enabled the government to enlarge the boundaries of any municipality by administrative order.[7]

The next day, 28 June, Israel's Minister of Interior issued an administrative order expanding the area of the Jerusalem municipality. It was extended to include the Old City, all of East Jerusalem and several nearby Arab villages. With the publication of the Jerusalem township's order, Israeli laws and ordinances became applicable to the new municipal area. On 29 June the physical barriers which had divided Jerusalem were removed and the two sections were opened to two-way traffic. The same day, the East Jerusalem municipality was formally dissolved and the new enlarged Israeli municipality set up a special liaison office in East Jerusalem.[8]

Jordanian officials insisted that in spite of Israel's measures, Jerusalem continued to be an Arab city. They claimed that King Hussein's protection of the holy places had not given rise to any criticism and they called upon all believers to come to the rescue of the holy places in Jerusalem. King Hussein himself condemned these measures as unilateral, arbitrary annexation and an outright provocation of UN authority and prestige. He called upon all nations to reject the Israeli aggression.[9] In early July, the UN General Assembly indeed adopted a resolution that declared Israel's measures to change the status of Jerusalem invalid. Given the universal attention that Jerusalem received and the unilateral nature of Israel's measures, it was easier to obtain international consensus on this issue than on any other consequence of the June war. Israel was called on to rescind those measures already taken and to desist from further unilateral steps. A further UN resolution deplored Israel's non-compliance with the first resolution and asked the Secretary General to send a personal representative to Jerusalem to report on the situation there. Ernesto Thalmann, a Swiss diplomat, was duly appointed. In later years, the General Assembly, the Security Council and other UN bodies adopted similar resolutions with which Israel did not comply.[10]

I. The Issue of Sovereignty

As indicated, Jordan's 'battle of Jerusalem' was indeed a unique battle within the comprehensive 'war' it waged to regain the lost territories. The city's religious importance to billions of believers sometimes blurred the line between the question of formal, political sovereignty as recognized by international law, and the emotional attitude of the believers who felt that Jerusalem *belonged* to them. The fact that the UN had originally envisaged the internationalization of Jerusalem and that its partition, as well as Israel's and Jordan's presence there, had never *de jure* been recognized – as even Crown Prince Hassan admitted [11] – added to the sensitivity of the question of sovereignty. Jordan, nevertheless, was persistent in its demand for the return of Jerusalem to full Jordanian sovereignty. Jordan's major argument was the rejection of Israel's claim to East Jerusalem, based on 'deeply-held religious beliefs and a sense of unique historical association deriving from religion', rather than on internationally-recognized legal foundations. Moreover, according to international law and conventions, Israel, as an occupying state, could not acquire sovereignty over the territory it occupied. Most of its activities in Jerusalem, such as the *de facto* annexation, the municipal unification and the destruction of private property, were therefore illegal.[12]

Simultaneously, however, probably due to the legal weakness of its own claims to sovereignty, Jordan, while insisting that Arab Jerusalem was, territorially speaking, an integral part of Jordan, did not deny others' non-political rights to the city. Moreover, Jordanian officials occasionally substantiated their claim to Jerusalem, as an inseparable and indispensable part of Jordan, by underscoring its importance to the Arabs and the Muslims. Immediately after the June war, King Hussein warned that if Israel insisted on holding Jerusalem, the Arabs and the Muslims would take all necessary steps to force it to evacuate the holy city. He also explained to Israelis, at clandestine meetings, that he could not compromise over Jerusalem as it was a trust bestowed upon him by the Muslim world.[13] Crown Prince Hassan used the same argument: 'Jordan's claim on Jerusalem is backed by the Muslim world. Jerusalem is not merely our own property but also the property of hundreds of millions of Muslims all over the world.' Prime Minister Bahjat al-Talhuni added: 'Jerusalem, in addition to being a Jordanian Arab city – in which Jordan insists on her full rights – is also a Muslim-Christian city.'[14]

Some of Jordan's arguments for regaining sovereignty in East Jerusalem were similar to those used to regain the West Bank. Namely, Jerusalem was an inseparable part of Jordan; it was an integral part of the occupied territories and 'there may be certain artificiality in treating . . . Jerusalem separately from the general questions of the West Bank', hence all Jordan's demands regarding these territories applied primarily to Jerusalem.[15] Jordan's adherence to the demand for full sovereignty in Jerusalem (a term which was not generally used regarding the rest of the West Bank where only a 'full Israeli withdrawal' was demanded) and its insistence on Jerusalem as an indivisible part of the occupied territories, reflected its concern about Israel's changing the status of Jerusalem. By annexing East Jerusalem, Israel signalled, to Jordan's chagrin, that the future of this area would be different and detached from that of the other occupied territories. Jordanian statements on this issue were designed to warn Israel that even if it gave up the entire West Bank, no settlement could be achieved unless East Jerusalem were returned in full. Messages in the same spirit were also conveyed privately to Israel.[16] Jordan was explicit in its rejection of the annexation of Arab Jerusalem and continued to perceive all the occupied territories as a whole and Jordan's demands as applying equally to all their parts.

Israel's withdrawal from Jerusalem was therefore a precondition as well as a *sine qua non* for a settlement and no peace could be achieved unless it was returned to Jordanian sovereignty.[17] It is worth noting that when addressing Western audiences, the King and his officials usually demanded the return of the *Arab sector* or the *Jordanian sector* of Jerusalem. When speaking to an Arab audience, they referred to the return of *Arab Jerusalem* to Jordan or to Jordanian sovereignty.[18] Even though 'Arab Jerusalem' could be construed as the Arab section of Jerusalem, the fact that Hussein did not mention an Arab or Jordanian *section* in his statements in Arabic, indicated that the King was reluctant to remind an Arab audience (and especially a Palestinian one) that Jordan had agreed to the partition of Jerusalem and to Jewish sovereignty in its Western part.

References to Jerusalem as Jordanian territory appeared until 1974 and Jordan took advantage of various events to enhance its claim. Immediately after the fire at the al-Aqsa mosque in August 1969,[19] Hussein cabled Arab and Muslim heads of state to inform them about the 'appalling event' which occurred when 'our sacred places . . . are under the yoke of the hated occupation'. The tone and content of the message implied that it was Jordan's responsibility to safeguard Jerusalem and its holy places. Even though Jordan had been deprived of authority there 'after the whole of

Palestine had been occupied',[20] it seems that King Hussein continued to consider himself morally responsible for the well-being of Jerusalem, of its Arab population and of its religious sites. A few weeks later, Deputy Prime Minister and Foreign Minister Abd al-Mun'im al-Rifa'i accused Israel of ignoring the international community and the principles of law and justice. He reiterated that Jerusalem was an inseparable part of Jordan and that it also carried religious and historical importance for all the peoples of the world.[21]

Hussein's United Arab Kingdom scheme of March 1972 also referred to the future of Jerusalem. It was designed to be the capital of the autonomous Palestinian region within the federal kingdom. Despite the criticism that publication of the scheme elicited, it provided the King with an opportunity to reiterate his insistence on full Jordanian sovereignty in Jerusalem. He repeated that Jordan would reject any solution that would not guarantee this sovereignty and would not recognize 'our rights in Arab Jerusalem'.[22]

Jordan also took advantage of the attempt to convene a peace conference in Geneva following the October 1973 war to enhance its claim to Jerusalem. When King Hussein and his officials outlined the points that Jordan was going to make at the conference, they emphasized, within their demand for full Israeli withdrawal, the withdrawal from Arab Jerusalem which they perceived as an integral part of 'occupied Arab lands'.[23]

Nevertheless, after early 1974, Jordanian spokespersons replaced the demand to reclaim *Jordanian* sovereignty over Jerusalem with the demand to return Jerusalem to *Arab* sovereignty. After that year, the reference to *Jordan's* rights in Jerusalem were rarely heard, while demands for regaining *Arab* rights and sovereignty there intensified.[24] The major reason for this conspicuous shift was probably the resolutions of the 6th Arab summit meeting in late November 1973 in Algiers. This meeting expressed, for the first time, an all-Arab commitment to guarantee the Palestinians' national rights in the spirit of the views of the PLO, which, according to the participants (with the exception of Jordan), was the sole representative of the Palestinian people. Moreover, in addition to the call for 'full liberation of all the Arab territories which were occupied in the aggression of June 1967', the meeting specifically insisted on 'the liberation of Arab Jerusalem and the rejection of any situation that might prejudice the full sovereignty of the Arabs over the Holy City'.[25]

In view of the inter-Arab consensus on the new role of the PLO and on the Arab nature of Jerusalem, Jordan's public demands for sovereignty over East Jerusalem seemed somewhat anachronistic. A few weeks later, on the opening day of the Geneva peace conference, Pope Paul VI publicly declared the special interest of the Holy See in Jerusalem as well as his readiness to take part in the efforts to solve the Middle East problem. The

Pope stated that any solution to the issue of the status of Jerusalem and of its holy places should take into account the urgent needs that emanated from the unique character of the city and the legitimate rights and aspirations of those who belonged to the three major monotheistic religions.[26] This declaration probably added to Jordanian policy-makers' understanding that insistence on their previous demands regarding Jerusalem might not be well accepted. They indeed ceased to publicly call Jerusalem a Jordanian city and no longer asked for its return to Jordanian sovereignty. Yet the pattern that developed in public statements of Jordanian officials regarding Jerusalem was markedly different from that towards the West Bank. In the latter case, in the first years after the June war, the King and his officials considered the West Bank Jordanian territory that should be returned to Jordan. Even after Jordan began to publicly acknowledge Palestinian rights, it did not relinquish the territorial claim to the West Bank. Only after the Rabat summit of November 1974 did Jordanian officials begin to ask for the return of 'Palestinian and Arab lands'. As of the second half of the 1970s, they more and more frequently insisted on the return of Palestinian land to the Palestinian people.

In the case of Jerusalem the pattern was different. The public demands to return Jerusalem to Jordanian sovereignty were replaced, as noted, in early 1974 with the demand for Arab sovereignty. This continued, with intensified frequency, throughout the period surveyed. *Palestinian* sovereignty in Jerusalem, or Palestinian rights therein, were rarely, if ever, mentioned or demanded by the Jordanians. The rare exceptions were when King Hussein and Crown Prince Hassan expressed support for the Palestinian people's right to an independent state 'on its national soil' in 'the West Bank, the Gaza Strip and Arab Jerusalem'.[27] Hussein made this statement when he was seeking to revitalize his decade-old federal scheme and this is probably the context in which it should be viewed. Hussein's speech of 30 August 1982 was delivered only two days before the announcement of the Reagan Plan in which the American President supported Palestinian autonomy but opposed an independent Palestinian state. Neither Hussein nor Hassan specifically demanded that East Jerusalem be handed over to the Palestinians, while they did make such a demand regarding the rest of the West Bank. The reason that King Hussein was not overly enthusiastic about Saudi Crown Prince Fahd's 'peace plan' of August 1981 was that it called for the establishment of a Palestinian state with East Jerusalem as its capital. The Arab consensus surrounding common Arab 'ownership' of the Holy City that caused Jordan to end its demands for sovereignty in Jerusalem constituted a two edge-sword. It indeed deprived the Jordanians of their coveted exclusivity over East Jerusalem, yet it simultaneously allowed them to refrain from recognizing Palestinian rights there.

Though in the late 1960s Jordan insisted that Jerusalem and the West Bank should be considered the same territory whenever their return to Jordan was discussed, this attitude changed after the mid 1970s. The PLO was then crowned as the 'sole legitimate representative' of the Palestinians and its right to sovereignty over the Palestinian territories occupied by Israel was recognized by the Arab world and, later, by the international community. Though on the declarative level, Arab Jerusalem was still considered an integral part of the West Bank, Jordanian public statements implied a clear distinction between the two areas. The term 'occupied Arab lands' included Jerusalem, while 'occupied Palestinian lands' referred to the West Bank (and occasionally the Gaza Strip).[28] These statements required the return of 'Palestinian lands and of Arab rights', the latter referring to Jerusalem. Sometimes Jordan demanded 'in addition to the [fulfilment of] Palestinian rights, the return of Jerusalem to *Arab* sovereignty'[29]. The distinction between Jerusalem and the rest of the West Bank was also reflected in the formula that King Hussein used in the 1980s. He often spoke of Jordan's duty towards 'the [Palestinian] lands, the people and the Holy Places' or of the need to liberate 'Jerusalem, Palestine and her people'.[30]

The message stemming from all these declarations suggests that even after Jordan was compelled to publicly acquiesce that, once Israel withdrew, the West Bank should be given to the Palestinians and to their representative, the PLO, Jerusalem should be treated differently. Though it was likely that 'any settlement of the future of the City will constitute part of a general settlement of the political future of the inhabitants of the occupied territories', Jerusalem still had a unique position as an 'Arab Muslim' entity within the 'Palestine question', and the Palestinian right to self-determination. Being defined as an Arab-Muslim issue implied an Arab-Muslim identity that should concern all Arab and Muslim countries and all peace-loving nations.[31] Yet Jordan, and the Hashemite family in particular, had special historical ties with Jerusalem.[32] Because of these ties, the Hashemites developed a special attitude towards the city and therefore deserved a special position there.

II. The Holy Places: A City of Peace

In view of the above, it is not surprising that Jordan never stopped trying to regain a foothold in Jerusalem. Even when it became obvious that the prospect for its return to Jordan's sovereignty was negligible, the Hashemite regime sought to be involved in decisions regarding its future and strove to maintain its influence there, especially via the Islamic establishment and institutions. It is reasonable to assume that the prospect of regaining influence in Jerusalem played a considerable role in the King's decision to enter into peace negotiations with Israel in 1993. Even after the peace talks began, the King was reluctant to sign a joint declaration with Israel until Jordan's special role regarding the Holy Places in Jerusalem was recognized. In late May 1994 Prime Minister Rabin undertook to acknowledge this role, and the joint declaration was signed two months later. The Jordan–Israel peace treaty of October 1994 indeed includes a provision regarding this.[33]

When Jordan realized that its demands for sovereignty in Arab Jerusalem were futile, it attempted to thwart the recognition of the rights of the other contenders – Israel[34] and the Palestinians – primarily by expanding the issue of Jerusalem. King Hussein and Crown Prince Hassan explained that Jordan could not give up its rights in Jerusalem: they were the 1000-year old rights of all Muslims. Jerusalem was not an exclusively Jordanian problem, nor an exclusively Palestinian or Arab one; it was the problem of the entire Muslim world. In a different context, when Jewish rights in the city were questioned and challenged, Jerusalem was depicted as a Muslim–Arab–Christian problem.[35] The argument regarding the Muslim and Christian holy places was indeed used against Israel's steps in East Jerusalem: Jordan and the Arabs could never give up Jerusalem because of the religious sites. Such a holy city could not and should not be in the hands of Israel. In an interview in 1981, King Hussein phrased this argument as follows: 'The question that has to be asked on the Arab, Islamic and world levels is this: Is it reasonable that we, as Arabs and Muslims, should agree to Jerusalem being so belittled as to become nothing more than the political capital of Israel?'[36]

After the publication of King Hussein's federal scheme in March 1972, this same attitude continued and focused around an old-new concept, previously raised mainly before the Western media, that Jerusalem, being sacred to the three [monotheistic] religions should be the *City of Peace* (a term derived from the meaning of its Hebrew name) as it belonged to all believers.[37] The use of this argument intensified after 1974, when the PLO was recognized as the legitimate representative of Palestinians and Jordan feared that Arab public opinion might be sympathetic to the PLO's claim to Jerusalem. Jerusalem again was portrayed as the *City of Peace* and as a possible meeting place for the three religions. In 1985 when Jordan negotiated with the PLO, following their 11 February agreement, King Hussein described the future of Jerusalem as the *City of Peace* from a different angle: 'Unlike what people are saying, Jerusalem is not an obstacle to peace but the key to peace. All those who believe in one God should unite around the sublime cause of peace. The Palestinians and the Jews will live in harmony on the land of peace, of faith and of hope'.[38]

Nevertheless, the frequent references to Jerusalem as the *City of Peace* and a sanctuary for all was not followed by any practical suggestion or operational proposal as to how to implement the idea. One exception was Crown Prince Hassan's statement that 'Legal arrangements of some intricacy are needed for the administration of the City, the access to, and worship at, the Holy Places'.[39] Yet he did not elaborate. Basically, the *City of Peace* remained an ideal and a slogan rather than a concrete, practical solution to a political problem. Moreover, most statements insisted that a precondition to Jerusalem's becoming a *City of Peace* was the return of its Eastern section to Arab sovereignty.[40] King Hussein indicated, however, that meeting this condition did not necessarily imply a return to the pre-1967 reality. He implied that a solution to the freedom of passage to *all* holy places could be sorted out without another partition of Jerusalem. While in the political context the King envisaged an Arab East Jerusalem and an Israeli Western one, he did not rule out the possibility of dual sovereignty: to 'open Jerusalem' as both a city and a symbol of peace.[41] Crown Prince Hassan expressed similar views. His main argument was that the spiritual reverence accorded to Jerusalem by the three religions placed the city above the demands of national politics. Exclusive control therefore would deprive Jerusalem of its spiritual soul. Hence 'Arab sovereignty over East Jerusalem must be restored while the legal status of the whole city remains undetermined, pending a final settlement of the Arab–Israeli dispute'. Hassan also maintained that, legally speaking, on the question of sovereignty, Israel as an occupant had only temporary limited authority in Jerusalem, subject to international obligations. Even though Israel considered itself guardian of the Holy Places in compliance with the 'Protection of the Holy Places' law of 27 June 1967, it enjoyed no territorial sovereignty over the Holy Places in East Jerusalem.[42]

Basically, Jordan opposed the internationalization of Jerusalem.[43] In certain contexts, however, Jordan was ready to discuss the possible internationalization of the City 'if this was what the international community wished' and if it promoted 'its transformation into a City of Peace'. Even then Jordan was only ready to change its traditional position providing two conditions were met: That 'such a plan has to be applied to the entire city and not only to its Arab sector'; and that it should be discussed only after Israel had withdrawn 'from the holy city and other occupied lands'.[44]

Jordan's perception, as shown, separated the national–territorial aspect from the religious aspect. Hence the idea of Jerusalem as a symbol of peace 'belonging' to all believers, neither replaced the demand for Arab sovereignty nor contradicted it. On the contrary, it was proposed in an attempt to enhance this claim. Yet the 'City of Peace' concept also served as a stimulus for Israel and an incentive for the international community to put pressure on Israel: It suggested no return to the *status quo ante* and recognized the religious importance of Jerusalem for the Jews as well.

III. Judaisation of Jerusalem

The distinction between issues of sovereignty and of religious sanctity was also designated to foil Israel's claims to East Jerusalem and to nullify its unilateral steps there. In the first years after the June war, Jordan supported the non-recognition of Israel's occupation and annexation of East Jerusalem by ignoring its sanctity to the Jews. Public statements by King Hussein and his officials emphasized Jerusalem's importance to Arabs, Muslims and Christians only. Even when Hussein later admitted to Jerusalem's sanctity to the three religions (and explicitly mentioned Jews), he occasionally connected opposition to Israel's sovereignty in East Jerusalem to his quarrel with a Jewish presence there; as he declared in 1974: 'Jerusalem will never be a Jewish city'.[45]

Jordan's main efforts regarding Jerusalem – besides demanding Israel's withdrawal and its return to Arab sovereignty – focused around Israel's *fait accompli* which Jordan construed as 'Judaisation' of the city. What particularly provoked Jordan, in addition to Israel's resolutions of June 1967, was the massive construction of new Jewish suburbs around Jerusalem on former Arab lands. By annexing these new residential areas to Jerusalem, Israel conspicuously tipped the demographic scale in favour of the Jews. The purchase and expropriation of Arab lands enabled Israel to surround the Arab-populated areas of Jerusalem and the nearby villages, to limit their expansion and to prevent Arab territorial contiguity. Jordan initiated a number of debates in the UN General Assembly and Security Council on these issues.[46]

On 30 July 1980 the Israeli Knesset passed a basic law which declared the 'whole and unified' Jerusalem as the capital of Israel. This law strengthened Israel's decrees of June 1967 which *de facto* annexed East Jerusalem. Jordan, clearly, never accepted this new law and called on both Israel and the international community to return the city to Arab hands. The most eloquent Jordanian spokesperson against Israel's control of East Jerusalem was Crown Prince Hassan. He frequently attacked Israel's illegal measures there by using international law and international conventions to refute Israel's claims and to challenge its self-proclaimed rights to the Arab part of the city.[47]

Israel was occasionally accused of taking actions designed to change both the status of Jerusalem and its Arab nature. As of the early 1970s, King Hussein claimed that Israel was banishing the Christian and Muslim population from the city, and warned against the alleged efforts to turn Jerusalem's mosques and churches into museums.[48] A major aspect of Israel's plot to Judaise Jerusalem, as Jordan saw it, was the renaming of Arab streets, quarters and historical sites with Hebrew names. The Amman daily *al-Ra'i* published a list of such names and charged that 'the changing of Arab names is systematically being carried out. They translate the land and its stones into Hebrew and publicise the new names, inside and outside the country, on maps, in atlases and in books. They are enthusiastically working to erase our heritage.' *Al-Ra'i* claimed that the new names had nothing to do with the old ones and that places that the Jews attributed to their ancestors had not been built by them. 'Solomon's stables', for example, were not built in King Solomon's time but by the Roman Emperor Adrian.[49] Hence, steps to prevent the Judaisation of Jerusalem were to be taken 'immediately', even before efforts to ensure an Israeli withdrawal and the reinstatement of Arab sovereignty, because the policy of Judaisation was allegedly designed to prevent the latter.

Towards the end of the period surveyed, Jordanian spokespersons frequently reiterated demands for an Israeli withdrawal from East Jerusalem, using all the arguments mentioned above. Israel was pressed to recognize the Arab rights to Jerusalem and not to ignore the fact that its Arab section had been illegally occupied since 1967. Jerusalem's Arab-Muslim identity should be respected, its holy shrines liberated, and the 'Arab flag should be hoisted over its hills'. The Jews enjoyed no rights over the al-Aqsa mosque, and they were attempting to Judaise the holy city.[50] Statements of this sort were made particularly after the outbreak of the 1987 *intifada*. The uprising once again placed Jerusalem in the limelight and provided Jordan with an opportunity to comment on one of its favourite topics without being suspected of competing with the Palestinians and the PLO.

By and large, the importance of Jerusalem to the Arabs, Muslim and Christian alike, and its return to Arab hands, was viewed by Jordan as the key to peace in the Middle East. Under Arab sovereignty, Jerusalem would constitute a symbol of peace and the guarantee for its implementation. This attitude was an attempt to place Jerusalem above and beyond any mundane, political and territorial issue. The need to hand it back to the Arabs, like its uniqueness and sanctity, was unquestionable.

7 SETTLEMENTS AND NATURAL RESOURCES

About three months after the June war, Israel began to settle the recently-acquired territories. In September–October 1967, four provisional settlements or 'outposts' (*He'ahzuyiot*) were established by *Nahal* soldiers. These were regular IDF soldiers who volunteered to combine military service with agricultural work; indeed, the *Nahal* had set up such settlements along Israel's borders since the early 1950s. Only one of the four settlements, Kefar Etzion, was built on territory occupied from Jordan.[1] Despite this fact and even though the settlements were merely considered military outposts, the Jordanians were alarmed. They realized that *Nahal* settlements in Israel were eventually transformed into ordinary civilian *Kibbutzim* or collective agricultural villages. Moreover, the area of Kefar Etzion, the Etzion Bloc, had formerly consisted of four Jewish settlements, occupied and destroyed by the Jordanian army in the 1948 war. Jordan was afraid that the Israeli government intended to re-establish these settlements and annex them to Israel. Hence it was quick to protest to the major powers about the establishment of Jewish settlements in the occupied territories and their illegality, as they contradicted international treaties and resolutions.[2]

In 1968, the construction of Israeli settlements in the Golan Heights and the West Bank intensified.[3] The location of West Bank settlements was not random. Their deployment already reflected the policy to which Israel would adhere up to 1977 (i.e., as long as Israeli governments were Labour-led coalitions). Settlements (both military outposts and civilian) were established mainly in the Jordan Valley or along the 'green line' (the pre-1967 demarcation line between Israel and Jordan's West Bank). Israel deliberately avoided establishing settlements in the densely populated areas of the Judean and Samarian mountains, in order not to violate the perception of a political settlement that it hoped to reach with Jordan on the basis of territorial compromise. The settlement map of Israel was drawn up by Yigal Allon, Deputy Prime Minister, Minister of Education and Foreign Minister in the Labour governments between 1967 and 1977, and was thus called the Allon plan. The plan advocated Israeli retention of the Jordan Valley as a buffer zone (with a corridor to Jordan) as well as the Jerusalem-Latrun area and the Etzion Bloc along the 'green line'. The rest of the West Bank, about 60 per cent, was to be returned to Jordan. Kiryat Arba (near Hebron) and Elon Moree (in Samaria) were, until 1977, the only settlements founded in the West Bank outside the lines of the Allon Plan.

Jordan, on its part, pursued the line of denouncing the settlements as illegal because they changed the status and the (Arab) nature of the occupied territories and constituted an Israeli act of defiance against the international community. The establishment of these settlements reflected Israel's greed for Arab land and its expansionist character. The on-going construction of settlements indicated, in the eyes of Jordanian spokespersons, that Israel was not seeking peace but rather, intensifying hostilities.[4]

References to dismantling the settlements, however, were less frequent than to the subject of withdrawal, for example, and Jordanian spokespersons rarely directly demanded tearing them down. It seemed that the hope was that continuous insistence on an Israeli withdrawal would eventually yield fruit and the question of the settlements would then become irrelevant. Hence, references to settlements were mainly in the context of criticism of Israel and an indication of the anti-Jordanian and anti-Arab intentions attributed to the Jewish state. This somewhat low-key attitude towards the settlements entirely changed in 1977 due to the political shift in Israel. Following the coming to power of the right-wing *Likud*, both its image and its policy brought the question of Israeli settlements in the West Bank into the limelight. Under the Labour governments, between 1967–1977, about 30 settlements had been established in the West Bank. Their total population, not counting the new residential quarters in Greater Jerusalem, was about 5000.[5] Aware of the political composition of the new government and of its ideological commitments, and even before the cornerstone for the first new settlement was laid, Jordan feared a massive construction drive that would, geographically and demographically, irreversibly change the Arab character of the West Bank. Jordan's reaction to Likud leader Menahem Begin's first cabinet reflected Jordan's apprehension regarding Israel's outright rejection of any territorial retreat, new settlements, and expansionism towards the East Bank of Jordan.[6]

Jordan continued to emphasize the illegality of the settlements. Claims were primarily made by Crown Prince Hassan who, in his books and articles, elaborated on the issue and maintained that the settlements violated the provisions and conventions of international law that forbade the acquisition of territory by war. The settlements had been established in defiance of certain provisions of the fourth Geneva Convention of 1949, of the Hague Convention of 1907 and of several UN resolutions. They were therefore often condemned by UN organs.[7]

One of the main overt explanations for Jordan's lack of enthusiasm about the Egyptian–Israeli peace process was that it could not effectively negotiate the issue of the escalating Israeli settlement in the occupied territories. Shortly after Sadat's dramatic visit to Jerusalem, King Hussein complained that the visit did not bring about a change in Israel's settlement policy. 'Nothing has changed. There are now 31 Israeli settlements on the West Bank, with 49 new ones planned. They have gone ahead with six of them since Sadat's visit.'[8] The King also criticized the idea of a Palestinian autonomy and the Camp David accords on the same grounds. When asked about the proposals for Palestinian autonomy in the West Bank over a transitional period (during which the permanent settlement would be negotiated), the King dismissed the notion as an impossible solution while Israel continued to set up new settlements. 'What will happen to the numerous settlements throughout and after the transitional period?', the King asked rhetorically, 'What will be the status of the Jewish settlers?'[9]

Apprehension about Israeli settlement intensified after Menachem Begin formed his second government in 1981, as most of Jordan's fears from 1977 had been realized. In 1981, at the end of Begin's first term as Prime Minister, there were about 80 settlements in the West Bank, some in the densely-populated Arab areas in Samaria and elsewhere. The new map reflected the policy of Ariel Sharon, Minister of Agriculture and later Minister of Defence in Begin's governments: the creation of Jewish blocs in the West Bank to be formed around the major cities in this area that would separate Palestinian enclaves. They would cut off Palestinian territorial contiguity and thus make the prospect of an independent Palestinian state a less viable option.[10] The settlements were portrayed as a serious obstacle to peace. They endangered the political situation and it was feared that their continued construction and enlargement would leave no hope to advance towards a peaceful solution.[11] Crown Prince Hassan noted that even the Americans opposed the settlement and that President Reagan had made an unheeded call on Israel to freeze the establishment of more settlements as part of his 1982 peace initiative.[12] Jordanian spokespersons also explained their vehement opposition to the settlements, claiming that they were perpetuating the Israeli occupation of Arab lands and thus paving the ground for their eventual annexation. The intensive construction of new settlements was designated to create a *fait accompli* and an irreversible new reality: 'creeping annexation' of the occupied territories.[13]

It seems that the Jordanians were more concerned about the new settlements in the 1980s not only because of their large number but also due to the composition of their population. Their settlers were 'no longer simply adherents of the extreme religious organization, Gush Emunim, which seeks the restoration of the promised land in accordance with Biblical provisions, but ordinary families seeking cheap housing away from the overcrowded urban centres of Israel. They receive encouragement and assistance from the government to move into these areas so that creeping occupation will turn annexation into a reality.'[14]

Moreover, while official Labour party policy regarded most of the West Bank as a bargaining card in future negotiations, as their settlement map showed, the Likud adopted a different stance. For them the settlements were creation of facts on the ground that would make future withdrawal practically impossible. Even though the West Bank had never officially been annexed, the Likud policy encouraged settlements in the West Bank, prioritized them in comparison to settlements within the 'green line' and bestowed upon their settlers financial benefits. It was obvious that for all intents and purposes, the Likud leaders regarded the West Bank as an integral part of Israel. It is not surprising, therefore, that during this period (after the early 1980s) a change could be detected in the emphasis and priorities of Jordan's public political statements. Demands for Israeli withdrawal became, if not less frequent, clearly less decisive, as a ritual or as lip service, due to the realization that such a withdrawal did not seem feasible in the foreseeable future. The settlements became the main target on which Jordanian spokespersons focused. They were portrayed both as an obstacle to peace and as indication that Israel preferred territory to peace.[15] Thus, statements about the need to liberate and save occupied Arab lands increased considerably. However, they usually referred not only to the intensive construction of new settlements, but to the comprehensive negative impact of Israel's policy on the Arab population, as well as on the geographical and human environment in the West Bank.[16]

Israel was accused of continuing its expansionist policy. Jewish settlements were established on every corner of occupied Arab land, in colonial fashion. Israel took over the natural resources, primarily the water, and expropriated Arab land and houses. Lands that were confiscated on the pretext that they were necessary for military purposes were eventually used for the establishment of new civilian settlements or residential quarters. The settlers terrorized the Arab population with the encouragement of the government, which urged its Jewish citizens to settle in the occupied territories. In this context, Israel was also accused of deliberately and arbitrarily changing the geography and the demography of the occupied territories and of their Judaization, by encouraging the Arab population to emigrate, and by expelling them for the sake of eventual annexation of the West Bank. Israel, according to the Jordanians, had, by 1985, taken over more than half of the West Bank lands and creeping annexation was occurring.[17]

Naturally, Jordan's actual demands of Israel, in this context, were, first and foremost, to put an end to the building of settlements. These demands were usually made in a general or indirect manner such as 'if Israel continues to build settlements in the West Bank, the prospects for peace will diminish'.[18] On other (relatively few) occasions, demands to stop the building of new settlements were made directly and even introduced as a precondition to political negotiation. Outright demands to remove existing settlements were also not frequent and mainly to Arab audiences.[19] The inclination to condemn Israel's settlement policy and the general quest to end it (rather than specific demands for the dismantling of existing settlements) seems to concur with the basic demand for a complete Israeli withdrawal. Adherence to the notion that the West Bank should be returned to Arab hands implied that once this occurred, the problems posed by the Jewish settlements would also be eliminated. On the other hand, an explicit and constant demand to dismantle the settlements could be construed as a goal in itself (i.e., not as a phase in the all-out struggle to regain the occupied territories) and hence to indirectly indicate acquiescence to something less than a total Israeli withdrawal. The settlement issue, however, remained a central one which was frequently referred to, one way or another, in the public statements of Jordanian spokesmen, particularly in the second half of the period surveyed.

8

CHANGING ISRAEL'S POLICY AND IDEOLOGY: THE HASHEMITE VIEWPOINT

CONCEPTUAL DEMANDS

A. Changing of Israel's Ideology and Policy

In the 1950s and 1960s, King Hussein, following the Arab consensus, had publicly viewed Zionism as a demonic movement of an expansionist and racist nature, that aimed not only to take over all of Palestine but to dominate the entire Arab Middle East and to subjugate its population to its imperialistic whims.[1] Hussein distinguished between Jews and Zionists. To the latter he attributed all of Israel's bad blood with the Arabs. The former he was willing to accept, yet only as members of a religious community and under Arab protection, not as members of an independent, political entity. Hence the King's reluctance to recognize Israel's legitimacy and right to exist as a nation-state.

Following the 1967 war, Hussein looked for a way to accommodate his earlier public statements within the new political reality that necessitated a certain recognition of Israel. Despite his adjustment to the changing conditions, he still toyed with the idea of possible Israeli 'de-Zionization'. Hussein's post-1967 statements, predominantly to Western audiences, indicated that he was willing to accept Israel as a Jewish state providing it gave up what he perceived as its Zionist nature. In a speech delivered in November 1967 at Georgetown University in Washington, King Hussein declared that 'Israel should "de-Zionisate" herself. The Jews of Israel should choose between living peacefully with the Arabs, or remaining an isolated outpost in the Arab world'. The King predicted that if a solution to the problems in the Middle East was not found, 'the struggle would go on until either the Arab world is subjugated by a Zionist empire or until the Arabs eventually destroy the State of Israel'. He called upon the Jews to give up Zionism and to integrate within the new society that the Arabs were striving to establish in the Middle East.[2] He believed that Israel had to change its political thinking and to decide whether it wished to merge into that part of the world or to live in isolation. The Israelis had to dissociate themselves from their 'siege mentality' and agree to live in the region as partners and not as masters. If Israel continued on the same path, it would become 'another Rhodesia'. How could Israel persuade the world it coveted peace and stability when it refused to change its outlook and methods in dealing with the environment around it? A major Arab force should be built up in order to impose a radical change in the thinking of Israeli leaders.[3]

It is not entirely clear what Hussein meant when he spoke about the 'de-Zionization' of Israel. What sort of transformation did he expect Israel's society and government to undergo? It seems that the first practical outcome of such a transformation would be withdrawal from the territories occupied in 1967 and repatriation of the 1948 Palestinian refugees. Since in Hussein's terminology Zionism equalled expansionism, carried out through forceful and violent means, giving up this ideology in whose name the Jews committed all their 'crimes' against the Arabs, might enable them to correct these wrongs. The King also expected Israel to keep a low profile, not to patronize the Arabs and to return to its natural dimensions, i.e., to recognize the fact that it was a small Jewish minority in an enormous Arab-Muslim region. Israel should not boast of its recent military victory and should not profit from it.[4] Hussein probably perceived non-Zionist Israel as a bi-national state rather than a Jewish one, devoid of territorial expansionism, probably within the 1947 UN partition lines. Such interpretations were substantiated in an editorial in *Al-Dustur* in early 1968:

> Israel insists on Arab recognition, yet such recognition requires fundamental changes, which Israel's current Zionist leadership cannot provide. In the long run, the future of the Israelis will depend on the Arabs since the Jews are a minority. The minority has to adapt itself to the will of the majority, otherwise it will be impossible [for the majority] to willingly accept it.[5]

Hussein even resorted to the generation-long rhetoric on peaceful Jewish–Arab coexistence in pre-Zionist epochs. Such coexistence could 'still' be achieved were it not for the expansionist and bellicose Zionist concept.[6] Prime Minister Bahjat al-Talhuni told a British delegation in 1970 that 'there is no hostility between us and Judaism as a religion and the Jews as a people. There is hostility, however, between us and Zionism which has been built on a political, racial and expansionist basis.'[7]

This attitude was typical of the first years after the 1967 war. From the 1970s it seems that in practice, Jordan accepted Israel's existence within the pre-1967 lines, and was willing to do so officially in return for certain Israeli concessions. Henceforth, the distinction between Judaism and Zionism served no purpose. Accepting Israel meant accepting Zionism as the state's ideology. The reference to Israel as the Jewish or the Zionist state continued and the Israelis were still called Zionists (with a negative connotation). The Israelis were still asked to change their mentality and political thinking, yet these calls were usually devoid of the demands for changing or abolishing the Zionist character of Israel ('de-Zionization'). References to Israel as a Zionist state were more frequent when addressing Arab audiences and were occasionally used to criticize Israel's activities: 'a Zionist plot', 'the Zionist occupation', etc.[8] These expressions seemed like lip service to the old Arab rhetoric and its traditional reluctance to use the term 'Israel' instead of the less antagonizing substitutes, 'the Jewish state' and 'the Zionist entity'.

As implied, the more Jordan publicly reiterated its readiness to accept Israel (in return for withdrawal and a solution to the Palestine problem), the fewer the references to and criticism of the Zionist character of Israel. This ideological compromise was not portrayed as a Jordanian concession. On the contrary, even if not specifically stated, it could be construed that if and when Israel withdrew from the territories occupied in 1967 and acquiesced to Palestinian self-determination, this would mean that Israel had undergone an ideological shift and given up its Zionist-expansionist nature. In the course of the years, Jordan indeed emphasized the changes it demanded and expected in Israel's practical *behaviour* and political thinking, rather than in its *ideological* perception. Following this approach, Israeli withdrawal from the occupied territories and recognition of Palestinian rights were not merely in compliance with the Arab demands, but also a gesture of appeasement, a manifestation of Israeli readiness to extend a hand to the Arabs and recognition that this was the only solution to the problem. When the prospects for peace and conciliation were at stake, the burden of proof lay on Israel. It was Israel that should change its attitude and meet the Arabs at least half way.[9]

B. Acknowledgement of the Central Position of the Hashemite Regime; Fear of Israel's Alleged Intentions

Jordan's demands of Israel reflected the complexity of its position *vis-à-vis* its Jewish neighbour. Hussein's determination to regain the West Bank led the King to hold direct clandestine meetings with Israeli officials, at considerable personal and political risk. Since Israel had always insisted on direct negotiations with the Arabs, Hussein believed that his gesture (though secret) would be reciprocated by Israeli concessions. He was infuriated by what he regarded as Israel's inflexible stance, its failure to appreciate Jordan's position and its reluctance to commit itself to anything beyond vague references to 'territorial compromise'. Its positions remained tough, stubborn and 'rejectionist' regarding any peace initiative.[10] King Hussein could not escape the feeling that the Israelis were taking him for granted and disregarding the central role that his country and his regime were playing in the quest for a political settlement. His brother, Crown Prince Hassan, publicly commented on this issue and noted that Jordan 'is critical to a settlement, to any settlement, of the Middle East problem . . . Jordanian views must be very seriously considered if any initiative is to have a chance at success'.[11]

These Jordanian views were exacerbated in the late 1970s, when the right-wing Likud came to power in Israel, and particularly after Menachem Begin formed his second government in 1981. During that period, several Israeli politicians advanced the slogan 'Jordan is Palestine' and advocated turning Jordan into the Palestinian state, given the fact that the majority of the population there were of Palestinian origin and that King Hussein himself had occasionally mentioned (albeit in different contexts) that 'Jordan is Palestine and Palestine is Jordan'.[12] West Bank Palestinians would migrate or be transferred to Jordan, as would the Palestinian refugees in Lebanon.[13] This could pave the way for Israeli annexation of the West Bank. These ideas were taken very seriously in Jordan, especially considering their unavoidable conclusion: that this would mean the destruction of Hashemite Jordan. A few weeks after the Likud's electoral victory in May 1977, Hussein warned that 'Israeli greediness' was expanding towards the East bank as well. Hussein occasionally repeated these accusations, adding that Israel intended to change the situation on the East Bank and wanted Jordan to solve the Palestinian problem.[14] Israeli references to the "Jordanian solution" intensified after the formation of the second Likud government in 1981. Hussein construed these statements not only as an indication of Israel's expansionist intentions, they also showed that despite the common interests and the various tacit understandings between Jordan and Israel (including against Palestinian militancy), Likud politicians were, for the sake of their own nationalistic interests, willing to sacrifice the Hashemite regime and to acquiesce to the transformation of Jordan into a Palestinian state.[15]

Hussein's comments in this respect became more frequent and more explicit. Israel, once again, was accused of intending to transfer the Palestinian problem to Jordan, and to make it a Jordanian problem, even at a price of military occupation of Jordan for that purpose. Jordan was not an empty country. It could not and would never be a substitute for the

Palestinian homeland. Jordan was thus portrayed not only as Palestine's defence line but also as the rampart that protected the Arab nation from 'Zionist expansionist ambitions'.[16] Jordan's disappointment with the Likud governments was thus twofold. Not only did they fail to appreciate Jordan's central position in the region and its pivotal role in any future settlement, but some Likud leaders were willing to turn their country into a Palestinian state, and even to dispose of the Hashemite dynasty. Prince Hassan's words reflect his bitterness:

> For their part, Israelis have consistently recognized the central role of Jordan in any viable settlement arrangements. Some propose to "bury the Palestinian problem in Jordan," others to transform our country into a Palestinian state, and still others to confer upon us what amounts to a policeman's role in a West Bank virtually incorporated into Israel. Mind you, these options scarcely scratch the surface of the catalogue of Israeli ideas. But all see in Jordan an important actor.[17]

It is difficult to determine to what extent Hussein was genuinely afraid that a 'substitute homeland' was an imminent Israeli course of action. He suspected some right-wing Israeli politicians of being unpredictable and it seems that at least during the second Begin cabinet, 1981–1984 (with Ariel Sharon as Minister of Defence), and particularly after Israel's invasion of Lebanon in 1982, he did not rule out that 'Jordan is Palestine' might become a viable Israeli option. At any rate, between 1977 and 1984, during the Likud governments, Hussein was reluctant to directly negotiate with its leaders, even though he signalled, shortly after Begin formed his first cabinet, that he was willing to continue the dialogue between the two governments.[18] All Jordanian statements in this respect obviously implied that a Jordanian precondition to any discussion of a political settlement with Israel required the latter's abandoning any considerations of a 'substitute homeland'.

9 THE PALESTINIAN ISSUE

Reference of Jordan's leaders to the 'Palestinian Problem' (*al-qadiyya al-filastiniya*), whether or not in the context of demands of Israel, was a most complicated and intricate issue. No other topic under discussion underwent such a metamorphosis in the statements of Jordanian officials. It clearly reflected political changes as well as developments concerning the Palestinian issue on the public agenda. Moreover, since the term 'Palestinian' referred both to territory and to people, it was difficult, if not impossible, to detach the former from the latter, even when Jordan's interests required such separation. As will be seen, immediately after the 1967 war, both the West Bank and its inhabitants were considered Jordanians by the government in Amman. A few years later, when Jordanian policymakers were forced to admit that the West Bank's population was Palestinian, great creativity was needed to explain why the West Bank should be considered a Jordanian realm and should be returned to Jordan, while its inhabitants were defined, nationally and politically, as Palestinians.

This raises several questions: What was the 'Palestine problem' in the eyes of the Jordanians? How did Jordan perceive its solution throughout the period surveyed? To what extent was Israel expected to solve the question and what exactly was Israel required to do in return for an Israeli–Arab political settlement?

In the first years after the 1967 war, Jordan continued to adhere to the same perception it had previously held. Namely, the *territorial* aspect of the Palestine question was confined to the area of the State of Israel within the 1949 armistice lines, where the Palestinians should exercise their rights and ambitions. The *human* aspect of the same problem concentrated on the 1948 refugees who should be repatriated to Israel.[1] In most cases, when

Jordanian officials used the term 'Palestinian' it was as an adjective describing the noun 'refugees' of the Palestinian diaspora.[2] When tension between Jordan and the Palestinian organizations mounted, in 1969–1970, King Hussein began to refer to the 'Palestinian people' and to its rights as well. Yet this was in specific contexts: Either as a 'people expelled from its homes and from its homeland'; or as '*our* Palestinian people' (author's emphasis). This people should, according to Hussein, regain its rights in the spirit of UN resolutions 194 and 242,[3] resolutions that referred to the Palestinians as refugees.

In other words, the solution to the Palestine question lay mainly, if not exclusively, with Israel. Both the West Bank and its inhabitants were regarded as Jordanians. 'The West Bank is an inseparable part of the Hashemite Kingdom of Jordan and its inhabitants are Jordanian citizens.'[4] Jordan's prime concern, like that of Egypt, in the wake of the 1967 war, was 'the liquidation of the traces of the aggression'; i.e., the retrieval of the territories recently occupied. The Palestinian identity (or at least the character) of both the 'territories' (the West Bank) and its population was at that time completely ignored. In a speech to the UN in October 1967, the Jordanian Foreign Minister referred to 'one million Jordanians who are living in the [occupied] West Bank of Jordan'. Even references to *fida'i* activity, which enjoyed extensive media coverage, did not mention its Palestinian affiliation and characteristics.[5]

While Jordanian spokespersons continued to pay lip service to their country's commitment to the Palestinian issue, in practice the issue was circumvented by the crucial territorial topic that was regarded purely as a domestic Jordanian matter. In early November 1967, Crown Prince Hassan told the Jordanian Parliament that 'the question of Palestine is the cornerstone of Jordan's internal, external and Arab policy. It is for us a matter of life or death.' Yet, he continued, 'The enemy occupied the West Bank and eternal Arab Jerusalem. Arab lands are endangered by the enemy.'[6] Only in the 1970s did Jordan admit that the West Bank and its indigenous population did not constitute a purely Jordanian matter. It was also a part of both aspects of the Palestinian problem. As of the summer of 1970, Jordanian officials began to refer to the Palestinian right to self-determination and even to the possibility of a Palestinian state in the West Bank.

According to Jordan's original perception, the demand for Israeli withdrawal in the aftermath of the 1967 war had nothing whatever to do with the Palestinian question. Henceforth, it became an inherent and inseparable part of this question. Even in the 1970s, however, Israeli withdrawal and returning the West Bank to Jordan were a precondition to any progress in the Palestinian arena. Once Jordan was back in the West Bank, the Palestinians there could exercise their rights and decide (via a referendum or otherwise) their fate: an independent state, a Palestinian–Jordanian federation, or some other entity.[7]

After the bloody encounter with the *fida'iyun* organizations in 1970/71, the right of the Palestinian people 'to fight occupation, injustice and aggression' was regarded by Jordanian spokespersons as 'legitimate and sacred'.[8] King Hussein's proposed federal scheme of a United Arab Kingdom in March 1972 was another telling instance. The King admitted that 'maybe the federal plan should have been introduced before June 1967'. Crown Prince Hassan also later admitted that the previous policy had been unrealistic: 'Today, we understand that the Palestinian problem must be dealt with in the context of the existence of Israel.'[9] Moreover, until that time, Jordan's demands of Israel were mainly for full withdrawal and recognition of the Palestinians' right to self-determination (i.e., the refugees' right of return). As of the 1970s Israel was also asked to endorse the establishment of a Palestinian state in the West Bank and Gaza and to recognize the PLO, demands that Jordan itself, only a few years before, had vehemently rejected. Indeed, Jordan's reluctant recognition of the Palestinian nature of the West Bank and of its inhabitants did not imply recognition of the PLO as their representative.

One has to bear in mind that the uniqueness of the 'Palestine problem' emanated from the particular political and demographic nature of the Hashemite Kingdom and from its 'special' affiliation to the Palestinian question. Not only had Jordan annexed and controlled about one-quarter of mandatory Palestine, but two-thirds of its population were Palestinians. Moreover, the Hashemite regime regarded itself as the guardian of the Palestinians, whom it had saved 'from the Israeli claws' and had offered them not only physical shelter and a safe haven, but also an alternative homeland and an alternative identity. Palestinian nationalism, however, incarnate in the PLO, that had begun to challenge Jordanian–Palestinian coexistence as early as 1964, gained more force and legitimacy after the June 1967 war. When all of mandatory Palestine came under Israeli control, the PLO was relieved of the need for its pre-1967 verbal acrobatics designed to explain why the Palestinians had no territorial claims to those parts of their homeland that were occupied by Arab states: the West Bank, the Gaza Strip and al-Hammah.[10]

Following the 1967 war, the PLO gradually contested Jordan's claim to the West Bank. The organization demanded to be recognized as the legitimate representative of the Palestinian people and insisted, to Jordan's chagrin, on being the lawful possessor of any Palestinian territory if and when Israel withdrew. Official Jordan continued to perceive the PLO as a military organization, a *fida'i* movement, and publicly supported its effort to liberate Palestine (i.e., the State of Israel). While Jordan took pains to portray the outcome of the war as an issue of occupied Arab territories

(Jordanian, Syrian and Egyptian) that should be recovered, the PLO managed to draw attention to its Palestinian aspects as well. As early as 1 September 1967, at the Khartoum Arab summit conference, together with 'no peace with Israel, no recognition of Israel, no negotiation with it', Article 3 also emphasized 'insistence on the rights of the Palestinian people in their own country'.[11] Though at that stage the reference to 'the Palestinian people's own country' referred, as it had prior to 1967, to Israel and not necessarily to the West Bank, Jordan was concerned. It was obvious that lip service to the 'Palestinian problem' had to be paid, even if in the style of pre-war rhetoric. Jordanian statements in that spirit could be construed as recognition of the existence of a 'Palestinian question' (without defining its exact nature) that should be negotiated. Yet, as noted, the Israeli occupation of the West Bank and of East Jerusalem was a another story; it constituted a Jordanian and an Arab problem.

Jordan continued to ignore the political aspirations of the PLO, particularly its declared intention to represent the Palestinians.[12] After the November 1973 recognition of the PLO as the sole legitimate representative of the Palestinians by the Arab summit in Algiers, Jordan still ignored the PLO. Hussein admitted that 'we do not represent the whole Palestinian people exclusively', yet he insisted that the Palestinians should (after Israel's withdrawal) decide who represented them. The King also criticized the recent summit for deciding on the Palestinian representation (i.e., recognizing the PLO) 'when the Palestinian people had not yet made their choice'.[13]

In the second half of 1974, in view of mounting Arab support for the PLO, Jordan somewhat changed its tune. Its spokespersons declared that Jordan had recognized the PLO when it was established in 1964, yet reiterated that the West Bank was occupied Jordanian land, 'so Jordan and Jordan alone was responsible for the retrieval of these territories'.[14] Jordan, however, was explicit regarding its future response if the Arab world transferred the 'Palestinian representation mandate' to the PLO. 'If the Arab heads of state decide that the PLO will be responsible for the occupied territories and will be the only legitimate representatives of the Palestinian people, we shall then respect their decision and consider ourselves relieved of our obligations and commitments, and henceforth we shall not take part in any discussions leading to a peaceful settlement.'[15]

Moreover, Jordan was infuriated by Israel's preliminary contacts with Palestinian notables and local leaders from the West Bank and East Jerusalem immediately after the war. These meetings were followed by rumours on bilateral negotiations to establish an Israeli-backed Palestinian state in the West Bank. King Hussein accused Israel of attempting 'to strike at the morale of the inhabitants in the occupied territories by describing the Arab–Israeli conflict as solely between the Israelis and the Palestinians, which was of no concern to other Arabs. This was done with the intention of establishing a weak political entity in the West Bank, which would be under Israeli control.' Hussein was also reported as saying, in another context, that 'anyone who doubts the unity of both banks of the Jordan is a traitor'.[16]

REFUGEES, RIGHTS, SELF-DETERMINATION

The fate of those Arab inhabitants of Palestine who had fled or been forced to flee their homes in 1947–9 developed into a controversial and bitter issue that made a solution to the Arab–Israeli conflict extremely difficult. They were estimated to number about 700,000; i.e., more than 50 per cent of the 1.3 million Arabs who lived in Palestine in 1947. The rest, 600,000 Palestinian Arabs who remained in their pre-1947 residences, lived in the newly-established state of Israel (about 180,000), in the West Bank that was incorporated into Jordan (about 400,000), and in the Egypt-occupied Gaza Strip (about 20,000). After 1949 most of the refugees resided in refugee camps in Jordan (West and East Bank), in the Gaza Strip, as well as in Syria and Lebanon.[17] Thus most Palestinian Arabs (over one million) continued to live within the boundaries of former mandatory Palestine, albeit under three different regimes; they enjoyed varied civil and political rights[18] and different residential status (refugees and non-refugees). Jordan hosted the lion's share of the refugees, about 450,000. Moreover, since Jordan considered itself the lawful suzerain of the Arab parts of Palestine and sovereign of the Palestinians whom it wished to integrate, Jordan facilitated the naturalization of all willing refugees and granted them full civil and political rights.[19]

As early as 11 December 1948, even before the fighting in Palestine had ended, the UN General Assembly adopted resolution 194, article 11 of which reads:

> [The General Assembly] resolves that the refugees wishing to return to their homes and live at peace with their neighbours should be permitted to do so at the earliest practicable date, and that compensation should be paid for the property of those choosing not to return and for loss of or damage to property which, under principles of international law or in equity, should be made good by the Governments or authorities responsible.[20]

Ever since, the implementation of this resolution has been a recurring Arab demand of Israel and the UN.[21] It was the source of the international legitimacy for insistence on the repatriation of the refugees (referred to by the Arabs as the 'right of return', *haqq al-'awda*). Various international efforts to solve the refugee problem failed. Israel agreed to the repatriation of 100,000 refugees as part of Israeli–Arab peace treaties, providing that the rest would be resettled elsewhere, i.e., in Arab countries. For their part, the Arabs demanded complete repatriation to Israel[22] and were reluctant to absorb any refugees in their own countries. On the contrary, Arab states that hosted refugees insisted that they remain in temporary camps and, with the exception of Jordan, discouraged their integration and opposed any rehabilitation projects whatsoever. They limited the refugees' freedom of movement and employment with the intention of perpetuating the refugees' plight as a bleeding wound, in order to keep Israel's guilt alive in world public opinion and, eventually, to get rid of the Palestinian refugees.

Post factum this approach did not serve the Palestinian cause well as it rooted the image of the Palestinian problem as merely a humanitarian one of deprived individuals, rather than as a national–political one. This attitude prevailed even after the establishment of the PLO, which took pains to uproot it, and even after the 1967 war. The most telling instance is UN resolution 242 of November 1967, which became the cornerstone of efforts to solve the Arab–Israeli conflict; its rationale (peace for territories) gained wider consensus than any other idea for a political settlement has won. But this resolution also perceived the Palestinian problem in the same way. It never mentioned either 'Palestine' or 'Palestinians' and the only, indirect, reference was its call 'for achieving a just settlement of the refugee problem'.[23]

This state of affairs suited Jordan's position, as resolution 242 did not threaten its national interest in the Palestinian realm. It could also provide an additional explanation as to why Jordan so consistently adhered to this resolution and why it considered it the best formula for a political Arab–Israeli settlement. It is not surprising, therefore, that Jordanian spokespersons so frequently expressed their support of 'Palestinian rights according to Security Council resolutions'. 'Palestinian rights' or their 'legitimate rights', in the early post-1967 period, were construed by Jordan as the right of return to their villages and towns in Israel. Jordan continued to view the question of Palestine as a refugee problem as long as possible. In September 1968 Prime Minister Bahjat al-Talhuni stated that 'the Palestine issue is not an Arab question but a humanitarian one'.[24]

During and after the 1967 war, between 200,000–250,000 residents of the West Bank left their homes and moved to the East Bank. Some of them, at least, were coerced into doing so.[25] More than half of them were 'old refugees' mainly from the camps near Jericho and some (15,000) from the Gaza Strip. Israel later allowed the repatriation of tens of thousands, but in practice only 14,000 returned to the West Bank.[26] Henceforth, demands for the repatriation of refugees were twofold: the return of the 1948 refugees (*lajiyun*) to Israel and the return of the 1967 refugees (*nazihun*) to the West Bank.[27] Generally speaking, however, the refugee question was usually portrayed as an issue related to the 1948 war and thus the quest for its solution was somewhat secondary to the more crucial demand: withdrawal from the territories occupied in 1967.[28] This reflected the attitude of the Khartoum summit meeting: first the traces of the 1967 aggression should be eliminated (i.e., regaining the occupied territories) secondly, by underlining the right of the Palestinian people over their homeland, the resolution had indirectly implied that the evils created in 1948 should be mended (repatriation of refugees and the destruction of Israel).

King Hussein used to depict this approach (particularly to Western audiences) in a more pragmatic and flexible manner than other Arab spokespersons. In November 1967 the King stated that if Israel absorbed one million refugees, the Arab would 'accept' it.[29] Even after president Sadat's journey to Israel, Hussein's declared precondition to join the Egypt–Israel negotiations was the repatriation of the Palestinian refugees in their lands.[30] In late 1968 and early 1969, world public opinion became more exposed to and more aware of the 'Palestine problem', mainly due to intensified *fida'i* activity from and within Jordan, and in view of the takeover of the PLO by al-Fatah and other *fida'iyun* organizations in February 1969. Jordan too had to adapt its public statements to the changing attitude. If, immediately after the war, Jordanian spokespersons insisted on the right of the *refugees* to repatriation, as of 1969 they spoke of the need of the *Palestinian people* to regain their full rights, including the right to self-determination (*taqrir al-masir*).[31] Henceforth the demand that Israel recognize the full rights of the Palestinian people became the Siamese twin of the demand for a complete withdrawal and both became a *sine qua non* for any future political settlement.[32] Later the King would note that, as a result of the Rabat resolution, 'the question of the restoration of the occupied territories and the national rights of the Palestinian people came to be merged into one whole'.[33]

Nevertheless, despite clothing the demands in more 'respectable' terminology, the substance of the rights in question, as the speakers explicitly explained, remained the same. The term 'Palestinian people' stood for 'refugees', and the homeland where their rights should be exercised was pre-1967 Israel; i.e., the refugees were entitled to either repatriation or compensation, in the spirit of UN resolution 194 of 1948. This change in terminology (but not necessarily in content) emanated from the public upgrading of the Palestine question. The *fida'iyun* organizations gradually become a dominant factor that kept the Palestine issue alive and active on the Arab and international public agenda. Since King Hussein had no intention of giving the West Bank to the PLO, he once again moved the ball into the Israeli court. The Palestine problem was depicted, in certain contexts, not only as a question of territories but also of refugees who had the right to return to their lands (in Israel) or be compensated.

The first deviations from this concept occurred on the eve of the major confrontation between Jordan and the Palestinian organizations in ('Black') September 1970. Addressing his new government in June 1970, the King stated: 'We have believed all along in one solution that we would accept. This is the solution that will give us [Jordanians] back our usurped land and will rescue our Palestinian people'.[34] It is possible that 'our Palestinian people' also referred to the non-refugee residents of the West Bank, under Israeli occupation. In response to American pressure to contain violent Palestinian activities against Israel from Jordanian territory, King Hussein was more unequivocal. He stated that 'the Palestinian people has the right to liberate what was usurped from its land. Jordan cannot function as an international police force to prevent this activity'. Simultaneously, he insisted on Israeli withdrawal from the occupied territories and their retreat to the pre-5 June 1967 borders.[35] It seems therefore that the term 'usurped land' that the Palestinians had the right to liberate, this time referred not to the State of Israel but to the West Bank. Indeed, the statement should be viewed in the context of the tension between Jordan and the Palestinian organizations and in light of King Hussein's efforts to prevent a showdown. It indicated that Jordan had no intention of limiting *fida'i* activity against Israel, yet it also implied that Jordan recognized, for the first time, a Palestinian right to a territory that Jordan also coveted. Though he spoke about the Palestinians as a collective, they still lacked national attributes. Hence Jordan's ambition to regain the West Bank did not contradict Palestinian rights there. A few weeks later the King went even further. In an attempt to allay the suspicions of the Palestinians regarding his intentions, he did not rule out that the solution to the Middle Eastern crisis would be the establishment of a Palestinian state in the West Bank. He pointed out, however, that after the liberation of the occupied territories (and their implied return to Jordan), the Jordanians and the Palestinians on both Banks should decide on their own fate and future relationship.[36]

These statements were certainly a precedent and, *post factum*, also a turning point. Indeed they were first uttered in a specific context and in order to achieve certain political goals. After the Jordanian army quelled the *fida'iyun* organizations, such ideas (and in particular, the possible establishment of a Palestinian state) were not discussed again for quite a while. But when Jordanian spokespersons returned to the earlier terminology – 'Palestinian rights' including the 'right to self determination'[37] – this was a clear shift away from refugee repatriation to the right of Palestinians to decide their own future, *in the West Bank*. It was emphasized, however – particularly after Hussein issued his March 1972 federal scheme – that the Palestinians could exercise this right only after the 'liberation of the occupied land' (i.e., after an Israeli withdrawal and the return of the West Bank to Jordan).[38] This stipulation was a *sine qua non* and, in return for its recognition of Palestinian rights, Jordan expected the Arab world to endorse its own right to first regain the occupied territories. That was also the essence of the federal scheme that, as noted, was to transpire *after* Jordan had regained the West Bank. In the speech that heralded the federal scheme, the King introduced it as a materialization of 'the pledge we made to allow our people the right of self-determination'.[39]

It seems that the entire move was designed to grant Jordan a double 'safety net' regarding the prospect of regaining a foothold in the West Bank. The first was the precondition of returning the West Bank to Jordan. The second, the idea that the Palestinians would decide on their own future, indicated that a sort of referendum would be held *after* Jordan controlled the West Bank. Under such circumstances, Jordan would be likely to influence the results of such a referendum. At any rate, these statements showed that Jordan could no longer separate the Palestinian question from that of the West Bank and was forced to admit that they were connected; i.e., after the West Bank returned to Jordan, its Palestinian inhabitants would negotiate with the government in Amman on the nature of their future relations. In the course of the coming years, various options would be discussed, from return to the *status quo ante*, to a federation, to a confederation, and to total separation and the establishment of an independent Palestinian state in the West Bank and the Gaza Strip.

In the course of the late 1960s and early 1970s Israeli Defence Minister Moshe Dayan toyed with the idea of a so-called 'functional compromise': an anti-thesis to the 'territorial compromise' concept. This was designed to prevent the partition of the West Bank and to perpetuate Israel's control there. He proposed to separate the sovereignty over the lands of the West Bank from sovereignty over its population. Such a division would leave the territories in Israeli hands while its population enjoyed Jordanian citizenship, and voted for the Parliament in Amman.[40]

The fact that the West Bank and its population were at the core of the Palestinian issue was later manifested in the Israel–Egypt peace process and the discussions on Palestinian autonomy. Jordan was clearly opposed to Israel's views as expressed in the Palestinian autonomy talks. They were perceived as Israeli refusal to recognize the Palestinians as a people entitled to self-determination. Israel was accused of separating the land from the people by confiscating the former and pressing the latter to emigrate. Jordan, on its part, insisted that Palestinian rights referred to a clearly-defined people inhabiting a clearly-defined territory. That had been the case for 'countless centuries'. King Hussein reiterated that the Palestinian cause was inseparable from the Palestinian lands.[41]

The political developments that preceded and followed the Yom

Kippur war and growing Arab and global concern about the Palestinian cause and the PLO as its representative, contributed to the erosion of Jordan's position *vis-à-vis* the Palestinians. In September 1973, the summit of 78 non-aligned countries in Algiers recognized the PLO as the sole legitimate representative of the Palestinian people. Similar resolutions were adopted by two additional meetings held there: that of Arab Foreign Ministers and the Arab summit conference, both in late November 1973.[42] Henceforth Jordan too publicly supported the legitimate, or constitutional (*shar'i*), rights of the Palestinian people and advocated a future referendum through which they would decide their political future.[43] Once again, that would occur only *after* Israel's withdrawal. Jordan's insistence on that sequence of events was explained by the fact that it was Jordan's responsibility to regain the occupied West Bank, as Jordan had lost it in 1967. In the summer of 1974, Hussein stated to *Newsweek* that his support of Palestinians' right to self-determination did not imply that he could not negotiate the return of the West Bank.[44]

In view of the regional and global change of attitude towards Palestinian rights, the Jordanian call for an Israeli withdrawal had an additional dimension after King Hussein had issued his federal scheme in early 1972 and particularly after the Rabat Arab summit of late 1974. Henceforth, withdrawal would not be demanded only in order to 'eliminate the traces of the aggression', to reverse the reality to the pre-1967 position or to satisfy Jordanian territorial ambitions. It was also demanded in order to enable the realization of Palestinian self-determination and to pave the ground for the establishment of their state in the territories. The demand for withdrawal was therefore described by Jordanian spokespersons as a service to the Palestinian people. This service should be rendered because Jordan still considered itself the representative of the Palestinians, since 95 per cent of them 'live in the East and the West Bank and the Gaza Strip'. 'We shall not give up even a grain of Palestinian rights,' King Hussein declared 'because it is our right and we shall not compromise on the Palestine problem as it is our problem.'[45]

Acknowledgement of Palestinian rights to repatriation, self-determination and to be masters of their own fate did not imply, however, that Jordan recognized the PLO as their representative. On the contrary, the Hashemite kingdom still perceived itself as the authentic and lawful representative of the Palestinians. Until the explicit and comprehensive Arab resolution of November 1974 at the Rabat summit meeting – and even afterwards – Jordan engaged in a futile rear-guard battle to prevent the recognition of the PLO as the 'sole legitimate representative of the Palestinian people'. When referring to Jordan's decision to grant the Palestinians freedom of choice regarding their political future, King Hussein stated, not without cynicism, that if they decided on an independent state they would have to elect their leaders, as 'I can not impose the PLO on them'.[46]

The issue of self-determination was very convenient for the Jordanians.[47] A general and unspecific term, it could always be construed in a way that would serve Jordan's interests and allow it to maintain its claim of representing the Palestinians *vis-à-vis* the PLO. Even as late as the mid-1980s, when Hussein concluded an agreement with Arafat for future cooperation, the possibility of a Jordanian–Palestinian confederal state in which 'the Palestinians will exercise their inalienable right of self-determination' was still being discussed.[48] Jordan therefore depicted itself as the banner-carrier of Palestinian rights. On the eve of the Geneva conference, Jordan conditioned its participation on granting to Palestinians the right of self-determination. Jordan did not oppose the participation of the PLO in Geneva, yet threatened to boycott the conference if a decision on the establishment of a Palestinian government in exile were adopted and if this government (i.e., the PLO) demanded sovereignty over the West Bank and Gaza.[49] Even after the Rabat resolution, Hussein believed that his country could still play a central role in the efforts to regain the occupied territories as he considered it unlikely that the Israelis would talk with the PLO.[50]

In Jordan's perception, its legitimacy as the representative of the Palestinians was not challenged by the mere fact that the West Bank and Gaza were Palestinian lands; its own claim was stronger than that of the PLO. Jordan no longer questioned the Palestinian nature of these territories, yet this reality did not *ipso facto* grant the PLO or any other Palestinian representative an advantage over Jordan, or the right to control the Palestinians as long as the Palestinians had not decided (by holding a referendum or otherwise) who their representatives were. Jordan's right to represent them was as strong, and perhaps stronger, than that of the other contenders. Jordan clung to the prospect that if the Palestinians were properly asked and within a suitable political context (i.e., under Jordanian control), they might choose to continue being represented by the Hashemites, as they had in the past, in view of the historical bilateral cooperation. The unification of the two Banks after the 1948 war reflected, according to King Hussein, a Palestinian choice that derived from the right to self-determination that Jordan had granted them.[51] Namely, the Palestinians had exercised this right as early as 1948, at the congress of Jericho.

Crown Prince Hassan traced the roots of this cooperation even earlier. In 1981, following the Egyptian–Israeli peace treaty and the suspension of autonomy talks, he published a book entitled *Palestinian Self-Determination*, in an endeavour to prove that Jordan never denied the Palestinians the right to self-determination (while Israel and post-Camp David Egypt did). He claimed that King Hussein bin Ali (founder of the modern Hashemite dynasty and father of King Abdullah) was 'the first voice to seek the right to exercise self determination in Palestine', while his son, King Abdullah, 'gave his life in attempting to preserve Arab identity in Jerusalem and Palestine'.[52]

These problems regarding Jordan's position on the question of Palestine did not, in practice, affect its demands of Israel. The Palestinian rights that Israel was required to honour remained the same as those in the wake of the June 1967 war. Only after Jordan itself was compelled to recognize the Palestinian rights was Israel asked to follow suit and, later, to agree to an independent Palestinian state, even under PLO leadership. King Hussein's speech before the UN General Assembly in September 1979 implied that mere repatriation of the refugees would not solve the Palestinian question. Israel therefore 'must withdraw from the territories it occupied in June 1967, must respect the right of the displaced Palestinians to return to their homeland and must stop its denial of the Palestinians' right to self-determination, including the right of their people to establish an independent state if they so wished'.[53]

As long as 'self-determination' and 'Palestinian rights' meant, according to Jordan, the repatriation of the refugees, they were basically aimed against Israel. Later, when these rights also included the Palestinians' right to decide their own future, it was Jordan that might become their potential victim, as the country that would, at the end of the day, have to pay the price if the Palestinians insisted on establishing an independent state in the West Bank. The demand that Israel recognize the Palestinian right to a state of their own was not made only because it was politically correct. Jordan also expected to benefit, hoping that this would precipitate an Israeli withdrawal. Even at the final stage, from the mid-1970s and onwards, when Jordan's prospects to return to the West Bank had dwindled, it still demanded that Israel recognize Palestinian rights and declare its willingness to let the Palestinians exercise their rights in the West Bank and Gaza.[54]

From Jordan's point of view, the Jordanian–Palestinian tug of war over the future of the West Bank was less relevant for Israel, since Israel's full withdrawal was a precondition to any action or discussion in this respect. Israel's position mattered only because Jordan's tactics to continue being involved in the West Bank were based on the assumption that under no circumstances would Israel give the West Bank to the PLO. The Jordanians still hoped that Israel might hand the West Bank over to King Hussein, or at least negotiate its return to Jordan. In order not to focus on the West Bank as the core of the Palestinian question and in order not to create the impression that if Israel withdrew the Palestinian problem would be solved, King Hussein took pains to underscore the other Palestinian rights 'beyond the West Bank and Gaza'. These concerned 'all the lands occupied since 1948'.[55]

After it was generally accepted that the Palestinians were not merely refugees, they were considered a people whose usurped rights should be regained.[56] This is the backdrop against which Jordan's intensified public calls should be viewed, as well as its insistence on Israeli recognition of mounting, diversified Palestinian rights. In addition to a complete withdrawal, Israel was required to allow the repatriation of the refugees, including the restoration of their lands and other property, to let the Palestinians exercise their right to self-determination, to recognize the Palestinian rights that had been ratified by the UN, to recognize their legitimate and national rights in their homeland and their right to establish their national home (*watan qawmi*), and even to create an independent Palestinian state on their national soil.[57] 'National rights' as Hussein later explained included 'genuine security' that Israel should grant the Palestinians, comparable to its own quest for security.[58] In one case at least, King Hussein even defined the 'legitimate soil' on which the Palestinians were seeking their rights as 'the West Bank and Gaza'.[59] These demands were portrayed, particularly to Western audiences, as the preconditions to any peaceful political settlement of the Middle Eastern conflict.[60] According to Crown Prince Hassan, there was almost universal consensus that the Palestine problem was 'at the core of the continuing Middle East tragedy' and its resolution constituted 'the sine qua non of any general and effective settlement of the Arab–Israeli conflict'.[61]

In the early 1980s, Palestinian rights were expanded once again. National self-determination, according to Crown Prince Hassan, was not a purely political act. 'It is a coalescence of legitimate rights – historical cultural, social and economic – that culminates in the exercise of political sovereignty by a distinct community in its ancestral homeland'. Hence Israel was asked to recognize these and other rights, in addition to the traditional demand for the Palestinians' right to self-determination on their national soil.[62] These far-reaching rights, which reflect national characteristics, implied the existence of a distinctive Palestinian people and the prospect of its forthcoming statehood. The mention of these rights is not so much a demand of Israel as Jordanian acquiescence to such an eventuality. Later Hussein added that the Palestinian people had the full right to *freedom* on its own land, a right that Israel should recognize and honour.[63]

In the second half of the 1970s, shortly before, and in the immediate aftermath, of President Sadat's visit to Jerusalem, Hussein raised another demand: that Israel concede to international supervision of the occupied territories. This was expected to precipitate an Israeli withdrawal or at least serve as a fallback in light of Israel's reluctance to withdraw. The King maintained that it was impossible to realize the Palestinian right to self-determination under Israeli occupation. This was also his view regarding the idea of autonomy to the Palestinians in the West Bank that was discussed between the Egyptians and the Israelis. He therefore proposed, as an interim measure, to place the West Bank and Gaza under international supervision to ensure that the inhabitants could determine their own future without pressure or interference by any external factor (i.e., neither Israel nor the PLO).[64] As of the second half of the 1970s, King Hussein began to add yet another component to his list of demands of Israel. Initially he suggested that Israel negotiate directly with the Palestinians. Later he insisted that Israel should recognize the PLO as interlocutor, and should negotiate its withdrawal from the occupied territories as well as seek a solution to the Palestinian problem with the PLO.[65] (At the time, these were still raised as two separate issues.) It is worth mentioning that these demands were made at a time when Jordan itself barely maintained contacts with the PLO, whose presence in Jordan had been banned since July 1971. Only after Sadat's visit to Jerusalem, the Camp David accords, and the Israel–Egypt peace treaty, did Jordanian–PLO ties and coordination resume. Henceforth Jordan emphasized the PLO's legitimacy as the sole representative of the Palestinians, and held that it should participate directly in any future peace negotiations and/or peace agreements.[66]

This declared adherence to the Rabat resolution and acceptance of the PLO as the Palestinian leadership was so compelling that King Hussein used it as another excuse to reject Israeli overtures for a political solution in the spirit of the so-called 'Jordanian Option'; i.e., the return of most of the West Bank to Jordan, while maintaining an Israeli presence along the Jordan Valley, the mountain tops and other strategic areas. Jordan had already rejected the idea because it entailed a territorial compromise to which Jordan was vehemently opposed. Officially, however, the notion was turned down because it meant that Israel intended to negotiate with Jordan and thus bypass the Palestinians, who should play the leading role in finding a solution. The King refused to take part in such a 'plot'.[67]

Hussein went even further to characterize UN resolution 242 – hitherto one of Jordan's most cherished documents, in that it provided international legitimacy for Jordan's demand for an Israeli withdrawal – as insufficient, as far as the Palestinian people and the Palestinian question were concerned.[68] This was an indication of the growing importance attributed to Palestinian rights, even, on the face of it, at the expense of the specific demand for Israel's withdrawal (particularly when it became clear that Jordan would not regain the West Bank). Jordan still insisted on demanding that Israel withdraw completely, notwithstanding that the withdrawal was only necessary to solve the Palestinian problem.

After Israel's invasion of Lebanon in the summer of 1982, Jordan tried to take advantage of the PLO's weakness. On the face of it, Jordan did not alter its previous positions,[69] yet it emphasized that Jordan and the PLO would coordinate activities to regain Palestinian rights.[70] Indeed, Jordan occasionally questioned the legitimacy of the PLO, particularly after the rebellion within al-Fatah movement in the summer of 1983, and the disappointment with Arafat's conduct after the conclusion of his agreement with King Hussein in early 1985. Yet even then, the King maintained that Jordan would honour any Palestinian decision regarding its leadership and undertook to accept the PLO as the legitimate Palestinian representative if the Palestinians so decided. Jordan's criticism of the PLO and their differences of opinion concerned the means that should be taken, not the issue of representation. Hence they did not dispute the organization's right to lead the Palestinians or to represent them at an international peace conference.[71] Not only did Jordan endorse its recognition of the PLO as the sole legitimate representative of the Palestinian people, but also insisted that Israel should follow suit. Israel was also asked to accept the organization as a participant in a future international conference that Jordan wished to convene in order to politically solve the Arab–Israeli conflict.

Israel rejected both the idea of the conference, which contradicted its unvarying demand for direct Israeli–Arab negotiations, as well as participation of the PLO. Jordanian spokespersons insisted that if Israel wanted peace it had to participate in the conference and abide by UN resolutions regarding withdrawal and the repatriation of refugees. Israel's reluctance to do so was viewed by the Jordanians as rejection of resolution 242, which they perceived as the cornerstone of any framework or mechanism for solving the conflict.[72]

King Hussein and other officials made it clear that Jordan had no intention of representing the Palestinians or substituting for the PLO at the expected international conference. In this way, the Jordanians enhanced the PLO's legitimacy as the sole representative of the Palestinians. They insisted on its participation at the conference either separately or as a part of a joint Jordanian–Palestinian delegation – saying that it was impossible to solve the Palestinians' problem without their participation.[73]

Jordan perceived the outbreak of the *intifada* in the West Bank and Gaza in late 1987 as enhancing its demands that Israel retreat from the occupied territories, grant the Palestinians their rights and thus put and end to the conflict.[74] The *intifada* also invigorated Jordan's initiative to end the conflict by means of an international conference. This time it was emphasized that the conference should bring about Israeli withdrawal from all occupied territories and solve 'all aspects of the Palestine problem'.[75] Even though this phrase had already been mentioned in the Hussein–Arafat agreement of 1985, it was frequently reiterated in the context of the reawakening idea of an international conference. Israel was now required not only to withdraw but also to accept the PLO as an interlocutor, to grant the Palestinians the right to self-determination and, probably, to solve the refugee problem. The PLO's contribution to the 'solution of all aspects of the Palestine problem' should be to abandon violence, acknowledge resolution 242 and 338, and acquiescence to a political solution of the Arab–Israeli conflict.[76]

Even after Hussein's decision to sever Jordan's 'legal and administrative ties' with the West Bank, in late July 1988, Jordan still felt a moral obligation and a sense of solidarity with its former citizens, West Bank Palestinians. Jordan undertook to assist and to support them until their national goals were achieved.[77] By and large, Jordan continued to put its earlier demands to Israel. Israel was asked to mend its ways and to respond positively to Arab peace initiatives. The Jordanian message was that Hussein's speech of the 31st of July had created a new reality in the Middle East. The Israelis should embrace this reality and adapt to it.[78]

PART III

JORDAN'S OPTIONS AND ITS QUID PRO QUO

10 A MILITARY OPTION?

Jordan's attitude towards the possibility and the advisability of a military option, throughout the period surveyed, was rather complicated. It was influenced by the course of political and military events and by domestic and regional developments. On the one hand, a factor that spurred King Hussein to prefer the political track, in the wake of the June 1967 war, was his evaluation that neither Jordan nor the other Arab states had a viable military option for regaining their territorial losses. In the following years, that assumption was occasionally questioned. On the other hand, the King, as well as other Jordanian spokespersons, noted that another Arab–Israeli war was immanent unless Israel withdrew to the 4th of June 1967 borders. Jordan, however, regarded the Arab military option as a last resort, to be considered only after all other efforts to make Israel give up its spoils of the 1967 war failed.

I. Justification of Palestinian Military Activity (1967–1970)

The activities of the Palestinian *fida'iyun* organizations after the June war, within and outside of the occupied territories, were generally acclaimed by Arab public opinion. The military defeat of three regular Arab armies in six days and the loss of territories three times larger than the Jewish state was a major humiliation for regimes and for the public, not only in Egypt, Syria and Jordan, but in the entire Arab world. The Palestinian organizations that continued to attack Israeli targets in the occupied territories and elsewhere were perceived by the Arab public as the only body that dared to challenge the Jewish state militarily, and to hoist the banner of resistance against victorious Israel. As such, they were regarded as redeemers of the lost Arab honour.

In view of the organizations' mounting popularity (and given that a considerable portion of the East Bank population were Palestinians), it was difficult for the Jordanian government to publicly criticize their activity even when the *fida'iyun* turned Jordan into their major base and implicated the country in Israeli retaliation. During most of the period between 1967 and 1970 Jordan was inclined to publicly sympathize with the organizations' activities, depicted as an alternative to the political option. Shortly after the June war, Hussein was quoted as saying that if progress towards a political solution were not reached 'within the next three months', Jordan would reassess its policy not to encourage *fida'i* activity and might consider new measures, regardless of the price it would have to pay.[1] At that stage, when Hussein was in the midst of a diplomatic campaign to mobilize world leaders to force Israel to withdraw, the support of the Palestinian organizations as well as the threat to resort to a military option were designed to put more pressure on his interlocutors and to imply that the Arabs still had an additional option.

In early 1968, while praising the spirit of the 'guerrilla', the King also warned that their activity might harm the Arab cause, unless coordinated with the general [Arab] strategy.[2] Yet after the Israeli raid on Karama on 21 March 1968, when the popularity of the Palestinian organizations reached a record high, the King was less reserved in his support for them. At a press conference shortly after the battle, in reply to a question as to whether the declared number of civilian casualties included *feda'iyun*, the King made his famous statement: 'It is difficult for me to distinguish between *fida'iyun* and others. We may reach a stage soon when we all become *fida'iyun*.'[3] A few months later, speaking to a British audience, he compared *fida'i'yun* activities to those of the various resistance movements against the Nazis in occupied Europe during World War II.[4] At this stage, while Jordan was insisting on the return of the West Bank and claimed it to be an occupied Jordanian territory, *fida'iyun* operations were introduced as legitimate resistance of people who had lost their homes and land. They were depicted as actions by individuals who had suffered a personal loss and not as an expression of national will. Whenever asked why Jordan did not put an end to the (anti-Israeli) activity of the *fida'iyun*, the King replied, 'I do not stop them because this is their land. Israel is occupying it and they [the *fida'iyun*] see no other way but to fight for their rights. It is their right to actively oppose the occupation.... There is no difference between my endeavours for a peaceful solution to their attempt to achieve a solution by struggle. What we all want is to regain our rights... When this is achieved there will be no justification for *fida'i* activity.'[5]

In the course of 1970, when the power, influence and popularity of the Palestinian organizations in Jordan reached unprecedented heights, they became a genuine threat not only to law and order but also to the authority of the regime. Hence, official expressions of support for *fida'i* activity (mainly to local audiences) were made more frequently and more explicitly in order not to antagonize public opinion and to appease the organizations. The general Arab military option, which Jordan should exercise together with the Palestinians, was occasionally mentioned. 'Jordan supports the *fida'i* activity with all her might. She neither opposes nor will she oppose it. We wanted this activity and made it possible. We want it to become stronger and to occupy its deserved place in the fateful battle (*ma'arakat al-masir*) . . . The power of our brothers the *fida'iyun* is our power and our power is theirs', and, 'The resistance is a legitimate right and a sacred duty. We have to close ranks and to stand united [in this battle]'.[6] It is worth noting that only in this context, on the verge of the September confrontation, were the *fida'iyun* referred to as acting on behalf of and in the name of the Palestinian people and that this people had the right to defend itself, to liberate its usurped land and to take up arms until its country was liberated.[7] These statements, though made in the midst of a national emergency and an existential crisis, did not necessarily imply that Jordan had given up its claim to the West Bank and to representation of the Palestinian people. After the September 1970 encounter and particularly after the elimination of the *fida'iyun*'s military and political presence in Jordan, in July 1971, the Palestinian military option was almost never mentioned by Jordanian spokespersons.

II. Jordan's (and the Arab's) military option

As already indicated, King Hussein and other Jordanian officials occasionally mentioned the danger of another cycle of violence if Israel did not withdraw to the pre-June 1967 lines. Such arguments, however, were not usually presented in the context of the viability of an Arab military option. It was often implied, or even explicitly stated, that if nothing is done to force a withdrawal and while Israel's arrogant and rejectionist attitude keeps pushing the Arabs into a corner, a war would break out, regardless of whether the Arabs had an adequate military option. As King Hussein put it to the Jordanian Parliament, 'We insist on the retrieval of our rights and on the rescue of our brothers in the occupied lands from the Zionist occupation. Our right is our goal and we shall not give it up, regardless of the circumstances, the price and whatever we have to sacrifice.'[8]

The threat that full-scale war would erupt ('If Israel keeps refusing to comply with UN resolutions and if the Powers fail to reach a peaceful solution'),[9] implied, in a way, that Jordan felt that the Arabs were indeed devoid of a military option. They still expected the Powers to extricate them from their dire situation. On other occasions, particularly after a few years had elapsed since the June war and no progress had been made in the realm of an Israeli retreat, King Hussein maintained that the Arabs did have a military option, albeit not an immediate one:

> If no progress is made towards a peaceful solution to the Arab–Israeli conflict, it is possible that the prospect of reaching such a solution may be lost forever . . . If [UN Secretary General's envoy] Jarring fails to implement Security Council resolutions, the only possibility is war. It might break out in a year, a couple of years or a decade [but will eventually break out].[10]

By the same token, Hussein warned against the Israeli-cultivated atmosphere of the unlikelihood of a forthcoming war, claiming that the Arabs 'are not yet ready for a war and will not be prepared in the foreseeable future'. Maybe an all-out war 'is currently not to be expected', the King said, but due to the political impasse, a war might break out 'next month or next year'. If a solution is not reached peacefully, 'no external power ... can prevent a long and continuous war'.[11] Some of Hussein's statements in the early 1970s, when the Arab–Israeli deadlock continued, implied that even though the Jordanians had a military option, they were reluctant to use force. They regarded it as a last resort not because they were afraid of war, but because they preferred and desired peace. In one case at least, the King admitted that Jordan had no military option of its own. When in 1971/72 an Israeli–Egyptian political arrangement was speculated, following President Sadat's feelers and initiatives, Hussein maintained that 'without Egypt we'll never have sufficient power [to wage war]', thereby eliminating the possibility that Jordan would confront Israel alone and on its own initiative.[12]

As became apparent in October 1973, Hussein was reluctant to confront Israel militarily even with the backing of Egypt and Syria.[13] On the one hand, this war showed that the Arabs did have a military option. Yet in view of their inconclusive achievements and their failure to force Israel to withdraw (save for the disengagement agreements between Israel and Egypt/Syria, achieved due to US pressure), the King was quick to conclude that this war might not be the last war between Israelis and Arabs. The decision on the future path, however, of making either war or peace, was, in his analysis, entirely in Israel's hands.[14]

Frequent speculation originated in Amman regarding the danger of a forthcoming war following Jordan's futile efforts to convince Israel to agree to a mutual disengagement of forces along the Jordan river. This speculation intensified after the Rabat Arab summit of late 1974 that denied Jordan's right to represent the Palestinians. Hinting at the importance of Jordan's involvement in the efforts to achieve a political solution, King Hussein reiterated the urgent need to renew the quest for peace in order to prevent another catastrophe. 'The next war will be different from the last one'. Not as limited, more comprehensive, 'a genuine disaster (*karitha*)'. 'Both parties,' he prophesised, would resort to 'horrible kinds of weaponry.' Moreover, such a war would have a greater impact on the global balance of power and would present a greater danger than the October war.[15]

Throughout the 1970s and the 1980s, Jordan continued to press the argument that as long as Israel clings to the territorial spoils of war, a new round of fighting is likely to break out.[16] After the mid-1970s, however, and particularly after the transformation in Israel politics in 1977, the fear of such an eventuality focused on Israel. The traditional warning that 'a war may erupt' was replaced by 'Israel might initiate a war'.[17] Such an intention was attributed by Hussein to Israel for two reasons:

A. The gap in the military balance of power between Israel and the Arabs had never been so wide, to the benefit of the former. Israel's strength was without precedent; it was stronger than all the 'confrontation Arab states' together.[18]

B. The coming to power of the right-wing Likud party. 'Menachem Begin is not a man of peace' and the new government may take advantage of its military superiority to try to change the status quo in the Middle East once again and to impose its policy on its neighbours.'[19]

The implied message that the Arabs had no military option was occasionally expressed explicitly.[20] Jordanians spokespersons maintained that this could be achieved only by means of close cooperation by Arab states. Only such a unified force would be capable of defeating the enemy and returning the usurped land.[21] The absence of such an option was sometimes explained by quasi-ideological reasons or global processes. As in the first years after the June war, the use of force was again depicted as a means that should be considered only as a last resort. Moreover, a military solution could by no means be considered the real solution. All concerned parties should abandon violence and seek international political assistance to solve the problem.[22] King Hussein outlined his views in this issue in a speech to Jordan's military academy in late 1987:

> The times when nations achieved their ambitions using the force of arms have long passed . . . Cooperation and good neighbourly relations, to which all countries of the world aspire, can only be maintained through dialogue and mutual understanding. Threats and the use of force should be abandoned. Those who adhere to obsolete ideas [i.e., the use of force] harm only themselves. Adherence to weapons will produce nothing more than continued pain and deeper wounds.[23]

As the King delivered this speech barely a week after the outbreak of the *intifada*, one can speculate that he also implied that, due to regional and global developments, Israel also had no military option.

11 THE PERCEPTION OF A COMPREHENSIVE PEACE

I. Peace as Jordan's *Quid Pro Quo*

In an article published in 1982 in *Foreign Affairs*, Crown Prince Hassan wrote, 'After the 1967 War, other Arab governments learned – and what a costly lesson – what we had known for almost two decades: Israel was to be an enduring reality of the Middle East.'[1] One can argue to what extent Jordan's political behaviour was indeed based on this assumption (unless Prince Hassan was referring to the policy of his grandfather, King Abdullah I). There is, however, no doubt that Jordan was the first Arab state to grasp the meaning of the changes generated by the 1967 war and to rapidly adapt to the new reality these changes created. While putting unequivocal demands to Israel, King Hussein was the first Arab leader who realized that a *quid pro quo* was needed in return. He was also the first (and for a long time, the only) leader who was willing to reciprocate with such a Jordanian *quid pro quo*.

In the first weeks after the war, Hussein believed that demilitarization of the West Bank (that had been discussed between Jordan, Israel and the US *before* the June war), might be considered a proper response to an Israeli withdrawal. Even Egyptian President Jamal Abd al-Nasser was convinced by the King that concessions would be necessary to secure the return of the West Bank. He gave Hussein a free hand to make such concessions, providing the King neither recognized Israel nor negotiated with directly.[2] As early as 28 June 1967, about two and a half weeks after the end of the hostilities, Hussein told US President Lyndon Johnson that he was willing to demilitarize the West Bank, in return for Israeli withdrawal to the pre-June 1967 borders. Demilitarization, as noted, was a concession that both he and Abd al-Nasser could live with. It could be construed as a merely technical issue, a sort of security arrangement of a limited military nature, rather than a political gesture. Nevertheless, Abd al-Nasser did not propose demilitarization of the Sinai peninsula, for example, in return for a similar Israeli retreat.

The King's efforts to obtain Israeli withdrawal in the aftermath of the June war have already been described. He then took pains to embark on a political initiative within the narrow margins between his willingness to make concessions (in order to regain the West Bank) and the Arab consensus (before and after the Khartoum summit meeting) that opposed peace, negotiations with, and recognition of Israel. Hussein was ready to carry those efforts to the limit, making declarative statements ('Israel's existence is a fact') as well as operative ones ('demilitarization'). According to the Beirut daily *al-'Amal* (mouthpiece of the Christian Phalanges), he also proposed to go as far as issuing a declaration that would put an end the state of belligerency with Israel.[3] A few years later, after the October 1973 war, Israeli withdrawal from the Jericho area was proposed and discussed, in order to provide Jordan with an enclave in the centre of the West Bank which Israel was willing to hand over, in the spirit of the Allon Plan. Israel asked Jordan for a declaration of 'non-belligerency' in return for such a withdrawal. This time the Jordanians refused,[4] considering such an undertaking too high a cost for a partial withdrawal.

The formulation of resolution 242 and particularly its acceptance by Jordan was considered by Hussein to be a major Arab concession and an appropriate *quid pro quo*. Termination of all states of belligerency and acknowledgement of the sovereignty and territorial integrity of every state in the area, including their right to live in peace within secure and recognized boundaries – all these were regarded as fair trade for the withdrawal of Israeli armed forces from the territories occupied in June 1967. The Jordanian (and later the Egyptian) acceptance of this resolution indeed marked a turning point in the Arab attitude towards Israel. It implied not only abandoning the pre-1967 approach according to which the Jewish state had no right to exist, but also a certain practical disregard of the Khartoum summit resolutions.

As noted, resolution 242 became Hussein's credo. He frequently quoted it like a mantra and perceived its implementation to be an instant remedy to the Arab–Israeli conflict, as it was designed to meet the basic demands of both sides. Its phrasing, 'the rights of every state in the area', with no specific reference to Israel, also made it easier for some Arabs to live with. The King regarded this resolution as a package deal, which specified the Arab demands as well as the exact price tag for their fulfilment. Henceforth, Hussein referred to this resolution as a simple equation: peace for territories. In return for a complete withdrawal, Israel was to enjoy a just, comprehensive and durable peace. Yet it was also the maximal concession that Jordan was ready to make for the sake of peace.[5] The Jordanian *quid pro quo* within the framework of 'peace for territories' was occasionally referred to in an indirect manner with the burden of the proof on Israel. If Israel sought peace, security, stability, etc., it had to retreat from the occupied territories and grant the Palestinians their rights. Peace was what Israel would get in return for honouring its part in the equation.[6] The symmetry, nevertheless, and the principle of reciprocity should be strictly observed. Israel withdrawal from the occupied territories should be 'synchronized with the termination of all conditions of belligerency and mutual respect for the sovereignty, territorial integrity and independence of all states in the area'.[7]

In a speech in 1985, King Hussein portrayed the resolutions of the Fez summit meeting (1982) as well as his accord with Yassir Arafat (1985), as 'the expression of the Arab commitment to live in peace with the people and the State of Israel – but only if Israel makes a similar commitment to live peacefully and on equal terms with its Arab neighbors, and particularly with a Palestinian people granted the right of self-determination'.[8] Hussein's public statements indicated that Jordan's acceptance of Israel did not derive from an ideological change but merely from its quest to regain the occupied territories. According to these statements, Jordan's willingness to achieve a just and lasting peace did not emerge before June 1967 but only after the war and directly stemmed from its results. 'If we [the Arabs] had agreed, before the outbreak of the war, to end belligerency, to allow freedom of navigation in the Suez Canal and to a final solution of the refugee problem, Israel would have consented. Now it refuses'; i.e., Israel had gained invaluable bargaining cards in the June war and thus the Arabs had to pay a higher price for a political settlement than what they would have been asked for earlier.[9]

The King admitted that 'If the Arabs could return to the lines of June the 4th, they would like to cross them' [and regain more territory] 'but the world would not allow it'.[10] In other words, the Arab demand for Israeli withdrawal to the pre-1967 boundaries was fair and realistic. The Arabs internalized the considerable changes that the Middle East had undergone and they should settle for a Jewish state within the 1967 borders. The question of recognizing Israel was usually negotiated by Jordanian spokespersons in rather vague terms. When asked in 1974 by a foreign journalist whether – in case of a total withdrawal – the Arabs would recognize Israel and establish formal relations, the King said, 'That's bound to happen'.[11]

One can discern three levels of references to this issue: Recognizing Israel as a fact (or an existing fact), recognizing Israel's right to exist, and recognizing Israel formally and diplomatically as a sovereign entity in the Middle East and as a legitimate member of the family of nations. On the first level, King Hussein referred to Israel's existence as a given fact. In 1969 he told an American audience that he 'recognize[d] that Israel is there in the Middle East and there to stay'. He also reiterated on several occasions that 'Israel's existence is no longer a question'. His brother Crown Prince Hassan emphasized that 'the Palestinian problem must be dealt with *in the context* of the existence of Israel' [italics in original].[12] The principle of reciprocity, however, was occasionally applied to this issue as well. Jordan's Foreign Minister Abdullah Salih asserted in May 1971 that recognition of Israel's existence should be traded for its withdrawal from all the occupied territories.[13] King Hussein maintained, 15 years later, 'To those in the West who seek Arab recognition of Israel's existence, we say this Arab commitment offers mutual recognition of Israeli and Palestinian national rights.'[14]

On the second level, resolution 242 was portrayed by Jordanians as recognition of Israel's right to exist. Even prior to its adoption, the King declared that Israel had the right to live peacefully and securely in the region.[15] Later, he repeated this more unequivocally. When asked in an interview to the BBC after the Fez summit in 1982 whether he recognized Israel's right to exist, the King said, 'I have recognized Israel since I helped in formulating Security Council resolution 242 and accepted it'.[16]

The third level was not actually reached even in the latter part of the period under discussion. Hussein was reluctant to commit himself to such an eventuality (i.e., *de jure* recognition and diplomatic relations), claiming it was 'premature at this stage to speak of that'. 'Obviously, at the end of the line, when we establish peace, one visualizes normal relations existing between all in the area'. Before this stage arrived, the King expected the solution of various practical questions such as the corridors that would link the West Bank to the Gaza Strip.[17] Hussein was also reluctant to elaborate on the nature of the future Jordanian–Israeli peace, its characteristics and components. When asked about this, he generally referred his interviewers to resolution 242, even though it provided the *framework* for peace and not its *substance*. These issues, if and when mentioned, were referred to in general and non-committing terms such as a 'peace that is based on [international] law and justice', a peace that takes into account 'the various interests of the concerned parties' and will provide 'security to the states and justice to the peoples'. Crown Prince Hassan perceived the peace that the Arabs desired as a genuine one, based on compromises that would enable 'Arab and Jew and Christian to live side by side in this region so important to all three faiths'.[18]

Throughout the entire period, Jordan insisted that the final result of Arab–Israeli negotiations should be a comprehensive peace, both in the sense that all problems should be solved prior to its signing and that it should embrace all Arab belligerent parties. Jordan categorically opposed a separate, partial or a piecemeal settlement. It desired a peace that would not only be acceptable to the Arabs in general, but also one to which future generations would consent to and could live with.[19] Jordan opposed the Egyptian–Israeli peace negotiations and their peace treaty in this context. As a separate, rather than a multilateral agreement, it posed a threat to the prospect of a just and durable peace and drove a wedge between Egypt and the Arab World.[20]

Whenever the issue of a political settlement was discussed, King Hussein occasionally assumed – particularly in the first years after the war – the role of an Arab spokesperson. He took pains to persuade his audience – usually foreign – that other Arab leaders shared his views and were also ready for a political *quid pro quo* in return for Israeli withdrawal. In his article in *Foreign Affairs*, Crown Prince Hassan endeavoured to create the impression that the Arabs had awakened from the illusion that they could have peace (or withdrawal) at practically no price. Hassan wrote that

> "peace on the cheap" . . . has been our biggest problem in the Arab world. . . . By "peace on the cheap" we mean the attempt to bring about a settlement at no cost to oneself. No problem that has endured as long, has cost as many lives, and has engendered as much distrust, hatred and discord as the Arab–Israeli conflict can have a cost-free solution. We in the Arab world know that now, for we have paid an inordinate price already, by anybody's accounting.[21]

The King and the Crown Prince frequently publicly viewed compliance with resolution 242, the Sadat initiative, as well as the various Arab summit resolutions and statements made by King Fahd, President Asad and Chairman Arafat, as an indication of the Arab commitment to a peaceful settlement of the conflict and as a token of their willingness to accept Israel and make peace with the Jewish state. Providing, of course, that it met their demands.[22]

Hussein speculated several times that an Israeli withdrawal would yield, in addition to other advantages, freedom of navigation [to Israeli vessels] through the Suez canal and in the Gulf of Aqaba.[23] Besides being a crucial issue from Israel's point of view (and one of the reasons for the outbreak of the June war), such statements created the impression that the King was speaking on behalf of Abd al-Nasser and maybe of other Arab leaders. As early as 1968, when asked whether the Arabs accepted the existence of Israel as a fact, the King said that while he was unable to speak for the entire Arab world, he felt that there was a 'general mood' for accepting Israel's existence. Minister of Information Adnan Abu Odeh claimed that following the Six Day war, more and more Arabs realized that Israel was a permanent factor in the Middle Eastern arena and it was in their interest to reach a peaceful settlement with it.[24] This argument was frequently advanced by Jordanian spokespersons who insisted that there was a strong and genuine desire on the part of the Arabs for a political solution to the conflict. The Arabs had committed themselves to such a solution and were willing to accept Israel's right to exist within secure and recognized borders. Moreover the Arab World had made far-reaching concessions for the sake of peace and 'now' it was Israel's turn to follow suit.[25] King Hussein and other senior Jordanian officials remained the most important Arab spokespersons, particularly outside the Middle East. In their statements they attributed to other Arab leaders moderate intentions and readiness to compromise far more than those leaders were willing to personally and publicly admit.

The above-mentioned statements indicated that Jordan (and the Arab world in general, according to the Jordanian claim) was willing to recognize Israel within its pre-June 1967 boundaries. Indeed, Hussein made it known that if he had to accept Israel he would rather do so within the demarcation lines of the 1947 UN Partition plan (i.e., a considerably smaller and weaker state than the one it became within the 1949 armistice lines). Yet this was wishful thinking rather than a point of departure or a precondition to political negotiations.[26] Jordan agreed that the pre-June 1967 lines (which were actually the lines of the Israeli–Jordanian armistice of April 1949 and constituted the *de facto* border between the two countries) would become an internationally recognized border. Moreover, a few months after the war, the King indicated, in private, that the Arabs might settle for something less than a full withdrawal and that 'Israel's ultimate borders could be open to bargaining'.[27] Hussein rarely mentioned such an eventuality again, yet Jordan did not rule out, even later, the possibility of certain border modifications providing they would be slight, mutual and acceptable to both parties.[28]

In the course of the years, Jordanian spokespersons publicly expressed their awareness of Israel's security needs. They referred to possible security arrangements in order to meet Israel's demands and to allay Jordanian. 'The Arabs cannot afford to ignore the inherent Israeli fears behind the country's obsession with the theme of security or expect these fears to disappear quickly.'[29] Throughout the entire period surveyed, the Jordanians indicated various 'arrangements' , such as border modifications, that they were willing to discuss in return for a full withdrawal. Another arrangement was demilitarization of the West Bank, which Jordan had already proposed as a test balloon immediately after the war.[30] Crown Prince Hassan even proposed to deploy international observers or a peacekeeping force there, and to limit the number of soldiers as well as certain kinds of weaponry along the border. He also proposed that demilitarization provisions be secured by collective multilateral guarantees provided by all states engaged in the [future] negotiations, and reinforced, if needed, by the permanent members of the Security Council.[31]

While recognizing Israel's security needs, Jordan was reluctant to accept Israel's demand for a secure border; i.e., a defensible line that would reflect neither historical, territorial, nor demographic realities, but merely Israel's security considerations, at the expense of Jordan's territorial demands. Such a line (i.e., the Jordan river or the Jordan Valley) would not necessarily constitute the formal, political border between the two countries. That idea was favoured by most Labour party leaders in Israel, yet Jordan categorically opposed it.[32] This was the major reason for Jordan's rejection of the Allon Plan and the various 'Jordanian Option' ideas that originated in Israel. These plans not only failed to meet the demand for a complete withdrawal but also stipulated Israeli presence along the Jordan river. The King and his officials, while acknowledging Israel's right to live safely within secure and recognized boundaries, insisted that these borders be far from the lines Israel had been holding since 1967. As Prince Hassan noted, Israel could not demand ultimate security. 'Each nation must enjoy some security as a result of a settlement, and none of us can have perfect security, for . . . one nation's perfect security, is another's perfect insecurity.'[33] Only withdrawal, and a political settlement that followed, would give Israel the security it desired.

Given the special place that Jerusalem occupied in Hashemite sentiments and politics, the King was ready to make particular concessions in order to secure the return of all of Arab Jerusalem to his sovereignty. Between 1949 and 1967 the Jordanian–Israeli border (or, more accurately, the armistice line) crossed Jerusalem, dividing it between the two countries. The Jordanian section included the 'old city' which contained, *inter alia*, the Jewish Quarter and the Wailing Wall, the most sacred Jewish site. Even though the general armistice agreement of April 1949 between Jordan and Israel guaranteed freedom of access to the holy places by both parties, the Jordanians denied Jewish worshipers access to the Wailing Wall and other sites. In June 1967 Israel occupied, together with the West Bank, the whole of Arab Jerusalem. Following the June war, and particularly after Israel changed the status of Jerusalem and *de facto* annexed it, Hussein was quick to offer to amend this past misconduct in return for a complete Israeli withdrawal that would include the whole of Arab Jerusalem.

As early as August 1967, even before the Khartoum summit meeting, a Lebanese newspaper reported that Hussein had offered free passage to the Wailing Wall, which would become an Israeli enclave.[34] No other source confirmed this report, though later, the King himself indirectly hinted at such a solution. Throughout the late 1960s and the early 1970s, Hussein reiterated, mainly in the western media, that the return of the Arab sector of Jerusalem [to Jordan] or the reintroduction of Arab sovereignty there, did not mean a return to the pre-1967 reality. 'I do not visualize a return to the conditions that existed pre-June 1967 war. We must find ways and means to insure the rights of all people living there. However, in this new context it should be clear that [Arab] sovereignty must be restored over the Arab part of the city.'[35] More specifically, he said that such a possible change should not deny the citizens of Jerusalem, 'Christians, Jews and Muslims', free passage to their holy places.[36] All these, as already noted, implied acquiescence to a certain future Israeli presence in the holy places.

The idea of transforming Jerusalem into a City of Peace, free and open to all denominations and all believers, also offered the Jews what they had been deprived of under Jordan's rule before 1967. Following Israel's withdrawal, Hussein stated, the city should be reunited and constitute a meeting place for the three monotheistic religions.[37] The King made it clear that he was willing to discuss new and creative ideas regarding the future of Jerusalem provided he regained control over its Arab section. He was ready for some sort of international supervision and/or for joint local government.[38] At a certain point, as noted, he even did not rule out the possible internationalization of Greater Jerusalem (both the Jewish and the Arab sections) as part of a comprehensive solution to the conflict. Soon, however, he relinquished this idea and openly renounced it.[39]

As of the second half of the 1970s, when the PLO's challenge to Jordan's claim to the West Bank and Jerusalem gained momentum, Jordan focused more on demands for Israeli withdrawal and on the return of East Jerusalem to Arab hands, rather than offering Israel new *quid pro quos*.

King Hussein, wrote Madiha al-Madfa'i in the early 1990s, '[t]ired of conflict and stalemate, and aware of the cost of continuing war . . . is determined to achieve a peaceful settlement with Israel, although not at any price'.[40] In other words, in the realm of the Arab realization that Israel's withdrawal should be adequately reciprocated, and the willingness to do so, Jordan was the pioneer, as both the earliest to acknowledge the fact and the most generous in its offer.

The framework for Jordan's diplomatic strategy of peace was based not only on the Security Council resolution 242, but also on resolution 338 of October 1973; as well as the 1974 Rabat summit resolution and the 1982 Fez summit peace plan.[41] With the exception of the Rabat resolution, the resolutions constituted international recognition of Jordan's position and offered a concrete definition of the price that both Israel and the Arabs should pay. Jordan took pains to make it clear that the maximal *quid pro quo* should be symmetric to Israeli concessions. King Hussein reiterated that Jordan's interpretation of resolution 242 was total Israeli withdrawal in return for total peace.[42] The acceptance of this resolution by additional Arab countries legitimized Jordan's approach. The Hashemite kingdom was then immune from accusations of having betrayed the Arab cause or of breaking down its consensus. Later adherence to other components of its diplomatic strategy further strengthened Jordan's inter-Arab legitimacy.

II. Peace as an End in Itself

According to King Hussein, he was ready, as early as 1967, to negotiate and make peace with Israel not only as means of precipitating the latter's withdrawal. Hussein still believed that, like in the late 1950s and early 1960s, the state of Israel was valuable, if not indispensable, to Jordan's national security (in spite of his official position that failed to recognize Israel's right to exist). Only the promotion of the 'Jordan is Palestine' slogan, by right-wing Israeli politicians in the late 1970s and the 1980s, temporarily and partially shook this belief.

When it became obvious on the public, declarative level that in order to regain the lost territories, King Hussein was willing to pay the ultimate price (i.e., peace with Israel), references to an eventual peace were more frequently made by Jordanian spokespersons. These spokespersons, and conspicuously among them, the King, endeavoured to explain to various audiences the importance of peace, and depicted it not only as a means (to regain the West Bank)[43] but also as an end. Since the 1970s, peace (that had hitherto occasionally been portrayed as an Israeli trap or an instrument to humiliate the Arabs) was presented as an asset, from which Jordan as well as the Arabs in general could gain economic and other benefits. Providing, of course, that Arab demands were met.

King Hussein took advantage of the Paris agreement, signed in late January 1973 by Henri Kissinger and Le Duc Tho to end the Vietnam war, to describe peace as the new global order of the day, into which the Middle East should also fit. Henceforth he took pains to connect the Arab–Israeli conflict to world affairs. 'The progress towards peace in the Middle East is a global interest, as the situation in this region contains greater dangers than Vietnam.' The King expressed his hope that 'after the end of the Vietnam war and the defusing of tension in Europe, this new atmosphere will reach the Middle East, as the world tends towards a general peace'.[44] On another occasion, Hussein reiterated that 'peace in the region would not only have an impact on regional stability, but would also influence global stability'.[45]

As of the early 1980s, Jordan's leaders, particularly when addressing western audiences, cultivated the idea of peace as a goal in itself. The attitude to peace as a most cherished and desired goal was expressed by King

Hussein when he spoke before the annual convention of the National Association of Arab-Americans in 1985. In a reference to President Reagan's address to the nation on America's economic problems, Hussein quoted him as saying, 'We have come to a turning point, a moment of hard decisions'. The President went on to say, paraphrasing the old Jewish saying, 'If not us, who? If not now, when?' The King maintained that 'that same message and that same action applies now to the conquest of peace in the Middle East'. He insisted that the Jordanian and the Palestinian peoples wanted peace: 'We are ready to pursue it now as earnestly and sincerely as is humanly possible. It is our hope and goal to turn our vision into a reality for all – Jews and Arabs alike . . . Let us attain our goal. Let us close the door on the bitter memories of the past and let us look to the future, that after all, is the promise of peace.'[46]

Another reason that the King desired peace so eagerly was that he wished to put an end to the 'no-war no-peace' situation 'that was imposed on us'. The King found this situation harmful to the Arabs and maintained that they should relieve themselves of its grasp and its suffocation. Peace, as indicated, was the only viable option for ending it.[47] Throughout the same period, the 1980s, Jordanian spokespersons occasionally referred to what was later called 'the fruits of peace'[48] and to the potential economic and practical advantages of such a peace. Foremost among these was Crown Prince Hassan who became the most dedicated advocate of the economic advantages that peace offered. In an article published in 1982, Hassan unfolded his own vision regarding areas of future Jordanian–Israeli cooperation that peace could promote:

> Israel and Jordan have vital interests in development of regional water resources in the Jordan River, but the importance of cooperation in the future cannot be overestimated. In other areas such as tourism, there is also substantial need for cooperation.
>
> After any settlement as before it, Jordan will share a long border with Israel. For us, development is not just an abstract goal, but a pressing need. We do not wish to continue to divert so much of Jordan's small resource base to a costly armaments program to defend our overexposed position or in order to reduce the risks along this extended border.[49]

Hassan advanced similar arguments in another article published two years later. Praising the benefits that might be extracted from a comprehensive peace, he wrote:

> A comprehensive settlement would release the constructive capabilities of both Jordanians and Palestinians to work for socioeconomic development that can consolidate the peace. It could easily turn the region into an advanced workshop and a maintenance center of modern technology. Such a settlement will have to

be supported by a Marshall-type plan for the region to enable its people to fully use their resources in peace and collaboration.[50]

The possibility of a large-scale international financial contribution to rehabilitate the Middle East was definitely an incentive likely to make the idea of peace with Israel more acceptable. It was also a sort of a test balloon, a hint to indicate to the Americans what the Arabs expected from them in return for making peace. The same idea was later also raised by Shimon Peres. Even though the Jordanians were not enthusiastic that it was the Israeli Prime Minister who had taken the initiative, they admitted that peace needed a healthy economic infrastructure, and supported it. On his part, King Hussein continued to forward the idea – even to local audiences – that it was probable that a peaceful solution to the Arab–Israeli conflict would solve Jordan's regional problems, and bring about economic prosperity as well as regional stability.[51]

III. A Comprehensive Settlement vs. a Separate or a Partial Settlement

As soon as a decision was taken in favour of the political option, Jordanian policy-makers did not rule out the possibility that a political settlement with Israel would eventually be finalized through a formal peace agreement. The Israelis had long insisted on this, and in practice, Jordan complied. The question of the nature of such a settlement then arose. Such a settlement could either be a (separate), bilateral, Israeli–Jordanian agreement, or part of a comprehensive, multilateral, Arab–Israeli settlement. To Jordan's leaders it was clear that the latter was preferable. The first option was never seriously discussed during the period surveyed. The fact that such a move was taken by Egypt in 1979 did not change Hussein's attitude towards a separate agreement.[52]

The King preferred an overall settlement since he believed that a unilateral venture leading to a separate, bilateral agreement was not feasible. He could not afford such an agreement for psychological reasons – the memory of the fate of his grandfather, King Abdullah, was probably still vivid in his mind – and for practical and political ones: Jordan was too weak and vulnerable to enter a course of action similar to the one that would be taken a decade later by Egypt's President Sadat. Even at his secret meetings with Israeli leaders, Hussein made it clear that even if they reached an understanding (based on a complete Israeli withdrawal), he could not and would not sign a separate peace treaty. It was precisely because of Jordan's weak and vulnerable regional position that Hussein always sought Arab cooperation and coordination. Jordan had always been one of the more enthusiastic and active advocates of Arab summit meetings.[53] The King sought the inter-Arab system's approval and backing for most of his political moves, to legitimize them in the eyes of his Palestinian subjects. Moreover, Hussein considered himself a pan-Arabist and an authentic Arab nationalist. He believed in the values and principles of Arab unity and cooperation. All these were not only part of a quest for the legitimacy of his policy, but also a part of the Hashemite heritage.[54]

Hence, the post-1967 efforts to regain the occupied territories should, in Hussein's perception, be coordinated with other Arab states, particularly with Egypt. Such coordination was occasionally praised in Jordan.[55] Egypt was not only the strongest and most important Arab state, it had also suffered the most substantial territorial loss in the 1967 war, and was eager to regain it. Yet, in the immediate wake of the war, the possibility of a comprehensive political settlement with Israel, not to mention a peace treaty, seemed out of the question.[56] The Khartoum resolutions removed 'peace' and 'negotiations' with Israel from the Arab public agenda as well as from its political vocabulary. Even a possible settlement in return for Israel's meeting of Arab demands was rarely mentioned. In the late 1960s there were occasional rumours that Hussein was meeting secretly with Israeli leaders and was negotiating a separate settlement. These not unfounded rumours were categorically denied by Jordanian spokespersons. They pledged that Jordan would never take unilateral steps and would neither negotiate nor conclude an agreement with Israel without the participation, backing and consent of its 'Arab brothers'.[57]

Jordanian leaders reiterated time and again, throughout the period, their insistence on cooperation and coordination not only with Egypt but with the other Arab countries as well.[58] Jordan's quest for a common Arab position stemmed in part from a desire to do away with suspicions regarding its alleged intention to negotiate separately with Israel; however, Jordan genuinely believed that a multilateral agreement was the only workable solution. In spite of the fact that Jordan had accepted resolution 242 and acquiesced to the Jarring mission, explicit references to an eventual peace settlement between Israel and the Arabs became common only in the early 1970s. These were intended to underscore Egyptian–Jordanian coordination rather than to elaborate on a possible peace settlement. Such references were first made when Jordan and Egypt were at odds regarding the Rogers plan and when separate Israeli–Jordanian or Israeli–Egyptian peace negotiations were speculated.

As early as March 1970, King Hussein stated that 'Jordan is fully and comprehensively coordinated with the [other] confrontation states, especially with Egypt'. With the issuing of the Rogers plan, it was officially decided that any agreement between Israel and Jordan would become effective only after an Egyptian–Israeli one.[59]

After the September 1970 encounter between the Jordanian army and the Palestinian organizations, Israeli officials invited Jordan to discuss peace talks through the good offices of Jarring without the recalcitrant Egyptians. King Hussein rejected the proposal and insisted that any talks to promote peace should be negotiated under UN auspices and that such talks should be held with a collective Arab body, not separately. The King and his Prime Minister pledged that Jordan would never initiate, negotiate or sign a separate peace with Israel. 'Jordan consented to UN resolution 242, that was also accepted by its sister Egypt . . . Talks on its implementation should be exercised by the UN and Jordan should not be isolated from the other Arab elements'. 'It is imperative to work for peace in this region and Jordan [like] Egypt [supports] neither a separate peace nor a separate action.'[60]

Because the September 1970 encounter resulted in the termination of the military and political presence of the Palestinian organizations in Jordan, the Hashemite kingdom was criticized and somewhat isolated by the other Arab states. It was therefore essential, from Jordan's point of view, to emphasize its coordination with Egypt to achieve a full and comprehensive peace settlement based on UN resolution 242. Jordan insisted that a solution to the Middle East crisis should be a comprehensive agreement or none at all.[61]

In early 1971 President Sadat proposed a partial Israeli–Egyptian agreement, under Jarring's auspices. It called for an Israeli withdrawal from the East Bank of the Suez canal to allow it to be cleaned and reopened to international navigation. Following this venture, and in response to Sadat's further initiatives regarding the Sinai peninsula, King Hussein made occasional statements concerning the importance of the cooperation of the two states to achieve a comprehensive peace, and that Jordan totally rejected any partial agreement. Hussein also pointed out that he had reached an agreement with Sadat's predecessor, Jamal Abd al-Nasser, that no separate solution would ever be considered and that they both would insist on an overall, multilateral settlement.[62] Yet it seems that Hussein's repudiation of a separate agreement did not stem only from ideological or political commitments. According to the King, 'Abd al-Nasser promised that the canal problem would not be solved as long as the question of Jerusalem was not solved'. Hussein suspected that if the Canal was going to be reopened, Sadat might detach his country from the Middle East crisis, and 'without Egypt's military might the rest of the Arab world would not be strong enough to confront Israel'.[63]

The October 1973 war and its outcome did not assuage Hussein's fear of a possible unilateral Egyptian initiative to regain its lost territory at the expense of the other Arab nations. Jordan viewed the post-war reality and the proposal to convene an international peace conference in Geneva as a means to achieve a comprehensive settlement. Spokespersons expressed their country's reluctance to reach a partial solution that 'would not take into account [the needs of] our Arab brothers'. This was also the declared reason why Hussein rejected Israel's 'Allon plan', as it entailed neither a full withdrawal nor a comprehensive settlement.[64]

When Egypt signed the second Sinai disengagement of forces agreement (the interim agreement) with Israel in September 1975, Hussein had some reservations. Still disappointed with Israel's reluctance to conclude a disengagement of forces agreement with Jordan, the King claimed that he was not sure whether such an agreement would lead to an overall peaceful solution. He construed it as capitulation to Israel's military superiority. Indeed, Hussein maintained, every state had the right to use any available means to regain its occupied land, but not by giving in to a stronger force. The prospect for a successful peace, as Hussein perceived it, depended on the power, ability and cooperation of all Arab parties.[65]

President Sadat's visit to Israel in late 1977, the ensuing Camp David accords and the Israeli–Egyptian peace treaty, added to Hussein's apprehension. Sadat's daring gesture of visiting Israel was received in Jordan with mixed feelings. On the one hand, it broke a psychological barrier, and paved the way for the political option to replace the military one in Arab–Israeli relations. Hussein depicted this step as 'a brave initiative that proves the world that there are people in the Arab world who desire a genuine peace'. 'This courageous move expresses hope'.[66] Yet, on the other hand, 'Sadat embarked on this initiative separately, without consulting any [of the Arab leaders]'. Moreover, he gambled on the last Arab card: acquiescence to a unilateral peace agreement with no consultation and without receiving any guarantees from Israel that this initiative would lead to a comprehensive settlement. Hussein maintained that 'prior to Sadat's journey we all worked together to go [to the Geneva international conference] in a joint Arab delegation'.[67] Hence Hussein implied that Sadat had broken the unified Arab front.

In the first half of 1978 Hussein was not optimistic regarding the prospect that the Egyptian–Israeli talks would be concluded successfully.[68] However, on the eve of the Camp David talks, when he still believed he would be invited to join, Hussein showed some sympathy for the process. He implied that he supported it as long as it was designed to bring about total withdrawal. Hussein expressed his hope that the talks would succeed and stated that the Sadat initiative was the maximal concession that the Arab side was ready to make.[69]

When the talks ended and their contents were published, Hussein continued to adhere to the line that Jordan believed in a just and comprehensive solution to the conflict and that such a solution should include all parties and all aspects involved.[70] These comments implied that the Camp

David accords did not meet Jordan's criteria. Hussein stated that Jordan was thus not committed, either morally or legally, to the accords, even though they assigned to his country a role in implementing the Palestinian autonomy.[71] He commented more openly and more directly on the flaws in the Camp David accords, particularly on their being vague regarding certain aspects of the future of the West Bank and Gaza, as well as the question of Jerusalem and the future of Israeli settlements. As the conclusion of the Israeli–Egyptian peace treaty drew near, Jordanian spokespersons pointed to what they considered the major flaw in the Camp David accords: they constituted a partial, separate agreement merely designed to solve bilateral Israeli–Egyptian problems. Because they provided no solution to other aspects of the Arab–Israeli conflict, the accords were unacceptable to Jordan, which still insisted on a comprehensive settlement, and thus did not wish to take any part in them. These bilateral discussions, Hussein maintained, would never solve the 'Middle East problem'.[72]

Jordan persisted with the same line after the Egyptian–Israeli peace treaty was signed on 26 March 1979. In Arab eyes, Egypt had committed a twofold crime: it concluded a separate bilateral peace treaty with Israel, and the agreement was achieved through direct negotiations. Hence Sadat had twice violated the Arab consensus. Jordan too, perceived this treaty as nothing but a separate agreement that 'gives nothing to the Arabs' and distanced the Arab world from a comprehensive peace. Hussein called it 'a dangerous and mistaken step' that played into the hands of Israel which hoped to isolate Egypt from the Arab world and to continue the occupation of Arab lands. The Egyptian people, like citizens in other Arab countries, opposed the treaty and the King was therefore sceptical about the prospects of its success.[73] In a speech at the UN, Hussein indirectly attacked the Egyptian–Israeli peace agreement as a partial arrangement from another angle. He maintained that 'all occupied territories constitute one indivisible unity and the principle of non-acquisition of territory by force applies to all of them'. There should be the same rule for the West Bank and the Gaza Strip as for the Golan and the Sinai. In the same speech, however, the King took pains to convince his audience that the Arab world was ripe for a comprehensive, multilateral peace with Israel. Despite the difference of opinion with Egypt, Hussein stated that the 'Arab countries today have sufficient confidence in themselves to consider all suggestions and ideas leading to a just peace'.[74] Crown Prince Hassan also tried to divert the major criticism from Egypt to Israel, accusing Israel of placing obstacles to the achievement of a just and comprehensive peace. 'A peace without justice is a peace built on sand'.[75]

Jordan's criticism of the Camp David track and of the Israeli–Egyptian peace treaty continued until the early 1980s, when Iraq's invasion of Iran and Israel's invasion of Lebanon somewhat distracted Arab public opinion and collective interest shifted elsewhere. Until then the criticism of Camp David focused – in addition to its basic flaws – on the following points:

1. The Egyptian–Israeli peace was not the peace that the people of the region sought. It differentiated and discriminated between the various Arab states (one regained its occupied lands, the others did not), and contradicted Arab interests.[76]
2. The separate bilateral agreement marginalized, if not ignored, the Palestinian issue.[77]
3. Egypt had dissociated herself from the Arab world.[78]
4. The accords could not be implemented and were doomed to fail.[79]
5. The accords constituted a plot against the Arabs, from which only Israel might benefit.[80]

Thus the government-inspired public image of Camp David in Jordan remained a symbol of a negative move that should be denounced as a wedge, designed to divide the Arab world. In a speech that revoked the 1985 agreement with Yassir Arafat, King Hussein stated that Jordan had been a keen and enthusiastic supporter of the peace process; it was a partner, or at least responded favourably, to most peace initiatives. 'The only initiative from which Jordan had excluded herself was that leading to the Camp David accords.'[81] Simultaneously, in order to underscore Jordan's stance as different from Egypt's 'deviation', spokespersons frequently emphasized their country's adherence to a just and comprehensive peace, which constituted the only viable solution to the regional problems, and the only way to guarantee a complete withdrawal from the occupied territories. By the same token, they reiterated Jordan's vehement opposition to partial and separate solutions. Such 'solutions' were considered impracticable, as the Arab–Israeli conflict could not be partially solved.[82] Moreover, following the Arab summit in Fez in September 1982, when an all-Arab peace plan was discussed and issued, Jordan was quick to support it. The Fez plan was introduced as the basis for regaining Arab rights and for a comprehensive, just and durable peace, for whose 'achievement we have struggled a long time'. As an Arab peace plan that underscored the genuine Arab attitude towards a comprehensive peace, Jordan supported it wholeheartedly.[83] The spirit of Jordanian expressions regarding the Fez plan, and the high frequency with which they were uttered, implied that the endorsement of this plan reflected an all-Arab consensus that supported Jordan's position. Namely, denouncement of the Egyptian–Israeli peace and of any other partial agreements, and support for the comprehensive solution concept.

Jordan continued to adhere to the comprehensive peace perception throughout most of the 1980s. Its leaders lost no opportunity to reiterate that position. When the Hussein–Arafat agreement was concluded and, later, when the idea of a joint Jordanian–Palestinian delegation (to an international peace conference) was discussed, they gave birth to rumours and speculations regarding possible future negotiations. The Jordanians then made it clear that they had no intention of entering into bilateral negotiations with Israel, with or without the PLO, unless they were a part of a comprehensive and coordinated Arab effort.[84] During this period Jordanian spokespersons occasionally referred to a comprehensive peace as one side of an equation whose other side was a full withdrawal. In other words, Jordan's peace perception was based on two pillars: a comprehensive, just and durable peace in the spirit of the UN resolutions, and a full Israeli withdrawal. This was not only Jordan's main goal but also the only feasible solution to the Arab–Israeli conflict, whose termination then seemed imminent.[85]

Throughout the twenty odd years that followed the June 1967 war, Jordan was consistent in its official position that opposed a separate peace agreement with Israel and insisted that such an agreement, if concluded, should be part of a comprehensive Israeli–Arab settlement. The reasons for adopting such an attitude as early as 1967, did not change in the course of the years. Jordan probably wanted and needed peace more than any other Arab state, a fact that its leaders did not deny. Yet it was obvious from the outset, even to the Israelis, that Jordan could not be the vanguard in embarking a separate peace initiative. Finally, it was Jordan that, contrary to its previous commitments, signed a bilateral and separate peace treaty with Israel in October 1994. This, however, occurred only after major changes had taken place in the region: After Egypt broke the taboo and concluded a peace treaty with Israel; after Jordan gave up its claim to the West Bank in 1988; after the Madrid peace conference in 1991; and mainly after the mutual recognition of Israel and the PLO in 1993 (that could be perceived as a move towards the solution of the Palestine problem – another Arab pre-condition for negotiating with Israel and recognizing it). Only then could Jordan enter into a bilateral peace treaty with Israel that would be considered less problematic in the eye of the Arab beholder.

12 FRAMEWORKS FOR A POSSIBLE AGREEEMENT

No less important than the nature of the final agreement were the frameworks and means through which it should be achieved. Two alternatives existed: either direct negotiations between the parties or indirect talks via the good offices of an external mediator or under international patronage which represents a sort of a combination of the two. Jordan was primarily interested in the substance, in an arrangement that would enable the resumption of its control over the West Bank. Yet it was forced to publicly concentrate on procedural principles and on frameworks in order to satisfy the consensual Arab position.

I. Rejection of the Israeli Demand for Direct Negotiations

Following the June 1967 war, the Israeli government as well as mainstream public opinion regarded the recent territorial gains as leverage to achieve peace with the Arabs.[1] Despite the different views of various cabinet members, there was a sort of consensus that stipulated withdrawal in return for peace. Prime Minister Levi Eshkol stated in the Knesset, as early as 12 June, that 'A new situation has been created which can serve as a starting point in direct negotiations for a peace settlement with the Arab countries'. On 30 July the government unanimously decided that 'Israeli forces would not withdraw from the cease-fire lines except as a result of direct negotiations with the Arab countries concerned'.[2]

The general Arab attitude not only opposed direct negotiations but regarded them as unthinkable and unacceptable. Since Israel insisted on direct negotiations as a *sine qua non*, compliance with this demand would constitute a humiliating Arab surrender and recognition of Israel (especially after Defence Minister Moshe Dayan's blunt statement: 'We are awaiting a phone call from the Arabs').[3] Direct negotiations became a symbol for both sides: Israel demanded this while the Arabs totally rejected direct talks. When Egyptian President Jamal Abd al-Nasser granted King Hussein a 'green light' to make concessions to Israel in return for the West Bank, he explicitly insisted that Hussein not enter direct negotiations with 'the enemy'. This Arab stance was institutionalized at the Khartoum summit conference, to whose resolutions the Arab leaders were committed. Indeed the uncompromising image of the Khartoum resolutions ('the three no's') was somewhat softened by Egypt's and Jordan's acceptance of UN resolution 242. This resolution, however, though it reflected the preference for a political option over a military one, neither specified nor implied direct negotiations.[4]

The first overt direct Arab–Israeli negotiations took place at the end of the October 1973 war, between Egyptian and Israeli officers. These were commonly known as the kilometre 101 talks (as they were held near the Suez canal, 101 kilometres from Cairo). Yet these talks were confined to military and technical matters that derived from the newly reached cease-fire. Since the disengagement of forces and interim agreements between Israel and Egypt and between Israel and Syria in 1974–5 had been reached through external mediation, it can be said that Sadat's visit to Israel and its aftermath constituted the first genuine and public direct Arab–Israeli negotiations after the June 1967 war.

These developments placed King Hussein in an extremely awkward position. As already stated, he was more interested in the content than in the framework. Had it not been for his public commitment to the Arab position that prohibited negotiations with 'the enemy', he would not have hesitated to negotiate publicly and directly with Israel as he did secretly in practice. Desperate to regain the West Bank, Hussein's pragmatic position, that in the course of the years turned into a semi-official one, was guided by two principles: (A) No framework for negotiation should be ruled out in advance, providing it takes into account Jordan's two preconditions (full withdrawal and solution of the Palestine question) and providing that Israel agrees to discuss these conditions in full; (B) Jordan should be recognized as an interlocutor and as a party to negotiations and its government should be given the authority to negotiate the future of the West Bank and its inhabitants. King Hussein indeed negotiated directly with the Israelis. Such secret talks commenced in early July 1967, about three weeks after the end of hostilities. In his public statements, however, King Hussein and his officials adhered to the collective Arab stance and denounced any attempt to bypass it.

Shortly after the war, the King totally rejected Israel's demand for direct negotiations. Negotiations with the enemy, Hussein maintained, were out of the question. The Arabs, as members of the UN, should deny the enemy's endeavour to dictate such preconditions.[5] He expressed his hope that 'now after we [the Arabs] changed our views regarding a political settlement' (his interpretation of the Khartoum resolutions), Israel should change its attitude towards direct negotiations.[6]

Simultaneously, and mainly to western audiences, Hussein introduced a less rigid version of the Arab position, according to which they would not indefinitely reject the concept of direct negotiations. As the King put it in early 1968, 'Jordan has adopted *for the time being* the Khartoum-made Arab position that opposed direct negotiations'.[7] The Arabs, according to Hussein, opposed Israel's demand only as long as Israel occupied their land. Instead of claiming that Israel's insistence on direct negotiations was an obstacle to peace, he preferred to maintain that the Israeli occupation of Arab lands was an obstacle to direct negotiations.[8] In 1969 Hussein even went so far as to declare: 'If Israel complies with resolution 242, we will agree to direct negotiations'.[9] The connection he made between direct negotiations and an Israeli withdrawal was designed primarily to create another source of pressure for such a withdrawal. It was based on the assumption that Israel might be willing to pay a high price for direct talks. On the other hand, conceding to Israel's conditions implied recognition of the Jewish state and thus granting Israel a considerable unilateral achievement without a proper *quid pro quo*.

Throughout 1968 and 1969 when Ambassador Jarring, the UN Secretary General's special envoy, took pains to advance his mission, Israel's insistence on direct negotiations (juxtaposed with the Arabs' rejection), was occasionally mentioned. Jordanian spokespersons took advantage of what they regarded as Israeli wrongdoing as an excuse for disregarding the demand which they had frequently criticized and discredited. King Hussein called it 'arbitrary', 'strange', and 'unjust'. Direct negotiations required the sort of Arab–Israeli common basis which 'does not currently exist'. It was impossible to conduct them while Israel held the occupied territories, declared certain issues (i.e., Jerusalem) non-negotiable, and ignored UN resolutions.[10] The frequent Jordanian references to this issue can also be explained against the backdrop of the constant rumours (most of them not unfounded) about direct meetings between King Hussein and Israeli leaders. Jordanian spokespersons not only totally denied these allegations but also took the opportunity to denounce the principle of direct negotiations and of Israel's insistence on them.[11]

A different position on this question was expressed by Hussein in late 1976. It was shortly after the 8th Arab summit conference in Cairo, which, under Egypt's leadership, was dominated by the inclination towards a political option, an option acknowledged even by Syria. Against this background, King Hussein said in an interview to the *Washington Post* that

Jordan was ready to take part in direct negotiations with Israel, providing all Arab states and the Palestinians gave such a venture their blessings.[12] No similar statements followed. About a year later, President Sadat set his political initiative in motion, a step that was criticized as a double violation of the Arab consensus: entering into direct talks with Israel and negotiating a separate peace agreement. Yet the fact that Hussein called Sadat's initiative (at its earlier stage) 'a courageous step that expresses hope',[13] implied that he was, publicly, more flexible towards the idea of direct negotiations than he had been a decade before.

Following Israel's invasion of Lebanon, the Reagan plan and the Fez summit plan, Jordan repeated the policy expressed in Hussein's 1976 statement, viz., joining in peace negotiations with Israel only if the latter agree to negotiate 'the Palestine question' with the PLO.[14] Even though formally Jordan persisted in its opposition to direct negotiations until the end of the period surveyed,[15] it seems that henceforth the possibility of direct negotiations, with or without an international umbrella, were more viable or at least less of a taboo than prior to Sadat's initiative. Moreover, Hussein began to regard the ban on direct negotiations as an anachronism. The Arabs, he believed, could live with direct negotiations and no harm would come to their cause, providing, of course, that such a step was taken only in return for an adequate Israeli concession.

After the conclusion of his agreement with Arafat in February 1985, the King was asked if he would accept Israeli Prime Minister Peres's invitation to visit Jerusalem. Hussein answered that he believed that even Mr. Peres was aware of the fact that he, personally, could not do that. Yet he did not rule out the possibility that the latter would visit Jordan.[16] Another indication of Jordan's flexibility appeared in 1987. Foreign Minister Tahir al-Masri credited King Hussein with bringing about US consent to an international conference, in spite of the fact that the Americans supported the idea of direct negotiations within that conference. Jordan was ready to form bilateral working groups, on a geographical basis, to do the actual negotiating at the conference. But Jordan still opposed Israel's demand for 'direct and unconditional negotiations'.[17] These principles were put to test at the Madrid conference in October 1991 with limited success. Two years later, however, following the mutual recognition of Israel and the PLO, Jordan commenced overt and direct peace negotiations which yielded, a year later, a Jordanian–Israeli peace treaty.

II. Indirect Negotiations: The Mediation by a Third Party

Generally speaking, according to Madiha Rashid al-Madfa'i, Jordan had always opposed foreign alliances and the internationalization of the

Arab–Israeli conflict. This opposition stemmed from the belief that inter-nationalization would not only endanger the Arab cause and constitute a threat to Arab identity, but would also mean that the principal world powers might at some stage wrest from the Arabs their right to settle their own affairs, so that the problem would become a question of what the superpowers agreed to or imposed on the Arabs. Al-Madfa'i quoted King Hussein as emphasizing that 'we in the Arab world reject the idea of a second Yalta'.[18] This, however, probably did not apply to the United Nations. As a multi-national organization, the UN somewhat offset the specific interests of the individual powers and was considered, as will be seen, an effective instrument in promoting an Israeli withdrawal. The involvement of the superpowers was regarded as more problematic, yet it had its own merit.

A. The Role of the UN

The collective, post-June 1967 Arab view, formalized at the Khartoum summit, rejected any negotiations whatsoever with Israel. Even the accep-tance of UN resolution 242 was explained by the fact that the resolution did not stipulate any kind of negotiations. The Arab states, Jordan included, sought some kind of international mechanism that would persuade Israel, by coercion or otherwise, to withdraw from the occupied territories. The mechanism they had in mind was the United Nations. They did not regard UN involvement as mediation, but expected the UN to pull the chestnuts out of the fire without any *quid pro quo* or even a gesture on their part. The UN track was primarily designed to bypass Israel's insistence on direct negotiations. Moreover, the organization was considered basically more pro-Arab than pro-Israeli, given the impressive number of Arab, Muslim and third world states among its members. Its resolutions regarding the Middle East, the Arab–Israeli conflict and the Palestine problem, since resolution 194 of December 1948 (on the Palestinian refugees' right of return), reflected its political composition and its pro-Arab bias. Anti-Israeli speeches and resolutions became almost a ritual at the opening of the sessions of the UN General Assembly.[19] Denouncing Israel for ignoring UN resolutions became a common Arab practice.

Preference for the UN was also Jordan's official position, at least in the wake of the 1967 war. Hussein not only declared that the Arab states would endeavour to solve 'the problem' through the UN, but also maintained that 'we [the Arabs] will discuss the problem only with the UN'.[20] This approach also explains why Jordan was quick to support the Jarring mission. Since Jordan considered resolution 242 the basis for any future arrangement, it expected the UN to work for its implementation through the Jarring mission or by any other means. If the implementation of resolution 242 entailed UN mediation between the Arabs and Israel, Jordan was probably ready to acquiesce, even if unwillingly, and without saying so explicitly. Its official stance was that 'Jordan accepted resolution 242 and wanted Jarring to discuss its implementation only, and not the implementation of anything else, as Israel wished'.[21] Moreover, when addressing Arab readership, Prime Minister Bahjat al-Talhuni stated that Jordan 'refused either to receive from or to give Jarring any written communications since that would mean that Jarring was departing from his mission as UN envoy and becoming a mediator'. Reports that Jordanian Foreign Minister Abd al-Mun'ain al-Rifa'i had given instructions to seek indirect negotiations with Israel through Jarring were flatly denied.[22]

This attitude suggested that Jordan viewed resolution 242 mainly as an instrument for achieving the withdrawal, and Jarring was expected to discuss its implementation. This is why Jordanian spokespersons who repeatedly committed themselves to the Jarring mission, accused Israel of its failure, or its lack of progress (because of Israel's insistence on direct negotiations), and praised the UN as the best way to solve international disputes and to achieve a just and lasting peace.[23] In March 1968, Jarring proposed that Israeli, Egyptian and Jordanian representatives be dispatched to his headquarters 'for separate consultations'. Jordan acquiesced (without a public admission), yet not before demanding a change in the wording of Jarring's invitation to read as follows: 'The parties declared their readiness to implement the resolution [242]'.[24]

A turning point, not so much in Jordan's position as in its public statements, can be seen in the second half of 1970, when attempts were made to reactivate initiatives for an Israeli–Arab settlement. Jordanian policymakers began to mention possible talks with Israel within the framework of these initiatives. They emphasized that such talks, if they took place, would be indirect. The revitalized next phase of the Jarring mission was referred to as indirect negotiations for peace.[25]

Jordan continued to perceive UN involvement as the best channel for a political settlement even after the October 1973 war. Hussein joined international efforts to turn the outcome of the war into leverage for a political settlement of the Arab–Israeli conflict. The idea of a peace conference in Geneva appealed to the King, who regarded the purpose of this conference as bringing peace to the region by means of an Israeli withdrawal.[26] The framework of an international conference became later, in Hussein's eyes, the most positive idea since 1973. He supported the various proposals to convene such a conference and even initiated certain moves in that direction.

Throughout the period, Hussein adhered to the UN's central (albeit not always exclusive) role in the efforts to bring peace to the Middle East. The commitment to the UN charter and resolutions was the best means, in Jordan's view, for achieving this goal.[27] The Arab–Israeli conflict was the UN's prime concern. Its efforts to find a proper solution and censure of Israel's 'illegal steps' in the occupied territories, were constantly praised.[28] Even the international conference was to be convened under UN auspices and the UN Secretary General would be its prime maker and shaker.[29]

Hussein persistently supported the idea of an international conference and became its most enthusiastic advocate. He viewed it as a concretization of the somewhat vague concept of UN involvement and a practical and tangible instrument to implement UN resolutions and eventually to bring about the long-awaited Israeli withdrawal. Hussein, who had regularly secretly negotiated directly with the Israelis, believed that the participation of Arab states in an international conference could be considered a gesture towards meeting Israel's demand (for direct negotiations) half-way. He hoped that Israel would reciprocate by adopting a more flexible attitude towards withdrawal from the occupied territories. Moreover, such a conference could grant some legitimacy to direct negotiations from which he, personally, might benefit *post factum*.

Jordan was thus among the first to respond favourably to the call to convene an international peace conference in Geneva in the wake of the October 1973 war. King Hussein expressed the hope that Jordan's participation in the Geneva talks would serve as an incentive for other Arab states.[30] The King received a formal invitation from the ambassadors of the US and the USSR in Amman. Prime Minister and Minister of Foreign Affairs Zayd al-Rifa'i represented Jordan at the opening ceremony of the conference in late December and announced his country's demands.[31] Yet, though Jordan supported the idea of third-party mediation, its acquiescence put Jordan in a rather awkward position regarding Palestinian representation and participation in the conference. Jordan wanted to take advantage of the invitation to Geneva to enhance its position as the representative of the Palestinians *vis-à-vis* the mounting inter-Arab tendency to bestow this title upon the PLO. On one hand, Jordan conditioned its participation in Geneva on recognizing and securing the Palestinians' right to self-determination. On the other hand, it threatened to boycott the conference if a decision to establish a Palestinian government in exile was endorsed (in other words, if the PLO was invited to Geneva).[32] In practice, the Geneva conference did not outlive its opening ceremony. Both the UN and Jordan sought to reconvene it. Though it had become a sort of imagined conference, throughout 1974 and 1975 policy-makers in Amman referred to it as a forthcoming reality and occasionally stated their conditions for participating.

The King and the Jordanian government tried to take advantage of their conditional participation in Geneva in order to mobilize Arab and international support for two Jordanian goals: The (rear-guard) struggle against recognition of the PLO as the sole legitimate representative of the Palestinians and the efforts to bring about an Israeli withdrawal in the Jordan Valley, by extending the post-October war disengagement agreements (on the Sinai peninsula and the Golan heights) to the Jordanian front as well. The efforts to achieve the first goal lasted until the Rabat summit conference in late 1974 denied Jordan representation of the Palestinians. Jordan, after having threatened, if the PLO participated in the conference, not to take part in any peace talks,[33] reversed its attitude in early 1975. Henceforth Jordanian leaders insisted on the participation of the PLO in Geneva while Jordan's own participation seemed of secondary importance. Jordan underwent a process of amending its political position: from refusal to take part in future peace talks on the pretext that they were contrary to the Rabat resolution, through possible Jordanian participation, providing that the Palestinians were represented there by their own delegation, to support for a joint Arab delegation in which both Jordan and the PLO were represented.[34]

As for the second goal, Jordan had threatened to boycott the peace conference unless Israel withdrew to an agreed-upon line east of the Jordan river.[35] Aside from Israel's rejection of this demand, no other party seems to have taken the threat seriously and Jordan soon stopped using it as a precondition for going to Geneva.

As indicated, Jordan's leaders indeed attributed utmost importance to an international peace conference. The failure of such a conference, King Hussein warned, could be disastrous for the Middle East and the entire world.[36] Until Sadat's initiative of 1977–78, Jordan's spokespersons, somewhat anachronistically, still adhered to the term 'the Geneva conference' and called for its reactivation under UN auspices.[37] They regarded it not as a goal in itself, but probably as the most efficient means to bring about an Israeli withdrawal. They believed that such a conference was a viable option and expressed their belief, as late as 1977, that the conference would soon convene. Jordanian's optimism was not groundless. Plans to reconvene the Geneva conference were indeed the order of the day in the latter half of 1977. The Americans together with the Soviets worked on preparing its framework and decided on its agenda and terms of reference. The joint US–USSR declaration of 1 October 1977 stated, *inter alia*:

> The United States and the Soviet Union believe that the only right and effective way for achieving a fundamental solution to all aspects of the Middle East problem in its entirety, is negotiations within the framework of the Geneva Peace Conference, specially convened for these purposes, with participation in its work of the representatives of all parties involved in the conflict, including those of the Palestinian people, and legal and contractual formalization of the decisions reached at the conference.[38]

President Sadat's visit to Israel a few weeks later and the ensuing events put that idea on hold. Following the Camp David accords and the direct Egyptian–Israeli talks that yielded a peace agreement, Hussein continued to regard a UN-sponsored and supervised international conference the best way to accommodate the demands of the Arabs and the Israelis. This time he promoted the idea in order to criticize the Egyptian–Israeli autonomy talks in which the former represented the Palestinian interests. The King demanded direct Palestinian participation in future peace talks and called for sending the problem back to the UN Security Council. The UN should return the international aura to the Middle East peace efforts and enable all the parties concerned to take part. 'It is unacceptable for the Arab future to be decided by the will of Egypt, Israel and the United States only.'[39] He suggested that the problem be treated within an international context with the participation of the USSR, the US and 'others'.[40]

Henceforth Hussein welcomed the participation of the Soviet Union in international efforts to solve the conflict. Despite his traditional pro-Western leanings on the one hand, and the Soviet invasion of Afghanistan on the other, the King who in the course of the years had become more sober and pragmatic found it politically expedient to warm up relations with the USSR. In the early 1980s he visited Moscow and concluded an arms deal with the Soviets. This reflected Hussein's dissatisfaction with US policy. The US was reluctant to sell Jordan an advanced anti-aircraft defence system and, according to Hussein, was unfairly pro-Israeli. Hussein did not intend to switch loyalties; he simply hoped to signal that the United States should adopt a more balanced stance. His willingness to view the Soviet Union as a part of the international mechanism to solve the Arab–Israeli conflict should also be viewed in this context.

In the 1980s Hussein considered the idea of convening an international peace conference with the participation of the five permanent members of the UN Security Council as the best, if not the only, framework for solving the conflict.[41] This was to some extent inspired by the September 1982 proposal by Leonid Brezhnev, leader of the Soviet Union, that the quest for a 'fair, just and realistic' solution to the conflict be made collectively, namely within a special international conference. Whatever settlement was achieved, Brezhnev maintained, should enjoy international guarantees that would be provided by the five permanent members of the Security Council. Like Hussein before him, he explicitly called for the convening of such a conference.[42]

The idea of an international conference gained momentum after the Israeli invasion of Lebanon in the summer of 1982 (operation 'Peace for the Galilee'). Efforts were made to bring an end to Israel's presence in Lebanon, and to reach a comprehensive solution to the Middle Eastern impasse. These yielded numerous proposals and ideas. During a period of just over a month (August–September 1982), at least four different plans were proposed: the plan of Saudi Crown Prince Fahd; the Reagan plan; the proposal of the Arab summit conference in Fez; and the Brezhnev plan. The latter, as noted, referred to an international conference as the most suitable vehicle for negotiating a political settlement. These plans and their offshoots created a suitable atmosphere for Jordan to intensively promote its credo regarding an international conference, to be chaired by the US, USSR, Britain, France and China. Hussein reiterated time and again that all concerned parties should take part in the conference. Occasionally he explicitly added 'including the PLO'. Jordanian spokespersons emphasized that they strove to revitalize the peace process by reconvening a peace conference in the spirit of the Geneva conference, in order to reach a comprehensive settlement to the conflict.[43]

One of Hussein's greatest achievements in this respect was the conclusion of an agreement for political coordination with PLO Chairman Yassir Arafat. In the agreement, the PLO not only agreed that a political settlement of the conflict should be sought and negotiated, but also that this would be done within the framework of an international conference with the participation of all those Jordan had proposed. Moreover, the PLO, 'the sole legitimate representative of the Palestinians', was to take part in the discussions within a joint Jordanian–Palestinian delegation.[44]

Even after that agreement proved futile and the King unilaterally revoked it and publicly suspended political coordination with the PLO in February 1986, and despite the ensuing deterioration in their bilateral relations, Hussein still adhered to the concept of an international conference, with the participation of the PLO.[45] In May, King Hussein disclosed that Jordan and the PLO were organizing a joint delegation to meet representatives of the five permanent members of the Security Council, as well as representatives of the Arab states, to discuss the possible convening of an international conference.[46] Two months later Jordan announced that the five powers had consented to Jordan's demand that the PLO be invited to the international conference on an equal level with the other participants. The PLO had to first recognize the international resolutions which constituted the basis for the convening of the conference (namely, resolution 242). At the last minute, the PLO leadership refused to accept the Security Council resolution without a written commitment by the United States to recognize the Palestinian people's right to self-determination.[47]

These developments did not weaken Jordan's determination to promote the idea of an international conference with PLO participation. Public statements by its leaders on the importance of such a conference became more frequent. Shortly after the suspension of their coordination agreement, Jordan accused the PLO of sabotaging the political option and of blocking the way towards a comprehensive settlement in the Middle East.

Yet in view of its failure to convince the PLO to change its uncompromising stance, Jordan made it clear that it had no intention of either sitting in for the PLO at the conference nor replacing it as the representative of the Palestinian people. Even if Jordan had wanted to do so, it was clear, in light of the Rabat resolution and the PLO's position in the Arab world, that this was not a viable option. Jordan then tried to persuade the US to reduce their preconditions for PLO participation at the conference. It turned out, however, that President Reagan was no less adamant than Yassir Arafat (see below).

Jordanian spokespersons continued to promote the international conference with growing frequency. Throughout 1986 and 1987, statements in favour of convening the conference were issued almost daily.[48] Jordan 'upgraded' its arguments to promote this idea not only quantitatively but also qualitatively. During this period official statements depicted the international conference as the only available means to achieve a comprehensive, just and lasting peace.[49] Occasionally they included even stronger wording: no such solution could ever be reached except through an international conference.[50]

The invitation of the PLO continued to be a *sine qua non* as far as Jordan was concerned. Yet in view of the gap between the American and the Palestinian positions, the option to include the latter within a Jordanian–Palestinian delegation seemed more and more appealing to the Jordanians,[51] not for political gain *vis-à-vis* the PLO, but to enable the convening of the conference in the first place. A joint delegation might serve as a formula that both the PLO, the Arabs and the Israelis could live with. For the Israelis, negotiating with a joint Palestinian–Jordanian delegation under an international umbrella could be regarded as direct negotiations, without the need to recognize the PLO. The Arabs, on their part, could claim that they were negotiating indirectly with the Israelis (due to the good offices of the five powers) and no recognition of Israel was involved. Foreign Minister Tahir al-Masri explained that since all the participating states would not be able to discuss all aspects of the Arab–Israeli conflict and be present at all sessions, a number of working committees, either bilateral or on a geographical basis, should be formed. According to al-Masri, even though this was customary at all international conferences, Israel objected as it wished to enter into direct, unconditional negotiations with the Arabs.[52]

Jordan did not refer to the conference as a hollow slogan or as a magic remedy. Spokespersons viewed it as a framework that would have the power to make decisions and would play an active role in their implementation. They also envisaged long and continuous debates and not merely ceremonial rhetoric (as, according the Jordanians, 'some Israelis demanded').[53] Though Jordan's officials focused on the future role of the permanent members of the Security Council and particularly on that of the superpowers, they envisioned that the UN would sponsor the conference and its Secretary General would play an active part in convening and running it. He was the one, for example, who would issue a special invitation to the PLO.[54]

The reluctance of the Israeli government to ratify the 'London agreement' between King Hussein and Shimon Peres in May 1987, the outbreak of the Palestinian *intifada* later that year, and Secretary of State George Shultz's support for an international conference in early 1988, all gave new impetus to Jordan's intensive efforts to convene a conference. Spokespersons emphasized Israel's negative attitude as the major obstacle to the initiative.[55] Throughout 1988 Jordan's call for an international conference (with the participation of the PLO) was as intensive as before and continued even after King Hussein officially withdrew his country's claim to the West Bank on 31 July. Despite the dissociation between the two Banks, Jordan was still willing to take part in a joint Palestinian–Jordanian delegation if this was what it took to convene the international conference.[56]

To sum up, on the public and declarative levels, King Hussein supported the idea of an international conference, regarding it as the best framework for reaching a solution to the Arab–Israeli impasse. In practice, however, he was more selective: he supported the idea as long as it served Jordan's interests; namely, the return of the West Bank. When President Carter sought to revitalize the Geneva conference with the active participation of the PLO, the King was definitely less enthusiastic. Yet even then he stipulated that Jordan would participate in a peace conference only if the PLO participated as the Palestinians' representative. On the face of it, this position manifested Jordan's adherence to the Rabat resolution, yet it was probably based on the assumption that Israel would reject the participation of the PLO. Hence Jordan expected Israel to pull the chestnuts out of the fire. If that was to be the case, the whole notion of a conference would be foiled by Israel and not by Jordan.

Jordan's ceaseless efforts throughout the 1980s to promote the idea of an international conference succeeded in mobilizing the Arab world to support the idea,[57] as well as Europe, the Soviet Union and the US. The idea eventually materialized in October 1991 with the Madrid peace conference. After the American-led coalition, supported by the Arab states, had liberated occupied Kuwait, President George Bush reciprocated by putting pressure on Israel to participate. Yet the Madrid talks and the ensuing meetings failed to reach a political solution to the Arab Israeli conflict. The real breakthroughs, the mutual Israeli–PLO recognition and the Jordanian–Israeli peace treaty were achieved (like the earlier Israeli–Egyptian peace) only via direct, bilateral negotiations as Israel had always insisted.

B. THE UNITED STATES

Following the June 1967 war, when Jordan sought any possible means to regain the West Bank, the United States seemed an important, if not a vital, channel. With its varied political, economic and strategic interests in the Middle East, the US sought to bring the region back to the pre-June 1967 territorial *status quo* as soon as possible. Failure to persuade Israel to withdraw might be exploited by the USSR to convince the Arabs that only the Soviets could help them to regain their losses. Since Jordan was within the Western sphere of influence, King Hussein believed that the Americans should do their best to back him. US officials, on their part, made it clear from the outset that they favoured a complete Israeli withdrawal (in return for recognition of Israel's right to exist). They promised Hussein in 1967 and in 1968 that their country would see to it that Israel handed the West Bank back to Jordan with 'minor border modifications'.[58]

At that stage, Jordan did not perceive the American role as mediation, but merely as the good offices of a friendly power. American involvement was intended to bring about a withdrawal, not to promote negotiations. On the other hand, Jordan was aware of the somewhat limited ability of the United States to coerce Israel to withdraw, due to domestic political constraints and strategic considerations. The US supported UN resolution 242 as well as the Jarring mission, and hoped that Jordan would return to the West Bank. Jordan wanted to see the US play a more active role in this direction, albeit under UN auspices.[59] As a matter of fact, only at the end of 1969 did the US set itself apart from the UN effort to put an end to the conflict when Secretary of State William Rogers submitted his plan for a negotiated and comprehensive Arab–Israeli settlement. The Rogers plan was initially designed to end the state of war between Israel and Egypt but it was accompanied by a proposal for a Jordanian–Israeli accommodation based, according to the consistent US position, on a complete Israeli withdrawal.[60] Jordan's initial reaction was cautious. Prime Minister Bahjat al-Talhuni defined Jordan's attitude towards the Rogers plan as 'not different from that of the other Arab States'. Information Minister Salah Abu-Zayd added that his government would not turn down any 'fair and genuine opportunity to achieve peace based on resolution 242'. In private, Jordanian officials even described the American proposals as 'interesting', and King Hussein regarded them as 'a step forward that renewed the prospects for a political settlement'.[61]

Egypt's rejection of the plan later elicited a less enthusiastic Jordanian reaction, explained by the fact that, for almost three years since June 1967, the Americans had done nothing for the sake of peace in the region, delivered no worthwhile plan and failed to produce an Israeli withdrawal.

Hussein and his officials particularly criticized the US for having supported Israel politically and militarily. They expected the Americans to play a more decisive and more positive role in the Middle Eastern conflict; i.e., to rectify their pro-Israeli policy. Jordanian spokespersons explained that because the Rogers plan was extremely ambiguous and unclear, Jordan would not take a stand. At a press conference in Washington in April 1969, Hussein hinted at his reservations regarding the Rogers plan, saying that he would rather have the 'powers' impose a settlement.[62]

In the summer of 1970, both Egypt and Jordan accepted the amended Rogers plan. Their consent indicated willingness to enter into negotiations with Israel through Jarring's mediation and according to the principles of resolution 242. The American initiative resulted in a cease-fire agreement that put an end to the Israeli–Egyptian war of attrition along the Suez Canal, that had broken out in March 1969. This time Jordanian spokespersons were less critical about American involvement, as they found it compatible with their interests. They were particularly pleased with the renewed reference to resolution 242, and maintained that the Rogers initiative did not go beyond this resolution, which Jordan had already accepted. Prime Minister Abd al-Mun'im al-Rifa'i described the new American initiative as merely 'procedural proposals' designed to reactivate the Jarring mission. In this spirit, King Hussein called upon the US to use its influence on Israel to persuade it to resume its participation in the Jarring discussions and to agree to the prompt implementation of resolution 242.[63] The changes in Jordan's attitude to the Rogers plan stemmed primarily from the Egyptian attitude and from Hussein's desire to keep in step with Abd al-Nasser. When Egypt accepted the plan, Jordan followed suit and the King wrote to the Egyptian President: 'We accept what you accept and reject what you reject'.[64]

Following the conclusion of the Israeli–Egyptian cease-fire agreement and after Abd al-Nasser's death and Sadat's coming to power, the Jarring mission was resumed and the Americans became partners in the (futile) UN effort in 1970–71 to achieve a political settlement. After the Yom Kippur war, Hussein was satisfied with the growing involvement of the US in the efforts to bring about an Arab–Israeli accommodation. The US first served as co-chair of the Geneva peace conference and then was the prime mover behind the disengagement of forces and the interim agreements between Israel and Egypt and Israel and Syria.

Hussein's hopes for an American-made breakthrough did not materialize. On the one hand, the Geneva conference turned out to be nothing but a one-time ceremonial show. On the other hand, Henry Kissinger's shuttle diplomacy indeed bore fruit on the Syrian and Egyptian fronts. To Hussein's chagrin, however, he failed to produce a Jordanian–Israeli disengagement of forces agreement along the Jordan river. Once again the King was disappointed with the American inability or unwillingness to coerce Israel into territorial gestures and concessions in the West Bank. At the same time, the King saw no other factor that could overcome the Arab–Israeli impasse. He was well aware that there were limits to the ability of the US to put pressure on Israel, yet he also knew that if anyone could persuade the Israelis to change their policy, it was the US. His preferred method to forward a political solution was still the international conference, but he realized that unless the US was the leading force behind it, the conference was doomed. It was against this background that Hussein declared in 1976 that the United States held the key to solving the Middle Eastern problem. 'We believe,' he said, 'that the US possesses a decisive influence on the [possible] making of a just peace in the Middle East.'[65]

The coming to power of Jimmy Carter as President of the United States raised hopes and expectations in Jordan. Not only did he seem to take more pains than his predecessors in his efforts to solve the Middle East conflict, but his actions and words implied a more balanced attitude towards the issue. In the course of 1977, however, it turned out that Carter attributed too much weight, in Jordan's view, to the Palestinians and to the PLO's role in the forthcoming peace process. Only two months after his inauguration, Carter publicly expressed his support for 'a homeland for the Palestinians'. In September he proposed to renew the international peace conference under UN auspices with the participation of the PLO. Jordan promptly accepted Carter's proposal and publicly supported it,[66] even though not overjoyed about the invitation of the PLO.

American involvement in the Egyptian–Israeli peace process was welcomed by Hussein as long as he believed that he too would be invited to take part in the negotiations in Camp David. He referred to Carter's activities as a positive step and the intended Camp David talks as a [suitable] framework for developing the principles of a just peace.[67] When he was denied participation at Camp David, and the role allotted to Jordan in the ensuing discussions over the future Palestinian autonomy did not meet his expectations, Hussein gradually changed his attitude. He believed that the US Middle East policy, based on the Camp David accords, was doomed. He was bitter and disappointed with this policy which, he claimed, was not likely to bring peace. After Jordan had supported all American peace initiatives, including those of Rogers and Kissinger, it discovered that depending on the US as a sole mediator did not yield the desired results.[68]

The basic bone of contention between Jordan and the US, according to Hussein, was the latter's unconditional military and political support for Israel. Hence the US was losing its position as an honest broker and could no longer serve as a mediator. 'The unlimited US assistance to Israel, as well as her overwhelming support and the approval of whatever

Israel is doing, make me feel that the US freedom of manoeuvering is limited than before.' He called upon the Americans to resort to a more balanced policy and to persuade Israel to amend its own positions and to adhere to a line that would produce a genuine peace.[69] This criticism of the US role in the conflict gave way to a more sympathetic attitude following the Israeli invasion of Lebanon and the issuing of the Reagan plan in September 1982. The American President still adhered to the Camp David process and framework that Jordan had rejected, yet he insisted that at the end of the day no independent Palestinian state would be established in the West Bank, but only a comprehensive autonomy federated with Jordan. Needless to say, policy-makers in Amman were delighted. King Hussein declared that the Reagan plan was 'the first and the most courageous plan adopted by the US administration since 1952'. He and his brother called it 'positive and constructive', and both looked forward to its implementation.[70] Nevertheless the King had to manoeuvre between his support for the Reagan plan and his commitment to the Arab consensus (recently reiterated at the Fez Arab summit meeting) regarding a PLO-led Palestinian state. The King hoped that the idea of an international peace conference might accommodate the two plans and would offer a formula for negotiation that all concerned parties could live with. When it turned out that the Americans preferred direct Israeli–Arab negotiations that would exclude the PLO, Jordan would not accept this, and its spokespersons once again expressed disappointment with the US position and its pro-Israeli leanings.[71]

Between 1986 and 1988 the Jordanians took pains to persuade the US to reverse its opposition to the proposed international conference and to adopt, once again, a more even-handed policy.[72] Crown Prince Hassan defined the US position (as well as that of the Soviet Union) towards the Arab–Israeli conflict as 'illogical', and called for its amendment. Prime Minister Zayd al-Rifa'i reminded the Americans that convening an international peace conference (i.e., the Geneva conference) was originally neither a Jordanian idea nor an Arab one. It was an American idea that the UN Security Council unanimously adopted in 1973.[73]

Foreign Minister Tahir al-Masri claimed that since the beginning of Reagan's presidency and particularly after George Shultz became Secretary of State, the US totally opposed the idea of an international conference. Hussein's efforts indeed contributed to ease some of the Americans' opposition, yet the US insisted that within the conference, Arab–Israeli negotiations should be direct and that the Palestinians should be represented by a joint Jordanian–Palestinian delegation without any PLO members.[74] The main US–Jordanian divergence of opinion over the international conference was basically a question of priorities. The US was ready to discuss various scenarios, including an international conference (as a framework for achieving a settlement), but wished to discuss the details first, before granting its approval to such a conference. Jordan, on the other hand, wanted an agreement in principle on convening an international conference, which would have power and authority, prior to the discussion of details.[75] In view of this alleged American attitude, King Hussein claimed that US policy in recent years had caused him 'pain and disappointment'. It reflected neither its own nor Israeli or Arab interests. The Americans had succumbed to the most extreme elements in Israeli society. And as it turned out, Israel and the US remained the only two states in the world that opposed the convening of an international conference.[76]

Throughout the entire period, a certain ambivalence in Jordan's attitude towards American mediation is evident. This ambivalence is well reflected in the statements above. On the one hand, Jordan appreciated the global role of the United States as a superpower, leader of the Western bloc, to which Jordan was affiliated. The US was sometimes seen as the only power capable of influencing recalcitrant Israeli governments, due to the 'special relations' the two countries enjoyed. Simultaneously however, these same 'special relations' reflected in the American commitment to Israel's security, and the public and political influence of the American-Jewish community, all raised serious doubts in Jordan as to whether the US could or would serve as an impartial mediator between the Arabs and Israel. The Jordanians perceived American support of Israel as inherent, support that transcended the lines of domestic political divisions. Hence the cautious and sceptical Jordanian attitude remained intact during both Republican and Democratic administrations.

C. The Soviet Union and Europe

On the face of it, Jordan's traditional good relations with the West stemmed from historical and practical considerations. The Hashemite kingdom had, in effect, been 'created' by Britain. Hence, Jordan's economic and political existence depended on the good will of the UK. Beginning in the late 1950s, the United States gradually replaced Britain as Jordan's main external guardian and provider. But Jordan's adherence to the Western bloc and its suspicious attitude towards the Soviet Union also had an ideological quality. While the toppling of the old pro-Western regimes in Egypt, Syria and Iraq in the 1950s and the 1960s was followed by a change in the political orientation, the *ancien régime* in Amman survived. While the revolutionary army officers, the new leaders of their countries, were being politically embraced and militarily aided by the Soviet Union, Jordan remained a conservative, moderate, pro-Western monarchy. For the Hashemite rulers, whose legitimacy derived, *inter alia*, from being descendants of the Prophet Muhammad, the atheistic communist message and its hostility towards dynastic monarchies were totally unacceptable. They perceived the Soviets as a severe threat to Muslims and Arabs and particularly to monarchies such as Jordan.[77]

The new reality created by the 1967 war had an impact on Jordan's attitude to the Soviet Union. King Hussein took pains to mobilize any available support for his efforts to regain his lost territories. In these efforts he could not disregard the second superpower, the USSR. Jordan had concluded diplomatic relations with the Soviets in 1963. Hussein arrived in Moscow (for the first time) in early October 1967 and met top Soviet leaders as part of his global grand tour to solicit whatever help he could obtain for Jordan's cause. In addition to his intention to mobilize the Soviet's assistance and sympathy, Hussein hoped that his visit to Moscow would exert indirect pressure on the US and even on Great Britain, not to take him for granted and to be more receptive to his political and military needs.

In the first years after the 1967 war Jordan did not seek Soviet mediation but rather US–USSR cooperation, hopefully under UN auspices, to find a solution to the Middle Eastern conflict. The King probably believed that such cooperation might offset American support for Israel. Hussein and his officials did not rule out an imposed solution by the two superpowers and was even ready to accept the creation of an international peace-keeping force in which Soviet and American troops would serve side by side.[78] In the aftermath of the October 1973 war, with the convening of the Geneva peace conference, Hussein's wish for Soviet–American cooperation in the Middle East under the aegis of the UN came true for a very short time. The two powers served as co-chairs of this short-lived conference. Henceforth, whenever Jordan discussed its preferred framework for ending the Arab–Israeli conflict – the international conference – Jordan emphasized the great importance it attributed to the role that the Soviet Union should play. Though the USSR was to participate in the conference as one of the five permanent members in the UN Security Council, Jordan hoped the USSR would take an active role, together with the US, whenever the conference was convened.[79]

Guided by these principles, Jordan welcomed the joint Soviet–American declaration on 1 October 1977 that called for the resumption of the Geneva peace conference under the co-chairmanship of the two powers. The declaration did not mention the PLO. After the Israeli–Egyptian peace process and the Camp David accords, Jordan sought, as noted, an alternative to the bilateral track, to implement the 242 resolution. The Jordanian idea was to return the Middle East problem to the UN Security Council or to Geneva, with the participation of all concerned parties. A major role was assigned to the USSR (together with the US).[80]

The King and his officials were also pleased with Soviet involvement following the Israeli invasion to Lebanon, in the form of the Brezhnev plan. This plan envisaged an international peace conference very similar to that which King Hussein had proposed. The King stated that the Brezhnev plan 'consolidated the Arab peace plan approved by the Fez summit' only one week before.[81] The Fez resolutions, however, failed to mention an international conference. In the second half of the 1980s (the latter part of Reagan's second term), the United Stated was less enthusiastic about the idea of an international conference and particularly about the role that Jordan assigned to the Soviet Union. Jordan managed to mobilize the latter's support for the idea and to persuade the US to be more flexible towards both the convening of the peace conference and the participation of the Soviet Union.[82]

The possible involvement of Europe (in the framework of the European Economic Community) as a mediator between the Arabs and Israel, was, in the period surveyed, only of secondary importance. Certain European powers like Britain, France and Germany indeed had economic and political influence over the conflicting parties. The EEC as a body had only taken its first steps as a European political power. Its active involvement in the Arab–Israeli conflict began after the 1973 war following a kind of 'European-Arab Dialogue' between the EEC and the Arab League established in July 1974.[83] Throughout 1977, both economic and political European–Arab relations on bilateral and multilateral levels intensified. The statements of the Council of the European Community in 1977, and later, supported a solution to the conflict based on Security Council resolutions 242 and 338; King Hussein viewed this kind of European involvement and the efforts to bring about a just peace in the region with favour. Nevertheless, European statements were also in the spirit of President Carter's comprehensive attitude and his 'homeland for the Palestinians' approach, regarding which the King had some reservations.[84]

The most conspicuous European statement, from an Arab point of view, was the Venice Declaration of 13 June 1980, at the conclusion of a summit meeting. The solution to the Middle Eastern conflict that the Europeans envisaged was based on two principles: the right of all the states in the region (including Israel) to exist in peace and security, and justice for all peoples in the region (i.e., recognition of the legitimate rights of the Palestinians). The proposed settlement should be a comprehensive one: the UN should provide guarantees for secure and recognized boundaries of all Middle Eastern countries, and the European Community was willing to take part in any international system that would provide these guarantees. The declaration did not suggest a framework for obtaining these goals. It merely undertook to contact the concerned parties and explore their views and responses. Only then would the European Community decide on the most appropriate form for a future initiative on their part.[85]

King Hussein expressed his satisfaction with the European initiative. He also commended the EEC members' attempt to understand the Palestinian question. The King perceived Jordan's relations with Europe, in part, as a means to put pressure on the US to adopt a more conciliatory attitude towards the Arab states. Hussein and other Jordanian spokespersons also underscored the importance of the European position (as expressed in the Venice declaration and further statements) and expected it to bring about more American (and European) pressure on Israel.[86] Crown Prince Hassan too, in his book in 1981, regarded the EEC as an important 'third party' whose mediation was as essential as that of the UN, the US and the USSR. Moreover, a European presence at an international conference might constitute an adequate balance between the two superpowers.[87]

Jordan had high hopes for the European initiative, and expected European assistance in reconvening an international peace conference under UN auspices that would create an alternative channel to Camp David. Hussein even sought European help in the amendment of resolution 242. Though the Jordanians did not seek the participation of the European community at the international peace conference, they hoped that Britain and France, the European members of the Security Council, would serve Jordan's interests at the conference. They took pains to mobilize the Europeans to the cause of the peace conference and wanted them to join forces with others to put pressure, mainly on Israel but also on the US, not to boycott the conference. They were delighted when the Europeans supported the convening of the conference.[88] However, Jordan feared that the participation of the EEC would increase Israeli and US opposition. Jordan was hoping for an effective conference with the power and authority not only to adopt practical resolutions but also to implement them. Participation of the EEC might enlarge the conference and was likely to contribute to its inefficiency. Hence Jordan wanted European support and sympathy for the *idea* of the international conference without their necessarily taking part in it. The Jordanians were probably also reluctant to have the Europeans at the conference *en masse* because they feared their pro-Palestinian stance.

CONCLUSION

Throughout the decade that predated the June 1967 war, and on the eve of the war itself, Jordan's declared views regarding Israel and the Arab–Israeli conflict were not basically different from those of the Arab consensus, i.e., Jordan rejected Israel's legitimacy and its right to exist.[1]

In the wake of the war, the aftershock caused by the loss of the West Bank and the sense of an urgent need to retrieve it, brought about a change in King Hussein's political and ideological thinking, as well as in Jordan's official position. The King realized that in order to regain the territories lost in June 1967, he, and the other heads of state, would have to offer Israel a suitable *quid pro quo*.

The public manifestation of this political shift in Jordan, beginning in the summer of 1967, was twofold:

1. A change in the content and style of the traditional statements that had been made by the King and his officials prior to June 1967.
2. A change in the views expressed by Jordanian spokespersons *vis-à-vis* the declarations of other Arab leaders.

King Hussein felt that he should not challenge the Arab consensus but instead attempted to make it more flexible. He endeavoured to persuade his peers that the June war was not a passing episode; it was a watershed which required that they adapt themselves to a new reality. Jamal Abd al-Nasser, leader of the strongest Arab state, became Hussein's first and most important convert: he approved Hussein's approach (embodied in the equation 'peace for territories'), at least as far as Jordan was concerned. Initially Abd al-Nasser gave the King a green light to try to regain the West Bank by political means. Later Egypt adopted the formula that Hussein was marketing. Eventually, even the Palestinians and the PLO acquiesced – to a certain extent – to some components of Jordan's perception.

Simultaneously, King Hussein remained a pioneer. He was ready, at the end of the day, to bypass the three no's of the Khartoum summit conference, and to negotiate with and recognize Israel, and to make peace, providing, of course, that Israel met his demands. First among these, and the most consistent and persistent demand, was complete withdrawal from the West Bank and East Jerusalem to the line of 4 June 1967. Yet the question of who was to regain these territories once Israel evacuated them underwent a salient change. In the immediate wake of the war, it was clear that they should be returned to Jordanian sovereignty. Due to post-war developments, Jordan was later forced to agree that the territories would be handed over to the Palestinian people and even to the PLO.

Other Jordanian demands called for Israeli recognition of Palestinian rights, of Jordan's special position in Jerusalem, and ending the intensive demographic expansion and building of settlements in the West Bank. Israel was also required to amend some of its policies and perceptions. If Israel complied, a political solution could be negotiated, indirectly, through the offices of a third party. Any settlement, however, had to be comprehensive, not partial or bilateral.[2]

It seems, however, that most of these demands were made, *inter alia*, in order to deal with Israeli reluctance to withdraw and to achieve that major quest, indirectly or from a different angle. If Israel withdrew completely, then issues of the settlements and of Jerusalem, for example, would become irrelevant.

In comparison to the clear-cut insistence on an Israeli withdrawal, the issue of recognition of Palestinian rights was more complex in view of the gradual decline in the Jordanian position in the West Bank, in both Arab and international public opinion, *vis-à-vis* that of the Palestinians and the PLO. Immediately after the war, when the King and his officials kept insisting that the West Bank and its population was Jordanian, they perceived only the territories west of the armistice line (i.e., the state of Israel) as Palestine. Hence the only Palestinians were Arabs who lived in Israel or the 1948 refugees, who fled from the areas that became Israel. Therefore, the only Palestinian-related demand of Israel at that time was the repatriation of the refugees. However, when Jordan was forced to admit that the West Bank and its inhabitants were Palestinians, its demands of Israel changed accordingly.

In the course of the years, the demand that Israel should recognize Palestinian rights paralleled the demand for complete withdrawal, and occasionally both demands were made together. Jordan then introduced the Israeli withdrawal and the return of the West Bank to Jordanian sovereignty as a precondition to any progress towards a solution of the Palestine problem. Once that occurred, the Palestinians would be able to decide their own future and exercise their right of self-determination. In other words,

Jordan's commitment to ensure Palestinian rights was designed to pressure Israel to withdraw.

As of late 1974, after the Arab summit conference in Rabat recognized, *inter alia*, the PLO's right to establish a state in the territories evacuated by Israel, Jordan amended its demand to the new circumstances: Israel should withdraw and give the Palestinians their rights (without the interim phase of Jordanian rule) in order to pave the way to an independent Palestinian state in the West Bank. Eventually, Israel was also expected to recognize the PLO and to negotiate the future of the West Bank with it (and not with Jordan), after the Rabat summit had recognized the PLO as 'the sole legitimate representative of the Palestinian people'.

The importance of the evolution of Jordan's perception of a political settlement did not stem from setting conditions and frameworks for such a settlement. To a certain extent, it was the other way around. On the face of it, in concluding a peace treaty with Israel in 1994, King Hussein broke most of the rules and the pre-conditions that he himself had set for such an eventuality. Indeed, Israel did recognize the PLO, but did not withdraw from the West Bank. Israel did not dissemble a single settlement and refused to give up East Jerusalem. No other Arab state (save Egypt, which made peace with Israel in the late 1970s) had joined the peace process. And to cap it all: the Jordanian–Israeli peace agreement was bilateral, not comprehensive, and was reached through direct negotiations.

The explanation for this inconsistency lies primarily in King Hussein's decision of July 1988 to sever ties with the West Bank and to relinquish the claim for its return to Jordan. The King made this decision after he realized that there was almost no prospect to regain the West Bank, not because of Israel's reluctance to withdraw, but due to the Arab and international recognition of the Palestinians and the PLO as the lawful possessor of the West Bank who should establish their independent state there. Hence, even if Israel withdrew, it was not Jordan that would control the liberated West Bank.

Jordan's decision to disengage from the West Bank was an upheaval, especially for the Jordanian–Palestinian–Israeli triangle. For one thing, it made a considerable part of Jordan's earlier demands of Israel irrelevant. Thus it paved the way, *inter alia*, to mutual Israeli–PLO recognition and to the Jordanian–Israeli peace treaty.

Until 1988 Jordan's ceaseless efforts to bring about an Israeli withdrawal, in which a tremendous amount of political energy and diplomatic endeavours were invested, were genuine. Once Hussein had given up the West Bank, this issue was eliminated from Jordan's agenda and it was, in a way, relieved of the Palestinian problem. Indeed, Jordan still demanded an Israeli withdrawal and the establishment of a Palestinian state under PLO leadership. The Hashemite Kingdom was even represented at the

1991 Madrid conference by a joint Jordanian–Palestinian delegation. This was mainly lip service. In practice, Jordan focused on its own interests, including those that derived from the new circumstances.

Israel's recognition of the PLO (September 1993), that in the recent past had constituted one of Jordan's preconditions to political negotiations, now assumed an entire different meaning. The Palestinian–Israeli rapprochement seemed to endanger Jordan's national interests and therefore served as a catalyst for Hussein's decision to enter overt peace negotiations with Israel. Moreover, peace with Israel, de facto or otherwise, was considered for several decades to be in Jordan's interest. The course of events between 1988 and 1993 created an opportunity to obtain such a peace at a rather low cost, with no territorial compromise or other problematic obligations on the part of Jordan. Jordan even regained some disputed territories (on the East Bank) from Israel and recognition of its future status in Jerusalem.

Jordan indeed failed to obtain any of its declared goals regarding a political solution to the Arab–Israeli conflict between 1967 and 1988. Yet the major importance of the evolution of its perception towards a political solution was in changing the atmosphere in the Arab world and in lessening its objections to Israel. The contribution of King Hussein and his officials to transforming the conflict, from one that depended on a military solution to one that sought a politically-oriented solution, was invaluable.

Once King Hussein realized that the traditional Arab attitude was anachronistic and that Israeli retreat had a price, Jordan positioned itself at the most moderate pole of Arab views (not without the acquiescence and, occasionally, the tacit blessing of Jamal Abd al-Nasser). Outside the Middle East, Jordan represented the rational and moderate side of the Arabs. Even within the region, at least till 1977 and Sadat's initiative, it played a leading role in gradually creating an atmosphere that encouraged a political solution. Its views on UN resolution 242 and advocacy of the political option had an accumulating impact. It was largely due to Jordan's activity that other Arab countries became ready to recognize Israel as a fact and not to rule out indirect negotiations. Hussein paved the way to Arab (and not only Arab) acquiescence to the Geneva and Madrid conferences, and to the general idea of an international conference.

King Hussein also contributed to the de-demonization of Israel in the Arab world and also, to a certain degree, to the 'normalization' of the conflict. He endeavoured to transform it from an ideological, religious and emotional conflict into a normal, or semi-normal, conflict over territorial rights and mundane assets. Today, more than a decade after the conclusion of the Jordanian–Israeli peace agreement, the most complicated component of the conflict between Israel and the Palestinians is gradually being channelled mainly (though not exclusively) into the territorial aspect: where the exact border-line between Israel and a Palestinian state will lie.

The conflict between Israel and its Arab neighbours has not yet been solved. Besides the direct territorial conflict between Israel and Syria and Israel and the Palestinians, more Arab states refuse to accept Israel than states that recognize it. Many in the Arab world (and in nearby Muslim countries) reject Israel on religious grounds. Even relations between Israel and those Arab states with which it concluded peace treaties, Egypt and Jordan, are problematic. On the formal level, between governments, the peace is depicted as 'cold' or 'lukewarm'. In the popular sphere, things are even worse: there are hardly any indications of normalization and of ties between people on the two sides of the border. Yet the current situation, despite the above-mentioned shortcomings, was un-thought of thirty-odd years ago. Only when comparing Arab–Israeli relations in 1967 and in the present, one realizes what a huge step the Arab world made towards Israel. This reality is the product of various developments and of the initiatives, policies and contributions of many individuals; however, the role of King Hussein was unquestionably overwhelming in its importance.

NOTES

Introduction: The Crystallization of Jordan's Perception

1   Crown Prince El Hassan Bin Talal, 'Jordan's Quest for Peace', *Foreign Affairs*, Spring 1982, p. 806.

2   Samir A. Mutawi, *Jordan in the 1967 War*, Cambridge University Press, Cambridge, 1987, pp. 2–3. For King Hussein's role in shaping his country's foreign and regional policy, see also Abd al-Majid Ali al-Ersan, *The Making of Jordan Foreign Policy under King Hussein*, PhD thesis, Claremont Graduate School, 1983 (printed by University Microfilm International Ann Arbor, 1997), pp. 101–32; Abdelfattah A. Rashdan, *Foreign Policy Making In Jordan, The Role of King Hussein's Leadership in Policy Making*, PhD thesis, University of North Texas, 1989 (printed by UMI Ann Arbor, 1995), pp. 51–83; Nasser Tahabub, *Jordanian Foreign Policy: A Case Study Analysis of the February 11th Agreement*, PhD thesis, Duke University, 1991 (printed by UMI Ann Arbor, 1997), pp. 140–53.

3   Mutawi, *Jordan*, pp. 4–5.

4   On the role of key position-holders as well as of other individuals in the decision-making process in Jordan, see Ra'ad Al-Kadiri, *Strategy and Tactics in Jordanian Foreign Policy 1967–1988*, D. Phil thesis, Oxford, 1995, pp. 13–18.

5   Elyakim Rubinstein, "Chapters in the Quest for Peace with Jordan" in *Yahasei Israel–Yarden* [Hebrew: Israel–Jordan Relations], Bar Ilan University Press, Ramat Gan, 1997, pp. 4–5.

I   The Special Relationship between King Abdullah and the Zionist Movement

1   Among the most conspicuous ones: Clinton Bailey, *The Participation of the Palestinians in the Politics of Jordan*, Unpublished PhD thesis, Columbia University, New York, 1966; Uriel Dann, *Studies in the History of Transjordan 1920–1949: The Making of a State*, Westview Press, Boulder, 1984; Avi Shlaim, *Collusion Across the Jordan: King Abdullah, the Zionist Movement and the Partition of Palestine*, Oxford University Press, New York, 1988; Yoav Gelber, *Jewish Transjordan Relations 1921–1948*, Frank Cass, London, 1997;

Mary C. Wilson, *King Abdullah, Britain and the Making of Jordan*, Cambridge University Press, Cambridge, 1987; Joseph Nevo, *King Abdallah and Palestine: A Territorial Ambition*, Macmillan, in association with St. Antony's College, Oxford, Basingstoke and New York, 1996; Dan Schueftan, *Optzia Yardenit* [Hebrew: A Jordanian Option], Yad Tabenkin, Ramat Efal, 1986; Anita Shapira, 'The Option of the Ghur al-Kibd: Contacts between Amir Abdallah and the Zionist Executive 1932–1934', *Studies in Zionism*, No. 2 (August 1980), pp. 239–83.

2   Nevo, *King Abdallah*, p. 6; Neil Caplan, *Palestine Jewry and the Arab question 1917–1925*, Frank Cass, London, 1978, pp. 171–2; Neil Caplan, *Futile Diplomacy*, Vol. 1, Frank Cass, London, 1983, p. 50; Dann, *Studies*, p. 52; *Ahram*, 14 January 1923.

3   Bailey, *The Participation*, p. 57.

4   Eli Shaltiel, *Pinhas Rotenberg* [Hebrew: Pinhas Rotenberg 1879–1942: Life and Times], Am Oved, Tel Aviv, 1990, pp. 213–14, 265–6, 375–6; Nevo, *King Abdallah*, pp. 18–19; Gelber, *Jewish–Transjordanian Relations*, p. 112.

5   At his meeting with Golda Meyerson, 10–11 May 1948. See below.

6   Report of Ezra Danin (Mrs. Meyerson's associate and interpreter) on the meeting with Abdallah on 17 November 1947, Central Zionist Archive (CZA) S25–4004.

7   One of the main bones of contention, for example, was a land corridor to connect the West Bank with Gaza (for the purpose of using its harbour as a Mediterranean outlet for Jordanian exports and imports). While Israel consented to a 100 m wide corridor that could accommodate a road and a railway, Jordan asked for a 10–12 km wide passage under Jordanian sovereignty that could be used for the resettlement of refugees. See Avraham Sela, *Mimaga'im LeMasa U'Matan* [Hebrew: From Contacts to Negotiation: Relations of the Jewish Agency and the State of Israel with King Abdullah, 1946–1950], Tel Aviv University, Tel Aviv, 1985, p. 45.

8   Nevo, *King Abdallah*, p. 198; Hussein A. Hassouna, *The League of the Arab States and Regional Disputes: A Study of Middle East Conflicts*, Oceania Publication, New York, 1975, p. 40.

9   There was speculation that on the day of his assassination in Jerusalem the King was to meet an Israeli associate there. Robert Satloff, *From Abdallah to Hussein: Jordan in Transition*, Oxford University Press, New York and Oxford, 1994, p. 4.

2   The Friendly Foe: Hussein and Israel prior to 1967

1   Yossi Melman, *Shutafut Oyenet* [Hebrew: Hostile Partnership: The Secret Ties between Israel and Jordan], Meitam, Tel Aviv, 1987, pp. 45–6.

2   Uriel Dann, *King Hussein and the Challenge of Arab Radicalism: Jordan 1955–1967*, Oxford University Press, New York and Oxford, 1989, p. 133.

3   See for example, *Jihad*, 19 May 1954.

4   In 1953 US president Dwight Eisenhower commissioned businessman Eric Johnston to sort out a just and agreed-upon plan for the distribution of the water in the Jordan river basin among its bordering countries. Johnston

proposed that Jordan receive 46.7% of the water, Israel – 38.5%; Syria – 11.7%; and Lebanon 3.1%. However, no agreement was signed as the Arab states refused to enter a joint agreement with Israel. See Peter Snow, *Hussein, A Biography*, Barrie and Jenkins, London, 1972, p. 198; Dann, *Challenge*, pp. 104–5; Satloff, *From Abdallah to Hussein*, p. 174; Adam Garfinkle, *Israel and Jordan in the Shadow of War*, St. Martin's Press, New York, 1992, p. 35.

5   Hussein Bin Talal, *Uneasy Lies the Head*, Bernard Geis Associates, New York, 1962, p. 84; See also Hussein, *Mihnati KaMalik, Ahadith Malikiyya*, Muassat Masri LilTawzi' [n. p.], 1987, p. 73.

6   The only difference, in this respect, between the various Arab states was, according to Mutawi, in their attitude to the West. While pro-Western countries like Saudi Arabia and Jordan saw no contradiction between their good relations with the West and their condemnation of Israel, the 'revolutionary' Arab states identified the struggle against Israel with the fight against imperialism. Mutawi, *Jordan*, p. 46.

7   *HaMizrah HeHadash* [Hebrew: The New East Quarterly], Vol. 5, No. 20 (4) 1954, p. 294. For similar expressions by other Arab leaders, see *Difa'*, 18 November 1952; *Ahram*, 27 September 1954; *Hamizrah HeHadash*, Vol. 4, No. 13 (1), 1952, pp. 41–2; Vol. 7 No. 25 (1), 1956, p. 49, No. 28 (4), pp. 301–2; Vol. 8, No. 29 (1), 1957, p. 63, No. 30 (2), p. 158, No. 31 (3), p. 231.

8   *The Middle East Record*, Vol. II, 1961, pp. 180–3, 185–7; Dann, *Challenge*, p. 105; Hava Lazarus-Yafeh, 'An Inquiry into Arab Textbooks', *Asian and African Studies*, Vol. 8, No. 1, 1972, pp. 1–19 (this article also studies Egyptian and Syrian textbooks); For samples of Nasser's views on the illegitimacy of Israel's existence, see his speeches in *Ahram*, 26 June 1962; 27 March, 23 July 1964.

9   Iris Fruchter-Ronen, *Yarden Ve'HaEtgar HaFalstini: Hitmodedota Shel Yarden Im HaSugiya HaFalastinit KeHelek MeTahlich Gibush Zehuta HaLeumit VeKefi SheHaNose Mishtakef BeSifrei Limud Yardenim 1964–1994* [Hebrew: Jordan and the Palestinian Challenge: Jordan's Handling of the Palestinian Issue as Part of the Coalescence of its Own National Identity and as Reflected in Jordanian Text Books 1964–1994], PhD thesis, University of Haifa, 2003, pp. 56, 60–1.

10 For a summary of these views, see Yehoshafat Harkabi, *Emdat Ha'Aravim BeSichsoch Israel-Arav* [Hebrew: The Arab Position in the Arab-Israeli Conflict], Dvir Publishing House, Tel Aviv, 1968, pp. 29–39. See also *Ha'aretz*, 22 April 1955, *HaMizrah HeHadash*, Vol. 6. No. 24 (4), p. 302. For Hussein's position, see *Ha'aretz*, 21 April 1959; his speech at the UN, 3 October 1960, *Uneasy*, p. 271; see also ibid., pp. 126–7; *Filastin*, 5 October 1960, *Manar*, 6 October 1960.

11 See for example, Egyptian and Syrian declarations to that effect, *Radio Ramallah*, 1 November, 1954, quoted in *HaMizrah HeHadash*, Vol. 6, No. 22 (2), p.134; *Ha'aretz*, 29 December 1954; Harkabi, *Arab's Position*, pp. 398–9.

12 Cecil Hourani, *An Unfinished Odyssey*, Weidenfeld and Nicolson, London, 1984, p. 86.

13 Avraham Sela, *Ahdut BeToch Perod* [Hebrew: Unity within Conflict in the Inter-Arab System], Magnes, Jerusalem, 1982, p. 54; Moshe Shemesh,

Mehanakba Lanaksa [Hebrew: From the Nakba to the Naksa: The Arab–Israeli Conflict and the Palestinian National Problem 1957–1967] Ben Gurion University Press, Beer Sheva, 2004, p. 494. Moshe Zak, *Hussein Ose Shalom* [Hebrew: Hussein Makes Peace, Thirty Years of Secret Talks], Bar-Ilan University Press, Ramat Gan, 1996, p. 73.

14 Another indication that a peaceful solution might also eventually lead to the liquidation of Israel was implied in Hussein's speech in November 1964 at a reception for the President of West Germany: 'Jordan and the Arabs sincerely hope to find a peaceful solution to the Palestine question, a solution that will guarantee the refugees' rights to their homeland', *Ha'aretz*, 27 November 1964.

15 Hussein, *Uneasy*, p. 271; Hassan Bin Talal, *The Palestine Question*, Department of Press and Publication, Ministry of Culture, Amman, 1968, pp. 22–3.

16 Hava Lazarus-Yafeh, "An Inquiry," pp. 15–16; Hassan bin Talal, *Palestinian Self-Determination: A Study of the West Bank and Gaza Strip*, Quartet Books, London, 1981, p. 38.

17 Hussein, *Uneasy*, p. 126.

18 Hussein, *Uneasy*, pp. 91, 126–7; Hussein Bin Talal, *Harbuna ma' Israil*, [Hebrew: Our War with Israel] Dar al-Jalil Li'Tabaat Wa'lnashr, Acre, n.d., p. 15; *The Middle East Record*, Vol. I, 1960, p. 174; Hassan, *The Palestine Question*, pp. 22–3.

19 Dann, *Studies*, p. 11; Nevo, *Abdallah*, pp. 12–15.

20 Hussein, *Harbuna*, p. 15.

21 Due to the urgency of the matter, the planes took off *before* the formal arrangements of securing Israel's permission were completed. Israel's official clearance was granted a few hours later. *Filastin*, 18 July 1958; Hussein, *Uneasy*, pp. 207–8; Snow, *Hussein*, p. 128; James Lunt, *Hussein of Jordan, Searching for a Just and Lasting Peace, A Political Biography*, Macmillan, London, 1989, pp. 77–8; John P. Glennon (ed.), *Foreign Relations of the United States 1958–1960*, Vol. XI: *Lebanon and Jordan*, US Government Printing Office, Washington, 1992, pp. 348, 383.

22 Snow, *Hussein*, pp. 124–5; Glennon, *Foreign Relations*, pp. 426–7.

23 See for example, *Ahram*, 18 July 1958.

24 Hussein, *Uneasy*, p. 204.

25 Melman, *Hostile Partnership*, pp. 48–9.

26 For a detailed discussion on that issue, consult *The Middle East Record*, Vol. I, 1960, pp. 132–7; Vol. II, 1961, pp. 109–10. See also: Moshe Shemesh, *The Palestinian Entity 1959–1974, Arab Politics and the PLO*, Frank Cass, London, 1988, pp. 19–28; Shemesh, *From Nakba to Naksa*, pp. 70–76.

27 Melman, *Hostile Partnership*, p. 49.

28 Garfinkle, *Israel and Jordan*, p. 37.

29 In the midst of this crisis, Israel's Prime Minister David Ben-Gurion asked President Kennedy to 'take steps to prevent the collapse of Hussein's regime,' Zak, *Hussein*, p. 36.

30 King Abdullah too had tried to use the good offices of the Jewish Agency in 1948 in an attempt to extract financial aid from the US. See Nevo, *Abdallah*, p. 111.

31 Zak, *Hussein*, pp. 70–1, 75, 80; Alexander Bligh, *The Political Legacy of King Hussein*, Sussex Academic Press, Brighton & Portland, 2002, pp. 22–3.

32 Melman, *Hostile Partnership*, pp. 58–61; Dann, *Challenge*, p. 105; Zak, *Hussein*, p. 253; Garfinkle, *Israel and Jordan*, pp. 38–9.

33 Moshe Zak, an authority on Jordanian–Israeli ties, claimed that Bourguiba, who made his proposals during a visit to Jordan, was disappointed with Hussein's reaction to his speech since it had been coordinated with the King in advance and he seemed to support it. Zak, *Hussein*, pp. 73–4.

34 *The Middle East Record*, Vol. 1, 1960, p. 174.

35 A small portion of south-west Palestine, occupied and administrated by Egypt since 1948. In addition to its indigenous population, it also accommodated a large number of refugees.

36 Al-Mamlaka al-Urduniyya al-Hashemiya, Wizarat al-Kharijiya, *Al-Urdun w'al-Qadiya al-Filastiniya w'al-'Alaqat al-'Arabiya* [Jordan, Ministry of Foreign Affairs, Jordan and the Palestine Problem and the inter-Arab Relations], Amman, July 1962, pp. 29–37; author's emphasis. See details and analysis: Shemesh, *From Nakba to Naksa*, pp. 68–70.

37 Al-Hammah, a narrow enclave of mandatory Palestine along the Jordanian–Syrian border, between the Yarmuq river and the Golan Heights. After the 1948 war it became part of the demilitarized zone between Israel and Syria but in the early 1950s the Syrians occupied it and, in practice, annexed it.

38 *Filastin*, 15 June, 17 July 1966.

39 Hassan, *The Palestine Question*.

40 R. Amman, 16 July 1966, quoted in Asher Susser, *On Both Banks of the Jordan, A Political Biography of Wasfi al-Tall*, Frank Cass, London, 1994, p. 103; *Radio Amman*, 12 March 1967; BBC 14 March, quoted by *The Middle East Record*, Vol. III, 1967, p. 161; Hussein, *Harbuna*, pp. 20–1.

41 Garfinkle, *Israel and Jordan*, p. 43

42 Moshe Shemesh, 'The IDF Raid on Samu': The Turning Point in Jordan's Relations with Israel and the West Bank Palestinians', *Israel Studies*, Vol. 7, No. 1, Spring 2002, pp. 139–67. See also Bligh, *Political Legacy*, pp. 27–46.

3 Adjusting to the New Reality: From June 1967 to Resolution 242

1 For an excellent analysis of King Hussein's position, see Mutawi, *Jordan*, pp. 100–3, 108–12; 123–6, 182–5; see also Zak, *Hussein*, pp. 103–20; and King Hussein himself, in *Harbuna*, pp. 44–57.

2 *Radio Amman*, 15 July 1986, *Ra'i*, 16 July 1986.

3 Ephraim Kam (ed.), *Hussein Pote'ach BeMilhama* [Hebrew: Hussein Starts a War: The Six Day War in Jordanian Eyes], Ma'arachot, Tel Aviv, 1974, p. 27 note; see also Zak, *Hussein*, p. 107.

4 See for example, *Dustur*, 25 November 1967. While the first stage, according to Arab spokespersons, might be negotiated by political means, the second stage would not. *The Middle East Record*, Vol. III, 1967, p. 255.

5 *Radio Cairo*, 9 June; BBC, 12 June 1967.

6   *Nahar*, 29 August 1967.

7   *Radio Amman*, 22 June; BBC, 24 June 1967.

8   Dan Bavly, *Halomot VeHizdamnoyot SheHuchmetzu* [Hebrew: Dreams and Missed Opportunities 1967–1973], Karmel, Jerusalem, 2002, pp. 35–6.

9   Dan Bavly, *Dreams*, p. 36.

10 A senior official in the Israeli military administration of the West Bank, who was involved in meetings with the local Palestinian leadership.

11 Dan Bavly, *Dearms*, p. 36.

12 *Jumhuriyya*, 6 July 1967. For similar Saudi, Kuwaiti, Iraqi and Syrian comments, see *The Middle East Record*, Vol. III, 1967, p. 256.

13 Sela, *Unity within Conflict*, p. 69.

14 *The Middle East Record*, Vol. III, 1967, p. 404; Mutawi, *Jordan*, p. 8.

15 *The Middle East Record*, Vol. III, 1967, p. 259.

16 *Nahar*, 27 July; *Risala*, 30 July 1967; Mutawi, *Jordan*, pp. 174–5.

17 Zak, *Hussein*, p. 151; *The Middle East Record*, Vol. III, 1967, p. 259.

18 *Radio Cairo*, 1 September; BBC, 4 September, 1967; author's emphasis.

19 *Radio Amman*, 13 September, 16 October, 1 November 1967; BBC, 15 September, 18 October, 3 November 1967; *Le Monde*, 20 September, 28 October 1967; *Jerusalem Post*, 1 November 1967.

20 *Dustur*, 10, 12 November 1967; *The Middle East Record*, Vol. III, 1967, p. 267.

21 *Dustur*, 7, 10, 12 November 1967; *New York Times*, 6, 8 November 1967; *Jerusalem Post*, 6, 10 November, 1967; *The Middle East Record*, Vol. III, 1967, p. 268.

22 Hourani, *Unfinished Odyssey*, p. 79; Nevo, *Abdallah*, pp. 14–15; *Le Monde*, 28 October 1967; *Dustur*, 25 November 1967.

23 *Dustur*, 1, 7, 25 November 1967; *New York Times*, 6, 8 November 1967. One has to bear in mind that at the same time that the King made such statements, he clandestinely met Israeli officials.

24 *Radio Cairo*, 23 November; BBC, 25 November 1967.

25 *The Middle East Record*, Vol. III, 1967, p. 267.

26 Hussein, *Mihnati KaMalik*, pp. 206–7; see also Mutawi, *Jordan*, pp. 2–3.

27 http://www.un.org/documents/sc/res/1967/scres67.htm.

28 *Dustur*, 17 October 1967; King Hussein's speech read by Queen Nur at Georgetown University, 15 March; Jordan TV, 16 March; *Daily Report* (DR), 17 March 1982. See also Lunt, *Hussein*, p. 166; King Hussein's speech, 19 February 1986, *'Asharat 'Aawam min al-Kifah w'al-Bina* [Arabic: Ten Years of Struggle and Building: King Hussein's Speeches 1977–1987], Markaz al-Kitab al-Urduni, 1988, p. 793.

29 *The Middle East Record*, Vol. III, 1967, pp. 271–2, 277.

30 The English version of the resolution reads: 'Withdrawal of Israeli armed forces from *territories* [author's emphasis] occupied in the recent conflict.' Nevertheless, the delegates of India, France and the Soviet Union to the Security Council asserted that their respective governments construed this provision as Israeli withdrawal from *all the* territories occupied in the June war. *The Middle East Record*, Vol. III, 1967, p. 89. This meaningful difference later became a bone of contention between Israel and the Arabs. Each party tended to prefer the version more favourable to its views.

31 See for example, Hassan, *Palestinian Self-Determination*, pp. 97–8, 118–19, 121; Hassan bin Talal, *Search for Peace: The Politics of the Middle Ground in the Arab East*, St. Martin's Press, New York, 1984, p. 107. See also below, chapter 5.

4 Political Activities and Initiatives, 1967–1988

1 Ra'ad al-Kadiri, *Strategy and Tactics*, p. 35.
2 Sela, *Unity within Conflict*, p. 87.
3 Ra'ad al-Kadiri, *Strategy and Tactics*, p. 49.
4 Garfinkle, *Israel and Jordan*, pp. 60–93.
5 The plan, named after its initiator Yigal Allon, Deputy Prime Minister who in 1968 proposed that Israel would annex the eastern part of the West bank (along the river Jordan and the Dead Sea, as well as the Etzion Bloc in southern mount Hebron and the Latrun area). The rest would be returned to Jordan which would be provided with a passage to the West Bank via Jericho.
6 *The Middle East record*, Vol. V, 1969–1970, p. 874.
7 Joseph Nevo, 'Tequfat Wasfi al-Tall BeYarden: 1970–1971' [Hebrew: Wasfi al-Tall's Era in Jordan 1970–1971: Endeavours to Create a Jordanian Entity], *Studies*, No. 18, Jewish–Arab Center, University of Haifa, Haifa, February 1979, pp. 2–9.
8 Kamal Salibi, *The Modern History of Jordan*, I.B. Tauris, London and New York, 1993, p. 247.
9 *Post factum* both fears turned out to be groundless. Most of the mayors and city councilors elected were Jordanian supporters.
10 Joseph Nevo, 'The Political Context of the Triangle: An Overview,' in Joseph Ginat and Onn Winckler (eds.), *The Jordanian–Palestinian–Israeli Triangle: Smoothing the Path to Peace*, Sussex Academic Press, Brighton & Portland, 1998, p. 17.
11 Ra'ad al-Kadiri, *Strategy and Tactics*, p. 78.
12 Zak Hussein, pp.103, 130.
13 Lunt, *Hussein*, p. 250; Henry Kissinger, *Years of Upheaval*, Little Brown, Boston, 1982, p. 506.
14 Hussein in *Newsweek*, 12 December 1977.
15 Schueftan, *Jordanian Option*, p. 333.
16 Sadat's statement was based on an Arab League resolution from July 1950 that *de facto* recognized the recent annexation of the West Bank, perceiving it as a temporary deposit in Jordan's hands, in return for the latter's suspension of peace negotiations with Israel.
17 Shemesh, *The Palestinian Entity*, p. 304.
18 It was reestablished in February 1976, but on a lower level: no longer a Ministry but a 'Bureau' for the Affairs of the Occupied Territories.
19 Before the Carter administration, the US undertook neither to recognize the PLO nor to negotiate with it, as long as the organization did not recognize Israel's right to exist and did not accept UN resolution 242. Under the Carter administration, the PLO was required only to accept resolution 242. An official US spokesperson maintained that endorsement of resolution 242

implied the recognition of Israel's right to exist. The PLO, as noted, failed to meet even this minimal requirement.

20   Kenneth W. Stein, *Heroic Diplomacy: Sadat, Kissinger, Carter, Begin and the Quest for Arab-Israeli Peace*, Routledge, New York and London, 1999, p. 248.

21   *Middle East Contemporary Survey* (MECS), Vol. 3, 1978/79, p. 637; Vol. 4, 1979/80, pp. 577–8.

22   See for example, Adnan Abu Odeh, *Jordanians, Palestinians and the Hashemite Kingdom in the Middle East Peace Process*, United States Institute of Peace, Washington 1999, p. 213.

23   In a confederation, the authority and autonomy of each component *vis-à-vis* the central government are greater than in a federation.

24   The PNC was due to convene in Algiers, but the Algerian government revoked the invitation following heavy Syrian pressure, as a part of their 'war' against Arafat.

25   See Zak, *Hussein*, pp. 201–2.

26   This time as Foreign Minister, after he and Likud leader Yitzhak Shamir switched roles in October 1986 according to the rotation agreement.

27   Even if that were the case and the US met Arafat's conditions, the PLO was not willing to specifically recognize resolution 242, but only 'all UN resolutions regarding Palestine'; i.e., all the extreme anti-Israeli UN resolutions including resolution 194 of December 1948 that recognized the right of Palestinian refugees to return to their homes and villages in the newly-established state of Israel.

28   The Egyptians, who controlled Gaza till 1967, did not claim it back. After the early 1970s, Jordanian spokespersons tended to refer to Gaza whenever they mentioned the West Bank, as did the PLO.

29   Shemesh, *The Palestinian Entity*, p. 344.

30   Abu Odeh, *Jordanians,* pp. 225–6.

31   Laura Zittrain Eisenberg and Neil Caplan, *Negotiating Arab Israeli Peace: Patterns, Problems, Possibilities*, Indiana University Press, Bloomington and Indianapolis, 1998, p. 66.

32   These territories and others in the Arava area were indeed regained by Jordan six years later as a part of the Jordanian–Israeli peace treaty in October 1994.

5   Withdrawal from the West Bank, East Jerusalem and the Gaza Strip

1   The major change, in this respect, evolved around the issue of *who* would control the occupied territories if and when Israel withdrew, Jordan or the PLO.

2   Hassan, *Palestinian Self-Determination*, p. 68.

3   Ibid., pp. 66–9; see also Hassan, *Search for Peace*, pp. 87–93.

4   The only exception to insistence on a complete withdrawal to the lines of 4 June 1967 was the acquiescence to minor mutual border modifications.

5   Zak, *Hussein*, pp. 146–7, 168, 226.

6   *The Middle East Record*, Vol. III, 1967, p. 410; *Dustur*, 18 October 1967; author's emphasis.

7 King Hussein, *Dustur*, 1, 12 November 1967; Foreign Minister Abd al-Mun'im al-Rifa'i, *Dustur*, 13 July 1968.

8 Hussein's speech at Georgetown University, *Dustur*, 8 November 1968; Hussein, *Dustur*, 16 March 1970.

9 Sela, *Unity within Conflict*, pp. 86, 92–3.

10 Hussein in the US, *Dustur*, 16 April 1969; Jordan's reply to Rogers' proposals, *Dustur*, 6 August 1970.

11 For example, Hussein to Parliament, *Dustur*, 2 November 1967; Prime Minister Bahjat al-Talhuni, *Dustur*, 24 October 1968.

12 Hussein, *Dustur*, 17 April 1970; Talhuni, *Dustur*, 25 July 1968. See also Talhuni, *Dustur*, 16 Sepember 1968; Hussein, *Dustur*, 16 April 1969, 1 March 1970.

13 *Dustur*, 28 June 1970.

14 Hussein's interview to the *Nouvel Observateur*, *Dustur*, 17 August 1970; Prime Minister Wasfi al-Tall, *Dustur*, 8 November 1970; Hussein, *Dustur*, 11 May 1971, 24 March 1972.

15 Prime Minister Ahmad al-Lawzi, *Dustur*, 19 April 1972, 6 November 1973; Hussein, *Dustur*, 11 June 1974.

16 *Dustur*, 7 February 1975.

17 Hussein, *Dustur*, 27 April 1975. See also Hussein, *Dustur*, 22 June, 27 July, 6 September 1977.

18 Hussein to *Newsweek*, 12 December 1977.

19 Hussein's statements, *Ra'i*, 20, 24, 27 September, 2, 9, 11, 24 October, 9 November 1978; Prime Minister Mudir Badran's statement: *Ra'i*, 17 October 1978.

20 Hussein, *Dustur*, 17 June 1979; 17 March 1982; 1 March 1984.

21 For Egyptian, Syrian and Iraqi views in this respect, see *The Middle East Record*, Vol. IV, 1968, pp. 205–9, 222–4, 228–9; Vol. V, 1969–1970, pp. 97–8, 106–7.

22 Foreign Minister Muhammad Adib al-Amiri, *Dustur*, 3 October 1967; Ambassador to the UN Muhammad al-Farra, *Dustur*, 4 October 1967.

23 *New York Times*, 7 November 1967.

24 Hussein, *Dustur*, 14 August 1970. See also *Dustur*, 20, 22 April 1969; 9 August 1970; 11 December 1970; Foreign Minister Antun Atallah, *Dustur*, 9 August 1970.

25 *Le Figaro*, quoted in *Dustur*, 18 August 1970.

26 See for example, *Dustur*, 17 November 1970; 18 October 1973; 5 June 1974; 15 March 1975.

27 Hussein, *Dustur*, 30 April 1969; Foreign Minister Antun Attallah, *Dustur*, 19, 28 July 1970.

28 See for example, Hussein, *Dustur*, 17 June 1976.

29 *Journal of Palestine Studies* (JPS), Vol. 9, No. 2 (winter, 1980), pp. 169–70.

30 Minister of Information Adnan Abu Odeh, 'Bridging the Peace Gap in the Middle East', *JPS*, Vol. 6, No. 2 (winter, 1977), p. 64.

31 *MECS*, Vol. 3, 1978/9, p. 638. See also *MECS*, Vol. 4, 1979–1980, p. 578.

32 *MECS*, Vol. 4, 1979–80, p. 578.

33 *MECS*, Vol. 3, 1978/9, p. 638.

34 *Radio Amman*, 14 December, DR, 18 December 1978; *New York Times*, 12 January 1979; *Jordan Times*, 4 June 1980, *MECS*, Vol. 4, 1979/80, p. 578.

35 Foreign Minister Marwan al-Qassim, *MECS*, Volume 5, 1980–1981, pp. 642–3.

36 Hussein, *Al-Watan al-Arabi*, 19 December 1980; Foreign Minister Marwan al-Qassim, *MECS*, Vol. 5, 1980–1981, pp. 642–3.

37 Hussein, *New York Times*, 25 January 1970. Hussein's speech at the UN, 25 September,1979, *JPS*, Vol. 9, No. 2 (winter 1980), pp. 169–70.

38 Prime Minister Zayd al-Rifa'i, *Dustur*, 15 March 1974; Madiha Rashid al Madfa'i, *Jordan and the United States and the Middle East Peace Process 1974–1991*, Cambridge University Press, Cambridge, 1993, p. 19; Hussein, in *Newsweek*, 12 December 1977; Lunt, *Hussein*, p. 256.

39 Hussein in *Newsweek*, 17 June 1974; Zak, *Hussein*, pp. 163–4.

40 Prime Minister Zayd al-Rifa'i, *Ra'i*, 15 March, 13 May 1974; Hussein, *Dustur*, 24 June 1974; Hussein (in the US), *Dustur*, 18 August 1974; Zak, *Hussein*, p. 164.

41 *Shuun Filastiniya*, No. 36 (August 1974), p. 193.

42 *The Middle East Record*, Vol. IV, 1968, pp. 243–4, 428, 431; *Radio Amman*, 9 July; BBC, 13 July 1968; Hussein, *Dustur*, 30 April1969, 15 May 1979, 17 March 1982, 11 March 1984; Hussein, *Ra'i*, 2 September 1978, 15 April 1979; Foreign Minister Antun Atallah, *Dustur*, 9 August 1970; Prime Minister Ahmad al-Lauzi, *Dustur*, 18 February, 19 April 1972; Minister for the Occupied Territories Affairs, Marwam Dudim, *Dustur, 26 August 1986.*

43 Jordan's ambassador to the UN Mohamad al-Farra, *Dustur*, 31 March 1968; Hussein, *Ra'i*, 24 March 1974; Hussein in *Newsweek*, 17 June 1974.

44 Hussein, *Dustur*, 1 October 1973.

45 Zak, *Hussein*, pp. 47, 130.

46 Hussein's speech read by Queen Nur in Georgetown, 15 March 1982; Jordan TV, 16 March; DR, 17 March 1982.

47 See for example, Hussein, *Dustur*, 10 January 1981; Queen Nur, at Princeton, *Ra'i*, 20 April 1985.

48 Jordan's UN envoy Abdallah Salih, *Dustur*, 7 November 1988 ; Chamber of Deputies speaker 'Akif al-Fayiz, *Ra'i*, 5 January 1988; Hussein, *Ra'i*, 15 January, 9 February 1988.

49 Hussein, *Ra'i*, 6 April, 10 May, 8 December 1982; *Dustur*, 24 January 1984; Hassan, *Ra'i*, 11 January 1982; 20 March 1983; 20 September 1985; Deputy Minister for Occupied Territories Affairs, Shaukat Mahmod, *Ra'i*, 27 July 1983. It is worth mentioning that after the summer of 1982 when Israel invaded Lebanon in operation 'Peace for the Galilee', the 'Arab occupied lands' which Jordan insisted be returned included south Lebanon.

50 Prime Minister Zayd al-Rifa'i, *Dustur*, 2 August 1986; Minister for Occupied Territories Affairs Marwan Dudin, *Ra'i*, 22 May 1987; Hussein, *Dustur*, 9 June 1987; Hussein, *Radio Amman*, 18 Sept. 1987; Hussein, *Ra'i*, 10, 14 October 1987, 2, 9 February 1988; Foreign Minister Tahir al-Masri, *Ra'i*, 13 July 1988; Chamber of Deputies speaker Ahmad al-Lawzi, *Ra'i*, 11 November 1988.

51 Hussein, *Ra'i*, 15 January, 10 October 1987; Minister Marwan Dudin, *Ra'i*,

27 July, *Dustur*, 26 August 1987; Prime Minister Zayd al- Rifa'i, *Dustur*, 12 February 1988; author's emphasis.

52 Zayd al-Rifa'i, *Dustur*, 14 February 1988; author's emphasis.

53 See for example, Minister Marwan Dudin, *Ra'i*, 14 February 1988; Foreign Minister Tahir al-Masri, *Ra'i*, 1 March 1988.

54 *The Middle East Record*, Vol. III, 1967, pp. 256, 296; Vol. IV, 1968, pp. 126, 210.

55 Ibid.

56 After the 1948 war the Gaza Strip was considered a possible outlet for Jordan to the Mediterranean. In 1949, while negotiating a peace agreement, Jordan and Israel discussed a corridor between the West Bank and Gaza that was to constitute a Jordanian-controlled port.

57 *Observer*, 1 October 1967; *The Middle East Record*, Vol. III, 1967, p. 266; Vol. IV, 1968, p. 210.

58 *Nahar*, 9 December 1968; *The Middle East Record*, Vol. IV, 1968, p. 80.

59 Reuven Padehzur, 'The History of Gaza since 1967' [Hebrew], *Ha'aretz*, 7 November 2003, p. B-7.

60 Shemesh, *The Palestinian Entity*, p. 104.

61 *'Amal*, 26 August 1967; *The Middle East Record*, Vol. III, 1967, p. 260. On a possible access road from the West Bank to Gaza, see also *The Middle East Record*, Vol. IV, 1968, p. 80.

62 Hussein, *Dustur*, 16 August, 1972; Hussein interview, *Nahar*, 24 August 1972; Hussein TV Interview, US, 11 February 1973. See also Prime Minister Zayd al-Rifa'i, *Dustur*, 5 June, 1974.

63 See for example, *Dustur*, 23 January 1978 (Hussein in the *New York Times*).

64 Hussein's press conference in Washington, 26 April 1977; Hussein TV interview to ABC, 29 August 1982.

6   The Question of Jerusalem

1 The Jordanian authorities ignored article 8 of the armistice agreement, which called, *inter alia*, for free access to the Holy places and for the use of the [Jewish] cemetery on the Mount of Olives.

2 The sanctity of the Temple Mount and Jerusalem for the Muslims derives from the fact that the prophet Muhammad made it the first *qibla* (the direction towards which Muslims should face during prayer), that was later replaced by Mecca. Moreover, Muhammad's legendary nightly journey to heaven (*al-mi'araj*) began on the Temple Mount.

3 See, for example, his speech on 19 February 1986, announcing the suspension of the 1985 agreement with the PLO, *JPS*, Vol. 15, No. 4 (summer 1986), p. 231. See also his eulogy at Yitzhak Rabin's funeral on 6 November 1995, *Ha'aretz*, 7 November 1995.

4 Zak, *Hussein*, p. 177.

5 Hassan bin Talal, *A Study on Jerusalem*, Longman, London and New York, 1979, pp. 5–8.

6 A few weeks later, in August 1967, Hussein made it known that, in return for East Jerusalem, he was ready to acknowledge the Wailing Wall as an Israeli enclave. *The Middle East Record*, Vol. III, 1967, p. 260.

7   Ibid., p. 290; Hassan, *Jerusalem*, p. 28.

8   Ibid.

9   Hussein and Prime Minister Sa'ad Ju'ma, 29 June, *The Middle East Record*, Vol. III, 1967, p. 295.

10 Hassan, *Jerusalem*, p. 50; Hassan, *Palestinian Self-Determination*, p. 70; *The Middle East Record*, Vol. III, 1967, pp. 82–3, 292.

11 Hassan, *Jerusalem*, p. 12.

12 Hassan, *Jerusalem*, pp. 3, 31–2, 40–1, 47.

13 Prime Minister Sa'ad Jum'a, *Dustur*, 9 September 1967; Hussein, *Harbuna*, p. 103; Zak, *Hussein*, p. 177.

14 Hassan, *Dustur*, 24 August, Prime Minister Bahjat al-Talhuni, *Dustur*, 16 September 1968.

15 Deputy Prime Minister and Foreign Minister Abd al-Mun'im al-Rifa'i, *Dustur*, 23 September 1969; Prime Minister Bahjat al-Talhuni, *Anwar*, 8 October 1968; Hussein, *Dustur*, 6 November 1973; Prime Minister Zayd al-Rifa'i, *Dustur*, 7 November, 22 December 1973; Hassan, *Jerusalem*, pp. 5–6.

16 Zak, *Hussein*, p. 180.

17 Hussein, *Dustur*, 24 March 1968; Foreign Minister Abdullah Salih, *Dustur*, 15 September 1971.

18 Hussein in the US, *Dustur*, 12 April 1968; Hussein in the UK, *Dustur*, 23 April 1969. See also Hussein, *Ra'i*, 31 March, 3 April 1972.

19 On 21 August 1969 a fire broke out in the al-Aqsa mosque on the Temple Mount. Besides the substantial damage caused by the fire, the incident elicited angry reactions in the Arab and Muslim world, and accusations that Israel had attempted to eliminate one of the holiest shrines of Islam. The fire was set by an Australian tourist, Michael Denis William Rohen, who was a member of a small Christian sect, 'the Church of God'. At his trial, he was judged insane and was sent to a mental hospital.

20 *Dustur*, 22 August 1969.

21 *Dustur*, 23 September 1969.

22 *Ra'i*, 16 March 1972; Hussein, *Dustur*, 24, 31 March, 3 April 1972.

23 Hussein, *Dustur*, 6 November 1973; Prime Minister Zayd al-Rifa'i, *Dustur*, 7 November, 22 December 1973.

24 See for example, Hussein's speech in Georgetown, 15 March 1982, read by Queen Nur. Jordan Television (English channel), 16 March 1982; DR, 17 March 1982.

25 Shemesh, *Palestinian Entity*, p. 272.

26 Pope Paul's declaration, 21 December 1973, in Dov Zakin (ed.), *HaSichsuch HaAravi–Israeli* [Hebrew: The Arab–Israeli Conflict, A Collection of Documents 1973–1984], Arab Studies Institute, Giva'at Haviva, 1985, p. 241.

27 Hussein, *Dustur*, 30 August 1982; Hassan, *Al-Ra'i*, 16 May 1986. See also Hussein's speech on 11 August 1882 on the occasion of the 30th anniversary of his accession to the throne, *King Hussein's Speeches 1977–1987*, pp. 389 ff.

28 Hussein, *Dustur*, 27 September, 9, 11 October 1978; 5 November 1981; Hassan, *Palestinian Self-Determination*, p. 38.

29 Hassan, *Dustur*, 20, 24 September 1978; 17 June 1979; author's emphasis.

30 Hussein to the Jordanian Parliament, 16 January 1984, *JPS*, Vol. 13, No. 3, 1984, pp. 202–3; Hussein at the 17th PNC in Amman, 22 November 1984, *JPS*, Vol. 14, No. 2, 1985, pp. 254–6.

31 Marwan Dudin, Minister For Occupied Territories Affairs, *Ra'i*, 15 September 1986; Hussein, *Dustur*, 1 November 1987.

32 Hassan, *Dustur*, 17 June 1979; Hassan, *Jerusalem*, p. 47; see also Hussein's speech of 19 February 1986, suspending the agreement with the PLO, *JPS*, Vol. 15, No. 4 (summer 1986), pp. 207ff.

33 Article 9.2 reads: 'Israel respects the current special role of the Hashemite Kingdom of Jordan in the Muslim holy sites in Jerusalem. When the negotiations on the permanent status take place, Israel will give high priority to the historic Jordanian role in these shrines.' Israel Ministry of Education, *Peace Treaty Between the State of Israel and the Hashemite Kingdom of Jordan, 26 October, 1994*, Government Printing House, Jerusalem, 1994, p. 12; Zak, *Hussein*, pp. 26–7, 173.

34 It is worth noting that even today (2006), more than a decade after the conclusion of Jordan–Israel peace treaty, the Jordanian press refers even to the Western (Jewish) part of the city as 'occupied Jerusalem' (*al-Quds al-Muhtala*).

35 Hassan, *Dustur*, 24 August 1968; Hussein, *Dustur*, 30 April 1969; Hussein, *Harbuna*, pp. 101–2.

36 Hussein, *Dustur*, 12 April, 24 August 1968; Hussein, *Ra'i*, 19 December 1974, 18 December 1976; Hussein, *Mustaqbal* (Paris), 5 September 1981.

37 Hussein to the *New York Times*, *Dustur*, 31 March 1972; Hussein to NBC, quoted in *Dustur*, 3 April 1972. See also Hussein, *Dustur*, 7 June, 5 October 1972; Prime Minister Ahmad al-Lawzi, *Dustur*, 15 September 1972.

38 Hussein, *Dustur*, 30 March, 18 June, 8 August 1974; 21 January, 15 March 1975. Hussein, *Ra'i*, 27 September 1985; see also Hussein (in France), *Dustur*, 4 February 1988.

39 Hassan, *Palestinian Self-Determination*, p. 128.

40 Hussein, *Dustur*, 30 March, 26 August 1974; 21 January 1975.

41 Hussein, *Shuun Filastiniya*, May, 1972, p. 242; Hussein, in the US, *Shuun Filastiniya*, May 1974, p. 194; Hussein, in *Newsweek*, 12 December 1977.

42 Hassan bin Talal, 'Return to Geneva,' *Foreign Affairs*, December 1984, p. 10; Hassan, *Jerusalem*, pp. 44–6.

43 *Middle East Record*, Vol. III, 1967, p. 260.

44 Hussein, *International Herald Tribune*, 19 March 1969; *Newsweek*, 26 August 1970; *New York Times*, 18 December 1970; Foreign Minister Abd al-Mun'im al-Rifa'i, *Dustur*, 1 February 1970; see also Queen Nur at Georgetown University, reading Hussein's speech, 15 March; *Jordan Television*, 16 March; DR, 17 March 1982; Hassan, *Jerusalem*, p. 47.

45 Hussein, *Dustur*, 15 September 1982; 4 February 1988; 19 December 1974.

46 Prime Minister Abd al-Mun'im al-Rifa'i, *Dustur*, 22 March 1970; Hussein, *Dustur*, 26, 27 June 1971; 8 March 1978; Foreign Minister Abdullah Salih, *Dustur*, 15 September 1971.

47 Hussein, *Dustur*, 3 August, 1 September, 1980; Hassan, 'Return to Geneva,' p. 10; Hassan, *Jerusalem*, pp. 12, 39–43.

48 Hussein, *Dustur*, 21 January 1972; Minister for Occupied Territories Affairs, Marwan Dudin, *Ra'i*, 15 September 1986.

49 *Ra'i*, 24 January 1986.

50 Hussein, *Dustur*, 18 September 1987; Hussein, *Ra'i*, 2, 4 February 1988; Minister Marwan Dudin, *Dustur*, 15 September 1986; Minister of Waqf, Abd al-Aziz Khayat, *Dustur*, 18 March 1988.

7 Settlements and Natural Resources

1 The other three were in Banias, on the slopes of Mount Hermon; near Quneitra on the Golan Heights and in Bardawil, on the northern coast of the Sinai peninsula, east of El-Arish.

2 *The Middle East Record*, Vol. III, 1967, p. 288; *Dustur*, 27, 29 September 1967.

3 For details, see *The Middle East Record*, Vol. IV, 1968, pp. 462–3.

4 Hussein, *Dustur*, 23 September 1969; 24 April 1975; Deputy Prime Minister, Abd al-Mun'im al-Rifa'i, *Dustur*, 23 September 1969.

5 The exact number of settlements as given by the various sources varies from 26 to 34. The differences are due to different definitions or methods of calculation. Geoffrey Aronson, *Creating Facts: Israel, Palestinians and the West Bank*, Institute of Palestine Studies, Washington, 1987, pp. xx–xxi; Meron Benveniste, *Lexicon Yahuda VeShomron* [Hebrew: West Bank Handbook], Kana, Jerusalem, 1987, p. 44.

6 See for example, Hussein, *Dustur*, 24 June, 7 September 1977.

7 Hassan, 'Jordan's Quest for Peace,' p. 809; Hassan Bin Talal, 'Return to Geneva', *Foreign Policy*, Winter 1984–1985, pp. 9–10; Hassan, *Palestinian Self-Determination*, pp. 71–3; Hassan, *Search for Peace*, pp. 113, 140. See also King Hussein's speech, *Ra'i*, 19 September 1985.

8 Hussein in *Newsweek*, 12 December 1977.

9 Hussein, *Dustur*, 30 May 1978 (interview in the *Chicago Tribune*); Hussein interview CBS, 1 October 1978, *JPS*, Vol. 8, No. 2, winter 1979, pp. 197–8.

10 Joseph Alpher, *Settlements and Borders*, Study No. 3, Final Status Issues: Israel–Palestinians, Jaffee Center for Strategic Studies, Tel Aviv University, 1994, pp. 10–11; Aronson, pp. xx–xxi; Hassan, *Palestinian Self-Determination*, p. 73. According to Israeli sources there were then about 16.000 settlers in 71 West Bank settlements, Benveniste, *West Bank*, pp. 43–4.

11 Hussein, *Dustur*, 20 March 1983; 1 February 1984 (interview NBC); Hassan, *Ra'i*, 17 May 1986; Prime Minister Mudhir Badran, *Ra'i*, 9 October 1983.

12 Hassan, 'Return to Geneva', pp. 9–10; Hassan, *Search for Peace*, p. 140.

13 Hassan, *Dustur*, 3 July 1978; *Ra'i*, 17 May 1986; Minister for Occupied Territories Affairs Hassan Ibrahim, *Ra'i*, 5 April 1982; Hussein, *Ra'i*, 27 February 1986. In 1983 the Jordanians claimed that 143 settlements had already been established and 25 more were on the way. A year later they placed their number at 165. A Jordanian official claimed in 1987 that there were 195 settlements in the West Bank and the Gaza Strip. Deputy Minister for Occupied Territories Affairs Shaukat Mahmud, *Dustur*, 27 July 1983. See also Hassan, *Search for Peace*, pp. 112–13; Minister Marwan Dudin, *Ra'i*, 29 March 1987. These numbers, however, were a gross exaggeration. In 1983 there were 76 settlements on the West Bank and in 1985, 105. At the end of

the period surveyed, in 1988, over 60,000 inhabitants lived in about 120 settlements throughout the West Bank. Benveniste, *West Bank*, p. 44; *Israel's Statistical Yearbook*, No. 39, Jerusalem, 1988, p. 36; No. 41, 1991, p. 44.

14 Hassan, *Search for Peace*, p. 113.

15 Hussein, *Dustur*, 3 July 1978; *Ra'i*, 24 January 1984 (interview to the BBC); 1 February 1984 (interview to NBC); Minister for Occupied Territories Affairs, Hassan Ibrahim, *Ra'i*, 5 April 1982; Prime Minister Mudhir Badran, *Ra'i*, 9 October 1983.

16 Hussein, *Ra'i*, 19, 20, 27 September 1985.

17 Hussein, *Dustur*, 10 February 1983; 19 September, 2 November 1985; Hussein, *Ra'i*, 19, 20, 27 September 1985, 26, 27 February 1986; Hassan, *Ra'i*, 7 January 1986; Hassan, 8 November 1983 (at Emory University, Atlanta), *JPS*, Vol. 50, winter 1984, pp. 7–9; Minister Mustafa Dudin, *Ra'i*, 26 March 1987; Chamber of Deputies' Speaker, Aakif al-Fayiz, *Ra'i*, 16 April 1987; Foreign Minister Tahir al-Masri, *Ra'i*, 13 July 1988.

18 Prime Minister Mudhir Badran, *Dustur*, 9 October 1983; Hussein, *Dustur*, 1 February 1984; Hassan, 'Jordan's Quest for Peace', p. 809.

19 Hassan, *Dustur*, 15 January 1984 (interview for British TV); *Ra'i*, 16, 17 May 1986.

8   Changing Israel's Policy and Ideology: The Hashemite Viewpoint

1 Hussein, *Uneasy*, pp. 126–7; Hassan, *The Palestine Question*, pp. 22–3; Harkabi, *Arab Position*, pp. 162–203.

2 *New York Times*, 7 November 1967.

3 Hussein's letter to the National Association of Arab-Americans, 15 May 1983; *King Hussein's Speeches 1977–1987*, pp. 454–61; Hussein at the UN, 25 September 1979, *JPS*, Vol. 9, No. 2, winter 1980, pp. 168–9; Hussein's speech, 17 March 1978, *King Hussein's Speeches 1977–1987*, p. 53. See also Hussein, interview to Jordan TV, 21 September 1988; DR, 23 September 1988; Foreign Minister Tahir al-Masri, *Ra'i*, 4 October 1988; Hassan, *Ra'i*, 17 May, 1986; Hussein, interview in *Newsweek*, 17 June 1974.

4 Prime Minister Bahjat al-Talhuni, *Dustur*, 21 June 1968; Hussein (in the US), *Dustur*, 12 April 1969.

5 *Dustur*, 13 March 1968.

6 Hussein (in the US), *Dustur*, 12 April 1969.

7 *Dustur*, 30 March 1970.

8 Hussein, *Ra'i*, 11 May 1971, 22 January 1972; 21 January 1975 (on Saudi TV), 15 May 1983; Ambassador to the UN Abd al-Hamid Sharaf, *Dustur*, 15 January 1976; Deputy Minister for Occupied Territories Affairs, Shaukat Mahmud, *Ra'i*, 27 July 1983.

9 Hussein interview in *Newsweek*, 17 June 1974; Hussein, *Ra'i*, 4 February 1977 (interview to the *Daily Telegraph*); 30 May 1978 (interview to the *Chicago Tribune*), Hussein's letter to the National Association of Arab-Americans, 15 May 1983, *King Hussein's Speeches 1977–1987*, pp. 454 ff.

10 Hussein, *Dustur*, 12 April 1969; 21 June, 1 November 1977 (interview to the *Washington Post*); Hussein interview in *Newsweek*, 17 June 1974; Foreign

Minister Antun Atallah, *Ra'i*, 12 August 1970; Jordan's ambassador to the UN Abdullah Salah, *Ra'i*, 7 July 1986.

11　Hassan, 'Jordan's Quest for Peace', pp. 804, 806. In this article, Prince Hassan accused not only Israel but also the US and 'frankly, many Arab countries' for overlooking Jordan or taking it for granted. See also His Royal Highness Hassan Ibn Talal, 'Jordan: The Quest for a Centrist Position', *JPS*, Vol. 50 (winter 1984), pp. 3–11.

12　Fruchter-Ronen, *Jordan and the Palestinian Challenge*, p. 180.

13　Many Jordanians believed that this was the ulterior motive underlying Israel's invasion of Lebanon (operation 'Peace for the Galilee') in June 1982. See for example, Foreign Minister Marwan al-Qassim, *Dusur*, 6 July 1982. See also *Ra'i*, 14 July 1982.

14　Hussein, *Dustur*, 21 June, 18 July 1977; 9 May 1978; Hussein at the UN, 25 September 1979, *King Hussein's Speeches 1977–1987*, p. 131ff; Hussein at the Amman summit, 24 November 1980, ibid., p. 232ff.

15　On earlier Arab ideas to turn Jordan into the Palestinian 'substitute homeland' (*al-watan al-badil*), see Fruchter-Ronen, *Jordan and the Palestinian Challenge*, pp. 181–2.

16　Hussein, *Ra'i*, 5 September 1981; Hussein, *Dustur*, 7 November 1981, 5 November 1983; Hussein's interview to the BBC, 13 September 1982, *JPS*, Vol. 12, winter 1983; Hussein's letter to the National Association of Arab-Americans, 15 May 1983, *King Hussein's Speeches 1977–1987*, pp. 454ff.

17　Hassan, 'Jordan's Quest for Peace', p. 806.

18　Zak, *Hussein*, p. 226. In August 1977, Hussein met Moshe Dayan who crossed the political line and became Foreign Minister in Begin's cabinet. Throughout his secret negotiations with Israeli leaders, the King never met either Menachem Begin or Ariel Sharon. He met Yitzhak Shamir in 1987, when Shamir was Prime Minister of the national coalition government and again in 1991.

9　The Palestinian Issue

1　During a UN debate on the refugees in 1960, a Jordanian commentator declared that the final solution [to the refugee problem] was an Arab Palestine and that this solution would be achieved on the soil of Palestine itself, *Filastin*, 11 October 1960.

2　Hussein, *Dustur*, 8 September 1968; 12 April 1969 (in Washington); 20 April 1969 (in Boston).

3　Hussein, *Dustur*, 16 April 1969 (in New York), 28 June 1970.

4　Prime Minister Bahjat al-Talhuni, *Dustur*, 25 July 1968. See also Hussein, *Dustur*, 8 September 1968, 30 April 1969.

5　Foreign Minister Muhammad Adib al-Amiri, *Dustur*, 3 October 1967; Hussein, *Dustur*, 12 April 1969 (in Washington), 15 February 1970.

6　*Dustur*, 2 November 1967.

7　Hussein, *Dustur*, 28 June, 17 August 1970.

8　*Dustur*, 28 July 1971.

9　Hussein, *Dustur*, 24 March 1972; Hassan, 'Jordan's Quest for Peace', p. 809. According to Said al-Tall, the federal idea was indeed discussed before 1967, following the Israeli raid on the village of Samu' in November 1966. Said al-Tall, *Al-Urdun wa Filastin* (Arabic: Jordan and Palestine). Dar al-Liwa Lil-Sahafat Wa'l-Nashir Wa'l-Tawzi' Amman, 1986, pp. 43, 147–8.

10 Article 24 of the Palestinian National Covenant of 1964. This article was omitted from the new 1968 version of the Covenant. As at that time Israel alone controlled the entire territory of mandatory Palestine, the PLO felt free to ask for their inclusion under future Palestinian sovereignty.

11 *The Middle East Record*, Vol. III, 1967, p. 264.

12 In the summer of 1973 King Hussein was asked for Jordan's response to the possible recognition of the PLO by the USSR. He answered vaguely, 'The Palestinian people is here, in the East and West Bank and in the Gaza Strip. Here is the steadfastness and not someplace else'. *Dustur*, 25 August 1973.

13 Hussein, *Dustur*, 4, 11 December 1973; see also Sela, *Unity within Conflict*, p. 108.

14 Prime Minister Zayd al-Rifa'i, *Dustur*, 5 June 1974; Hussein, *Dustur*, 24 June, 30 August 1974.

15 Prime Minister Zayd al-Rifa'i, *Dustur*, 13 September 1974.

16 *The Middle East Record*, Vol. IV, 1968, p. 220; see also Shemesh, *The Palestinian Entity*, pp. 167–179.

17 Consult Benny Morris, *The Birth of the Palestinian Refugee Problem, 1947–1949*, Cambridge University Press, Cambridge, 1989, Appendix I, pp. 297–8. See also Rony E. Gabbay, *A Political Study of the Arab-Jewish Conflict: The Arab Refugee Problem (A Case Study)*, Librairie E. Droz, Genève, 1959, pp. 166–8, 174–5.

18 The Palestinians in Jordan (refugees and non-refugees alike) who wished to be granted Jordanian citizenship enjoyed full political and civil rights like Transjordanians. In Israel, even though Arab citizens were granted political rights, they lived (until 1966) under a military administration and their freedom of movement was limited. Hence their work and education opportunities were also impaired. The Palestinians in the Gaza Strip were under Egyptian military administration that barely allowed them to travel out of the Strip to Egypt or elsewhere. On the status of the refugees in different host countries, see Gabbay, *A Political Study*, pp. 202–17.

19 On the intricacy of this policy and on its economic and political implications, see Avi Plascov, *The Palestinian Refugees in Jordan 1948–1957*, Frank Cass, London, 1981, pp. 41–50.

20 <http://www.un.org/documents/ga/res/3/ares3.htm>.

21 It is worth noting that all Arab state-members of the UN voted *against* this resolution (since it also included a clause on Jerusalem to which they objected).

22 This attitude fit Jordan's perception of Israel as Palestine.

23 *The Middle East Record*, Vol. III, 1967, p. 89; <http://www.un.org/documents/sc/res/1967/ scres67.htm>.

24 *Dustur*, 16 September 1968.

25 Crown Prince Hassan estimated their number as 234.000. Hassan, *Palestinian Self-Determination*, p. 99.

26 *The Middle East Record*, Vol. III, 1967, pp. 310–12.

27 Prime Minister Sa'ad Juma', *Dustur*, 11 September 1967; Prime Minister

Bahjat al-Talhuni, *Dustur*, 12 January, 22 May 1968, 2 June 1969; Hassan, *Dustur*, 4 July 1968; Hussein, *Dustur*, 12 April 1969 (speech in the US).

28 Hussein, *Dustur*, 25 November 1967 (interview in *Le Monde*), 12, 20 April 1969 (in the USA).

29 *Dustur*, 12 November 1967 (quoting an interview in the *New York Times*).

30 *Dustur*, 23 January 1978 (interview in the *New York Times*).

31 Hussein, *Dustur*, 14, 24 April 1969, 14 August 1970, 4 April 1976; Chief of the Royal Court, Abd al-Hamid Sharaf, *Ra'i*, 13 May 1979.

32 See for example, Jordan's comments on the Rogers Plan, 6 August 1970; Foreign Minister Antun Atallah, *Dustur*, 9 August 1970.

33 Hussein's speech, 19 February 1986 (the suspension of his agreement with the PLO), *JPS*, Vol. 15, No. 4 (summer 1986), p. 216.

34 Hussein, *Dustur*, 28 June 1970.

35 *Dustur*, 28 July 1970, Jordan's response to the Rogers Plan.

36 Hussein, *Dustur*, 17 August 1970 (interview in the *Nouvel Observateur*).

37 Prime Minister Wasfi Tall, *Dustur*, 8 November 1970; Hussein, *Dustur*, 17 November, 11, 15 December 1970, 4 May 1971.

38 Prime Minister Wasfi Tall, *Dustur*, 8 November 1970; Hussein, *Dustur*, 24, 31 March 1972 (interview to the *New York Times*); Prime Minister Ahmad al-Lawzi, *Ra'i*, 19 April 1972.

39 Hussein speech of 15 March 1972, *JPS*, Vol. 1, No. 4 (summer 1972), p. 166.

40 See Moshe Dayan, *Avnei Derech* [Hebrew: Story of My Life], Idanim, Jerusalem, Dvir, Tel Aviv, 1976, pp. 490–1, 503; Dan Schufftan, *Korach HaHafrada* [Hebrew: Disengagement: Israel and the Palestinian Entity], Zmora-Bitan and University of Haifa Press, Haifa, 1999, p. 44.

41 Hussein's speech at the UN, 25 September 1979, *JPS*, Vol. 9, No. 2 (winter 1980), pp. 169, 170; Hussein's speech, 19 February 1986 (suspension of the agreement with Arafat), *JPS*, Vol. 15., No. 4 (summer 1986), pp. 208, 209.

42 The Arab conferences also called on nations to respect the Palestinian national rights and supported their right to decide their own future by means of an internationally supervised referendum 'after Jordan completed her role in the liberation of the West Bank and Jerusalem', Sela, *Between Unity and Conflict*, pp. 104, 108, 112ff.

43 As late as 1974, when Hussein was asked what the legitimate rights of the Palestinians were, he answered: The right to return to their homeland or to be compensated, according to UN resolutions. Hussein in *Newsweek*, 17 June 1974.

44 Prime Minister Zayd al-Rifa'i, *Ra'i*, 22 December 1973, 13 September 1974; Hussein, *Ra'i*, 4 December 1973, 11, 24 June, 26, 30 August 1974; Hussein in *Newsweek*, 17 June 1974. Three years later, when asked by the same weekly if Jordan could negotiate Israel's withdrawal from the West Bank, the King said that it was no longer Jordan's problem but that of the PLO. Hussein in *Newsweek*, 12 December 1977.

45 Hussein, *Dustur*, 19 April, 7 June, 2 November 1972. This is one of the first instances when a Jordanian spokesperson implied that the Gaza Strip was likely to share a common future with the West Bank and that Jordan was the legitimate representative of the residents of Gaza as well.

46 Hussein, *Ra'i*, 18 August 1974.

47 Hussein, *Dustur*, 23 November 1973; *Ra'i*, 28 November, 10, 12 December 1976.

48 Jordanian–Palestinian Accord (released 23 February 1985), *JPS*, Vol. 14, No. 3 (spring 1985), p. 206. See also Hussein's speech in Washington DC at the 13th Annual Convention of the National Association of Arab Americans (NAAA), 4 May 1985, *JPS*, Vol. 14, No. 4 (summer, 1985), pp. 16, 21.

49 Hussein, *Dustur*, 28 November 1973; *Ra'i*, Official Jordanian spokesperson, 24 January 1974.

50 Hussein, *Dustur*, 4 November 1974 (interview to British Television).

51 Hussein, *Dustur*, 30 August 1974 (interview to *al-Hayat*).

52 Hassan, *Palestinian Self-Determination*, p. 12. Prince Hassan was probably referring to King Hussein Ibn Ali's reluctance to sign an Anglo-Hijazi treaty in which he would have to recognize Palestine as a British mandate. He adhered to this stance, *inter alia*, due to pressure levied on him by Palestinian Arab notables.

53 Hussein at the UN, 25 September 1979, *JPS*, Vol. 9, No. 2 (winter 1980), p. 169.

54 Ibid.

55 Hussein, *Dustur*, 23 April, 11 July 1975.

56 See for example, Hussein, *Ra'i*, 23 September 1980 (in Parliament).

57 Hussein, *Dustur*, 20 January, 15, 27 April 1975, 5 March, 11 November 1976; *Ra'i*, 9 February, 29 April, 22 June, 27 July, 8 August, 6 September 1977; *Dustur*, 23 January 1978; Prime Minister Mudhir Badran, *Ra'i*, 29 August 1979; Hassan, *Palestinian Self-Determination*, pp. 103, 123. Regarding the refugees, Hassan did not rule out their resettlement, if they wished, and their compensation.

58 Hussein, *Ra'i*, 19 June 1986 (quoting *Radio Amman*).

59 Hussein on the BBC, 13 September 1982, *JPS*, Vol. 12, No. 2 (winter 1983).

60 Hussein, *Dustur*, 5 March (in Australia); 16 March (Japan), 4 April (the US); 17 June, 1976 (Austria); 20 February, 22 June 1977; Foreign Minister Hassan Ibrahim, *Ra'i*, 7 October 1976 (at the UN); Hussein, *Ra'i*, 4 February 1980 (interview to the *Observer*), 12 July 1980.

61 Hassan, 'Jordan's Quest for Peace', pp. 804, 811–12.

62 Hussein, *Ra'i*, 21 January 1982; Hassan, 'Return to Geneva,' p. 9. See also Hussein at Emory University, Atlanta, 8 November 1983, *JPS*, Vol. 14, No. 50 (winter 1984).

63 Hussein, *Dustur*, 9 June 1987; author's emphasis.

64 Hussein, *Dustur*, 1 November 1977; 4, 23 January, 30 May 1978 (interview to the *Chicago Tribune*).

65 Hussein, *Ra'i*, 14 February 1976 (interview to the *Guardian*); 8, 10 April 1976 (in the US).

66 Prime Minister Mudhir Badran, *Dustur*, 29 August 1979; Hussein, *Dustur*, 14 June 1979 (in France).

67 Hussein, *Dustur*, 12 December 1977, 16 February 1981. See also Hussein's announcement on the suspension of his agreement with Arafat, 19 February 1986, *JPS*, Vol. 15, No. 4 (summer 1986), p. 210.

68 Hussein, *Dustur*, 16 February 1981. The first Jordanian official to express this notion was the Minister of Information (of Palestinian origin) Adnan Abu Odeh. As early as 1976 he claimed that resolution 242 was insufficient, being too vague and too general, in regard to two of its most important components: The Palestinians and Israel's security. Adnan Abu Odeh, 'Bridging the Peace Gap in the Middle East,' *JPS*, Vol. 6, No. 2 (winter 1976), p. 64.

69 One year earlier Crown Prince Hassan stated that 'If, at the end of the day, the Palestinians propose to act jointly with the Jordanians in their search for peace – so be it'. Hassan, *Palestinian Self-Determination*, p. 130.

70 Hussein, *Ra'i*, 31 August, 4 September 1982.

71 Hussein, *Ra'i*, 22 August 1983, 24, 26, 27 February, 4 March 1986.

72 Prime Minister Zayd al-Rifa'i, *Ra'i*, 16 September 1986, *Dustur*, 21 August 1986; Information Minister Muhammad al-Khatib, *Ra'i*, 17 May 1987; Hussein, *Ra'i*, 10 October, 9 November 1987 (his speech at the Amman Arab summit conference); Foreign Minister Tahir al-Masri, *Ra'i*, 10 August, 2 October 1987.

73 Hassan, *Ra'i*, 30 January 1987; Hussein, 16 January 1987; Information Minister Muhammad al-Khatib, *Dustur*, 5, 17 May 1986; Senate President Ahmad al-Lawzi, *Rai*, 20 March 1987; Hussein, *Ra'i*, 15 January, 2 February 1988; See also Hassan, *Palestinian Self-Determination*, pp. 118–19. Jordan was willing to include West Bank Palestinians in a joint delegation, while the PLO failed to meet the minimal US conditions for participating in such a conference (i.e., accepting resolution 242).

74 Hussein, *Dustur*, 21 December 1987; Prime Minister Zayd al-Rifa'i, 25 December 1987; Hussein, *Ra'i*, 15 January (on British TV), Foreign Minister Tahir al-Masri, 25 January 1988.

75 Hussein, 18 September 1987, *Hussein's Speeches, 1977–1987*, p. 1024; Hussein, *Ra'i*, 2, 4, 9 February 1988; Prime Minister Zayd al-Rifa'i, 10 April 1988; Foreign Minister Tahir al-Masri, 13 July 1988.

76 See for example, Hussein, *Ra'i*, 28 January 1988 (interview on German TV).

77 Hussein, *Ra'i*, 27 August 1988; Foreign Minister Tahir al-Masri, 4 October 1988.

78 Hussein, *Ra'i*, 21 September 1988; Foreign Minister Tahir al-Masri, 4 October 1988 (in the UN).

10   The Military Option

1   *Dustur*, 18 October 1967.

2   Hussein, 8 March 1968, *The Middle East Record*, Vol. IV, 1968, p. 588.

3   Hussein at press conference, 23 March 1968, ibid.

4   Hussein, quoted in *Difa'*, 9 May 1968.

5   Hussein (in Washington), *Dustur*,19 April 1969.

6   Hussein (in Jordan to tribal leaders), *Dustur*, 15 February, 22 February 1970; see also Hussein (to a military unit), *Dustur*, 17 April 1970.

7   Government statement, *Dustur*, 28 July 1970; Defence Minister Abd al-Wahhab al-Majali, *Dustur*, 9 August 1970.

8   Hussein, *Dustur*, 11 May 1971.

9   Foreign Minister Abd al-Mun'im al-Rifa'i, *Dustur*, 17 July 1968, 23 September 1969.
10 Hussein (in the UK), *Dustur*, 23 April 1969.
11 Hussein (in the US), *Dustur*, 12 April 1969; see also Hussein (in France), *Dustur*, 24 October 1967.
12 Hussein, *Dustur*, 19 January, 6 February, 24 March 1972. See also: Shemesh, *The Palestinian Entity*, p. 219.
13 On Jordan's token participation in the October war, see chapter 4.
14 Hussain's interview to Lebanese *al-Nahar*, quoted by *Dustur*, 6 November 1973; see also Hussein, *Newsweek*, 17 June 1974; *Dustur*, 5 November 1974.
15 Hussein, *Dustur*, 14, 25 January, 24 April, 7 August 1975.
16 See for example, Hussein, *Dustur*, 7 September 1977; Hussein, *Ra'i*, 4 August, 1 September 1980; Hassan, *Dustur*, 10 January 1981; Minister of Information Muhammad al-Khatib, *Dustur*, 5 May 1986; Foreign Minister Tahir al-Masri, *Dustur*, 11 June 1986.
17 Hussein *Dustur*, 14 February 1976 (quoting an interview in *The Guardian*), 31 July, 26 August 1977, 9 May 1978.
18 Hussein, *Dustur*, 25 November 1975 (interview in *US News and World Report*); 14 February 1976 (interview in *The Guardian*); 4 February 1977 (interview to the *Daily Telegraph*).
19 Hussein, *Dustur*, 31 July, 26 August 1977.
20 Foreign Minister Tahir al Masri, *Dustur*, 4 August 1986 (interview in *al-Usbu' al-Arabi*).
21 Hussein, *Dustur*, 17 March, 4 November 1978; See also Joint Syrian-Jordanian Communique, 22 August 1975, *JPS*, Vol. 5, No. 1–2 (autumn 1975–winter 1976), pp. 262–3.
22 Hassan, *Ra'i*, 17 May 1986 (interview in *al-Usbu' al-Arabi*); Hussein, *Dustur*, 9 April 1987; Hussien, *Nahar*, 29 January 1972, quoted by *Shu'un Filastiniya*, No. 9, May 1972, p. 243.
23 Hussein, *Ra'i*, 14 December 1987.

11   The Perception of a Comprehensive Peace

1   Hassan, 'Jordan's Quest for Peace', p. 807.
2   *The Middle East Record*, Vol. III, 1967, p. 259.
3   *Amal*, 26 August 1967, quoted by *The Middle East Record*, Vol. 3, 1967, p. 260.
4   al-Madfa'i, *Jordan and the United States*, pp. 25–6.
5   Hussein, *Dustur*, 4 March 1970 (interview to AP).
6   Foreign Minister Antun Atallah, *Dustur*, 9 August 1970; Hussein, *Dustur*, 18 August, 17 November, 11, 12 December 1970, 7 April, 30 September 1975, 16 March, 29 June 1976; Hussein, *Ra'i*, 15 January, 10 October 1987, 4, 8 February 1988.
7   Hassan, *Palestinian Self-Determination*, p. 98.
8   Hussein's speech at the Annual Convention of NAAA, 4 May 1985, Washington DC, *JPS*, Vol. 14, No. 4 (summer 1985), p. 17.
9   Hussein, *Dustur*, 12, 30 April 1969, 3 September 1978.

10 Hussein press conference, *Dustur*, 30 April 1969.

11 Hussein interview to *Newsweek*, 17 June 1974.

12 Hussein, *The Middle East Record*, Vol. V, 1969–1970, p. 103; BBC interview, 13 September 1982, *JPS*, No. 46 (winter 1983); Hassan, 'Jordan's Quest for Peace', p. 809. One should recall that prior to the June war and even afterwards, Jordanian spokespersons implied that the Palestine problem should be solved within the 'green line' of pre-1967 Israel, not on Jordan's West Bank.

13 *Shu'un Filastiniya*, No. 2, May 1971, p. 155.

14 Hussein's speech in Washington DC, 4 May 1985, at the Annual Convention of the NAAA, *JPS*, Vol. 14, No. 4 (summer 1985), p. 17.

15 *Dustur*, 12 November 1967 (quoting Hussein's interview to the *New York Times*); see also *The Middle East Record*, Vol. 5, 1969–1970, p.103.

16 Hussein interview to the BBC, 13 September 1982, *JPS* , Vol. 12, No. 2 (winter 1983), p. 204. See also *The Middle East Record*, Vol. 5, 1969–70; Hussein, *Ra'i*, 5 March (in Australia), 16 March (in Japan), 4 April 1976 (in the US), 15 May 1983; for Crown Prince Hassan's views, see Hassan, *Palestinian Self-Determination*, p. 14; Hassan, 'Jordan: The Quest for a Centrist Position', his speech at the Carter Center, Atlanta, GA, 8 November 1983, *JPS*, Vol. 13, No. 2 (winter, 1984), pp. 8, 9.

17 Hussein's interview to the BBC, 13 September 1982, *JPS*, Vol. 12, No. 2 (winter 1983), pp. 203–5; Hussein interview in *Newsweek*, 12 December 1977.

18 Hussein, *Dustur*, 6 November 1973; Hassan interview to the *Times*, 5 September 1982; Hassan, 'Jordan's Quest for Peace', p. 811.

19 Hussein to the *New York Times*, 25 January 1970, quoted in *The Middle East Record*, Vol. V, 1969–1970, p. 40; Hussein, *Dustur* (in France) 16 December 1970; Hussein, *Radio Amman*, 13, 15 July 1986; Prime Minister Mudhir Badran, *Dustur*, 30 October 1977; Minister Marwan Dudin, *Ra'i*, 29 November 1986; Speaker 'Akif al-Fayiz, *Ra'i*, 23 February 1987; Hassan, *Palestinian Self-Determination*, p. 123.

20 Hussein, *Ra'i*, 7 April (in France), 6 September 1979 (in Cuba); Hassan, 6 May 1982 (interview to the *Times*).

21 Hassan, 'Jordan's Quest for Peace', p. 803; see also Hassan, *Palestinian Self-Determination*, pp. 121–2; Hussein, *Mihnati KaMalik*, p. 241.

22 Hussein, *Dustur*, 18 December 1976 (to the *Washington Post*); 19 August 1978 (to a Japanese newspaper); Hassan, *Palestinian Self-Determination*, pp. 122–3; Hussein's speech, 19 February 1986 (suspension of agreement with PLO), *JPS* (summer 1986), p. 208; Hussein, 4 May 1985, Washington, his speech to the NAAA, *JPS* (summer 1985), pp. 16, 17.

23 Hussein, *Dustur*, 10 November 1967, 12 April 1969 (both in Washington).

24 *The Middle East Record*, Vol. IV, 1968, p. 221; Abu Odeh, 'Bridging the Peace Gap', p. 54.

25 Hussein, *Dustur*, 19 December 1974; 6 March 1976 (in Australia); 30 May 1978 (interview to the *Chicago Tribune*), 19 August 1978; Hussein's speech in Washington (to the NAAA), 4 May 1985, *JPS* (summer 1985), pp. 16, 17.

26 See for example, Hussein to a French journalist, *Dustur*, 25 November 1967; Hussein (in Parliament), *Dustur*, 4 April 1971.

27 Foreign Minister Zayd al-Rifa'i (at the opening of the Geneva conference), *Dustur*, 22 December 1973; *The Middle East Record*, Vol. III, 1967, p. 267.

28 *The Middle East Record*, Vol. V, 1969–70, p. 104. As of the mid-1970s, the issue of border modification was somewhat problematic, since Jordan then stated that it could not negotiate territorial issues on behalf of the Palestinians and obviously not undertake any concessions 'not even on one inch'. Prince Hassan, therefore, when discussing such a possibility, very carefully stated that 'it is clear that in some cases security requirements may dictate minor modifications to specific lines previously disputed'. Moreover, he referred to an Israeli-Arab peace, not to one between Israel and Jordan, Hassan, 'Jordan's Quest for Peace', p. 812.

29 Abu Odeh, 'Bridging the Peace Gap', p. 59; see also Hussein, *Ra'i*, 19 June 1986.

30 *The Middle East Record*, Vol. IV, 1968, p. 220, quoting the *Christian Science Monitor*, 1 February 1968; Hussein, *Dustur*, 12 April 1969 (in the US).

31 Hassan, 'Jordan's Quest for Peace', pp. 809, 812; Hassan, *Palestinian Self-Determination*, p. 125.

32 See for example, Schueftan, *A Jordanian Option*, pp. 300–1; Hassan, *Ra'i*, 6 February 1984.

33 Hassan, 'Jordan's Quest for Peace', p. 809.

34 *The Middle East Record*, Vol. III, 1967, p. 260, quoting Lebanese paper *al-Amal*, 26 August 1967.

35 Hussein in *Newsweek*, 17 June 1974.

36 *The Middle East Record*, Vol. V, 1969–1970, p. 105 (interview to *Le Monde*, September, 1970); *New York Times*, 16 March 1974.

37 Hussein, *Ra'i*, 26 August 1974, 27 September 1985 (at the UN); *Dustur*, 27 January 1975; Hussein, *Mihnati KaMalik*, p. 241.

38 Hussein, *International Herald Tribune*, 19 March 1969; *Dustur*, 26 August 1974.

39 Hussein, *Dustur*, 11 July 1975.; Hussein speech at Georgetown (delivered by queen Nur); Jordan TV, 16 March; DR, 17 March 1982. Internationalization was the favoured UN solution for the future of Jerusalem in 1947–1949, to the chagrin of both Israel and Hussein's grandfather Abdullah. Both parties preferred to divide Jerusalem between themselves rather than internationalize it.

40 al-Madfa'i, *Jordan and the United States*, pp. 11–12.

41 Ibid., p. 12.

42 *Middle East Contemporary Survey*, Vol. 6, 1981–1982, p. 679.

43 Hussein, *Dustur*, 30 January 1987 (speech at a European Union meeting).

44 Hussein, *Dustur*, 16 February, 5 April 1973.

45 Hussein, *Ra'i*, 10 March 1976.

46 *JPS*, Vol. 14, No. 4 (summer 1985), p. 22.

47 Hussein's speech of 19 February 1986, *JPS*, Vol. 15, No. 4 (summer 1986), pp. 207, 212.

48 This term was used extensively by King Hussein, particularly after the conclusion of the Jordan–Israel peace treaty in October 1994, in order elicit the support of the reluctant Jordanian public for the peace process.

49 Hassan, 'Jordan's Quest for Peace', p. 805.

50 Hassan, 'Return to Geneva', p. 13.

51 Information Minister Muhammad al-Khatib, *Dustur*, 5 May 1986; Hussein, *Dustur*, 14 December 1987.

52 Even though at the end of the day, in 1994 Jordan signed a peace treaty with Israel that was, indeed, a separate bilateral agreement.

53 At the first Arab summit meeting in 1964 Hussein proposed to institutionalize this forum and to summon it annually.

54 See Hussein, *Uneasy*, pp. 83–100.

55 *The Middle East Record*, Vol. 4, 1968, pp. 218–20 (quoting Hussein in the *New York Times*, 25 February 1968, and Prime Minister Bahjat al-Talhuni, in *Jumhuriyya*, 1 August 1968); Hussein, *Anwar* (Beirut), 18 January 1968; Hussein, *Jarida*, 20 January 1968; Hussein, *Harbuna*, pp. 97–100.

56 *The Middle East Record*, Vol. 3, 1967, p. 260.

57 *The Middle East Record*, Vol. 4, 1968, pp. 219–20; Vol. 5, 1969–1970, pp. 104–5; *New York Times*, 25 February 1968. Such negotiations indeed took place, yet Hussein, as shown, insisted that a separate settlement was out of the question, even if Israel met all his conditions.

58 Hussein, *Ra'i*, 30 August 1974, 30 September 1975; Prime Minister Zayd al-Rifa'i, *Ra'i*, 13 September 1974; Hassan, *Ra'i*, 22 October 1977; Senate President Ahmad al-Lawzi, *Dustur*, 23 March 1987.

59 Hussein, *Dustur*, 16 March 1970 (in Pakistan); see also Hussein, *Dustur*, 25 August 1970 (after talks with Abd al-Nasser).

60 Hussein, *Dustur*, 17 November, 16 December 1970; *The Middle East Record*, Vol. 4, 1968, p. 105.

61 Hussein, *Dustur*, 4 April 1971 (in Parliament); 29 April 1971 (in *Die Welt*), 19 January 1972.

62 Hussein, *Dustur*, 29 April 1971 (in *Die Welt*), 6 February, 25 August 1972; 9, 12 February 1973.

63 Hussein, *Dustur*, 6 February 1972 (in *al-Syassa*, Kuwait).

64 Prime Minister Zayd al-Rifa'i, *Ra'i*, 22 December 1973; Hussein, *Ra'i*, 24 June 1974, 18 December 1976.

65 Hussein, *Dustur*, 25 November 1975; 12 January 1977.

66 Hussein, *Ra'i*, 23 January, 8 March 1978.

67 *Newsweek*, 12 December 1977 (Hussein interview); Hussein, *Dustur*, 2 January, 8 March 1978.

68 Hussein, *Dustur*, 23 January 1978.

69 Hussein, *Ra'i*, 13, 19 August 1978.

70 Hussein, *Ra'i*, 20 September, 2, 11 October 1978: Jordan government statement on the Camp David agreements, 19 September 1978, *JPS*, Vol. 8, No. 2 (winter 1979), p. 180.

71 Hussein, *Ra'i*, 20, 29 September, 9 November 1978.

72 Hussein, *Ra'i*, 2 October, 9, 10 November 1978, 13 January 1979.

73 Hussein, *Dustur*, 26 March, 5, 7, April, 6 September 1979; Minister of Information, Lila Sharf, *Ra'i*, 28 September 1984.

74 Hussein at the UN, 25 September 1979, *King Hussein's Speeches 1977-1987*, p. 139.

75 Hassan, *Dustur*, 14 June 1979.

76 Hassan, *Ra'i*, 21 April 1980; Hussein, *Ra'i*, 20 June 1980; Joint Soviet–Jordanian statement, Moscow, 29 May 1981, *JPS*, Vol. 11, No. 1 (autumn 1981), p. 236; Hassan, 'Back to Geneva'.

77 Hussein, *Ra'i*, 4 February 1980; Senior Jordanian official, *Dustur*, 5 August 1981; Hussein, *Dustur*, 5 September 1981; Minister of Information, Lila Sharf, *Ra'i*, 28 September 1984.

78 Hussein, *Ra'i*, 18 April 1980 (interview to the *Washington Post*); Hassan, 'Jordan's Quest for Peace', p. 802.

79 Hussein, *Dustur*, 8 July, 19 November, 1981.

80 Hussein at the UN, 25 September 1979, *JPS*, Vol. 9, No. 2 (winter 1980), p. 169; Hussein, *Dustur*, 12 January 1981.

81 Hussein's speech, 19 February 1986, *JPS*, Vol. 15, No. 4 (summer 1986), p. 207.

82 Hussein, *Dustur*, 12 June 1979, 20 June 1980 (in the US); Prime Minister Mudhir Badran, 29 August 1979; Hussein, *Dustur*, 6 May 1982 (in the USSR). Hussein, *Mustaqbal*, 5 September 1981, in *JPS*, Vol. 11, No. 2 (winter 1982), pp. 164–7.

83 Hussein, *Dustur*, 15 September, 11 December 1982; 18 February, 19 March 1983; Hussein, *Ra'i*, 15 May 1983; Hussein (in the USSR), 3 December 1983, *JPS*, Vol. 12, No. 3 (spring 1983), pp. 242–3; Hussein, to the BBC, 13 September 1982, *JPS*, Vol. 12, No. 2 (winter 1983), pp. 203–5; Hussein, 19 February 1986, *JPS*, Vol. 15, No. 4 (summer 1986), pp. 217–18.

84 Hussein's speech, 4 May 1985 (NAAA, Washington), *JPS*, Vol. 14, No. 4 (summer 1985), p. 16; Minister Marwan Dudin, *Ra'i*, 26 August 1986; Hassan, *Ra'i*, 7 January 1986.

85 Hussein, *Ra'i*, 8 May 1984; Hussein, *Jordan Times*, 19 August 1986, *Ra'i*, 2 December 1986; Chamber of Deputies Speaker 'Akif al-Faiz, *Ra'i*, 16 April 1987; Senate President Ahmad al-lawzi, *Ra'i*, 26 March, 4 July 1987, Foreign Minister Tahir al-Masri, *Dustur*, 1 March 1987.

12   Frameworks for a Possible Agreement

1 For overt and covert government resolutions, see Dan Bavly, *Dreams and Missed Opportunities*, pp. 35–6.

2 *The Middle East Record*, Vol. III, 1967, pp. 273–5.

3 *Ma'ariv*, 13 June 1967.

4 See for example, Prime Minister Abd al-Mun'im al-Rifa'i, *International Herald Tribune*, 19 March 1968; Hussein, *Kifah* (Beirut), 19 July 1969.

5 Hussein, *Dustur*, 9 September 1967 (in Turkey), 1 November 1967 (in the UK).

6 *New York Times*, 8 November 1967.

7 *The Middle East Record*, Vol. IV, 1968, p. 218; author's emphasis.

8 Hussein, *Dustur*, 1 November (in the UK), 7 November (in the US), 12 November 1967 (interview to the *New York Times*).

9 Hussein, *Dustur*, 16 April 1969 (in the US).

10 Hussein, *Dustur*, 12, 16 April 1969 (in the US); *The Middle East Record*, Vol.

V, 1969–1970, p. 104; *Difa'* (editorial), 13 October 1969; Hussein interview to *Stern*, 24 May 1970.

11 Foreign Minister Abd al-Mun'im al-Rifa'i, *Dustur*, 13 July 1968; *The Middle East Record*, Vol. IV, 1968, pp. 221–2, Vol. V, 1969–1970, p. 105; Hussein, *Ra'i*, 31 March, 3 April 1972; 12 February 1973; 24 March 1974.

12 Hussein, *Dustur*, 18 December 1976 (interview to the *Washington Post*).

13 Hussein, *Ra'i*, 23 January 1978.

14 Minister of Information Adnan Abu Odeh, *Dustur*, 27 November 1982.

15 Foreign Minister Tahir al-Masri, *Ra'i*, 16 June, 16 August 1987.

16 Hussein's speech in Washington, 23 February 1985, *JPS*, Vol. 14, No. 3 (spring, 1985), p. 207.

17 Foreign Minister Tahir al-Masri, *Ra'i*, 2 May, 16 August 1987.

18 al-Madfa'i, *Jordan and the United States*, p. 64.

19 See for example, *The Middle East Record*, Vol. I, 1960, pp. 177–9, 210–13; Vol. II, 1961, pp. 188–93, 228–39.

20 Hussein, *Dustur*, 9 September 1967 (in Turkey) 27 October 1967 (in Spain), 7 November 1967 (in the US).

21 Prime Minister Bahjat al-Talhuni, *Dustur*, 22 May, 21 June 1968; *The Middle East Record*, Vol. IV, 1968, p. 217.

22 Prime Minister's Talhuni interview in *al-Ahram*, 26 October 1968, quoted in *The Middle East Record*, Vol. IV, 1968, p. 219, see also p. 222.

23 Hussein, *Dustur*, 23 October 1968 (in France), 12 April 1969 (in the US), 16 March 1970 (in Pakistan), 7, 17 November, 8 December 1970; Foreign Minister And al-Mun'aim al-Rifa'i, *Dustur*, 8 November 1970; Foreign Minister Antun Atallah, *Dustur*, 19 July 1970.

24 *The Middle East Record*, Vol. IV, 1968, pp. 122–3.

25 Foreign Minister Antun Ataallah, *Dustur*, 19 August 1970; Hussein, *Dustur*, 17 November, 8 December 1970.

26 Hussein, *Ra'i*, 16 March 1974.

27 Hussein, *Ra'i*, 19 September 1985.

28 Hassan, *Palestinian Self-Determination*, pp. 125–6; Hussein, *Ra'i*, 16 June 1987; Jordanian ambassador to the UN, Abdullah Salih, *Ra'i*, 7 July 1986.

29 Hussein, *Ra'i*, 15, 16, 26 January, 1 July 1987.

30 Hussein, *Ra'i*, 24 June 1974 (interview in *al-Anwar*).

31 *Ra'i*, 28 November, 22 December 1973.

32 Hussein and Prime Minister Zayd al-Rifa'i, *Ra'i*, 28 November 1973. Jordan received the formal invitation to Geneva on 27 November. At that time, the sixth Arab summit conference was meeting in Algiers. The next day, the concluding resolutions of the meeting recognized, *inter alia*, the PLO as the sole legitimate representative of the Palestinians. Jordan's delegate disapproved of the clause.

33 Prime Minister Zayd al-Rifa'i, *Dustur*, 5 June 1974; Hussein, *Ra'i*, 4 November 1974 (on British TV), 25 January 1975 (interview to *al-Ahram*).

34 Prime Minister Zayd al-Rifa'i, *Dustur*, 16 February 1975; Hussein, 16 June 1975, (in *al-Usbu al-Arabi*), 16 December 1976 (in the *Washington Post*); Prime Minister Mudhir Badran, *Ra'i*, 21 February 1977; Hussein, *Ra'i*, 22 June 1977, 2 January 1978 (in Iran).

35 Hussein, *Dustur*, 18 August 1974 (in the US); 26 August 1974 (to *US News and World Report*).

36 Hussein, *Dustur*, 12 January 1977 (in Kuwait), 8 August 1977.

37 Adnan Abu Odeh, 'Bridging the Peace Gap', pp. 53–65.

38 Kenneth Stein, *Heroic Diplomacy*, p. 215.

39 Hussein, *Ra'i*, 10 January 1980 (to *Newsweek*), 4 February 1980 (to the *Observer*).

40 Hussein, *Dustur*, 12, 14 June 1979 (in France).

41 See for example, Hussein, *Ra'i*, 23 May 1984 (in *Le Figaro*), 18 June 1984 (to British TV), *Dustur*, 19 August 1984 (to CNN), 25 March 1985 (in Spain), 31 May 1985 (in the US), 1 June 1985 (in the US), 8 June 1985 (in the UK).

42 For the Brezhnev plan, see *New Outlook*, May 1983. More than a year earlier, in May 1981, Hussein stated that Jordan welcomed the Soviet Union's invitation to a special international conference. Hussein, *Dustur*, 27 May 1981 (in Moscow).

43 Hassan, 'Return to Geneva', pp. 11–12; Hassan, *Ra'i*, 7 January 1986.

44 Hussein, *Dustur*, 25 March 1985, *Ra'i*, 26 March 1985.

45 Hussein's speech on 19 February 1986, *JPS*, Vol. 15, No. 4 (summer 1986), pp. 206–32; Hussein, *Ra'i*, 26 February 1986.

46 Hussein, *Jordan Times*, 1 May 1986.

47 Prime Minister Zayd al-Rifa'i, Dustur, 24 July 1986.

48 See, for example, Hussein, *Ra'i*, 26 March, 12 July, 7 October, 12, 14 December 1986; 15, 16, 26 January, 16 June, 1 July, 15, 17, 18 September, 1 October 1987; Hussein, *Dustur*, 9 April 1987; Hassan, *Ra'i*, 18 May 1986; Prime Minister Zayd al-Rifa'i, *Ra'i*, 19 June 1986, 29 March, 9 April, 25 December 1987, *Dustur*, 2 August 1986; Foreign Minister Tahir al-Masri, *Ra'i*, 3 April, 2 May, 16 June, 10, 16 August 1987; Senate President Ahmad al-Lawzi, *Ra'i*, 20, 26 March 1987; Speaker 'Akif al-Fayiz, *Ra'i*, 16 April 1987.

49 Hassan, *Ra'i*, 18 May 1986; Director General, Ministry of Foreign Affairs Taysir Tuqan, *Ra'i*, 10 March 1987; Speaker Ahmad al-Lawzi, *Ra'i*, 26 March 1987; Hussein, *Ra'i*, 16 June, 1 July 1987, 20 February 1988.

50 Prime Minister Zayd al-Rifa'i, *Ra'i*, 19 June 1986, 29 March, 9 April 1987; Hussein, *Ra'i*, 14 December 1986.

51 Foreign Minister Tahir al-Masri, *Ra'i*, 10, 16 August 1987; Hussein, *Ra'i*, 2 February 1988; Prime Minister Zayd al-Rifa'i, *Ra'i*, 10 April 1988.

52 Foreign Minister Tahir Al-Masri, *Ra'i*, 16 August 1987.

53 Foreign Minister Tahir al-Masri, *Ra'i*, 9 April, 2 May 1987; Prime Minister Zayd al-Rifa'i, 9 April 1987; Information Minister Muhammad al-Khatib, *Ra'i*, 3 August 1987.

54 Hussein's speech in the 17th PNC in Amman, 22 November 1984, *JPS*, Vol. 14, No. 2 (winter, 1985), p. 256; Hussein, *Ra'i*, 1 July, 18 September 1987, 20 February 1988; Foreign Minister Tahir al-Masri, *Ra'i*, 16 June 1987.

55 Foreign Minister Tahir al-Masri, *Ra'i*, 16 August 1987, 1 March 1988; Jordan's ambassador to the UN Abdullah Salih, *Ra'i*, 7 September 1987; Hussein, *Ra'i*, 10 October 1987, 8 February 1988.

56 Hussein, *Ra'i*, 7 August 1988; Speaker Ahmad al-Lawzi, *Ra'i*, 11 November, 16 December, 1988.

57 Hussein (at the UN), 25 September 1979, *JPS*, Vol. 9, No. 2 (winter, 1980), p. 170; Hussein, *Ra'i*, 28 October 1988.

58 Scheuftan, *A Jordanian Option*, pp. 304–5. See also Dan Bavly, *Dreams and Missed Opportunities*, p. 54.

59 Prime Minister Bahjat al-Talhuni, *Anwar* (Beirut), 8 October quoted in *The Middle East Record*, Vol. IV, 1968, p. 219.

60 Kenneth Stein, *Heroic Diplomacy*, p. 57; Schueftan, *A Jordanian Option*, p. 305.

61 *The Middle East Record*, Vol. V, 1969–1970, p. 40.

62 Hussein, *Dustur*, 25 February (interview to the *Times*), 4 March, 3 May 1970; Foreign Minister Abd al-Mun'im al-Rifa'i, *Dustur*, 25 April 1970; *The Middle East Record*, Vol. V, 1969–1970, p. 104.

63 The Jordanian government's response to the Rogers plan, *Ra'i*, 6 August 1970; Hussein, *Ra'i*, 8 December 1970; *The Middle East Record*, Vol. V, 1969–1970, p. 72.

64 *The Middle East Record*, Vol. V, 1969–1970, p. 72.

65 Hussein, *Ra'i*, 4 April 1976 (in the US).

66 Hussein (at the UN), 25 September 1979, *Hussein's Speeches 1977–1987*, pp. 138–9.

67 Hussein, *Ra'i*, 13 August 1978.

68 Hassan, 'Jordan's Quest for Peace', p. 802; Hassan, 'Return to Geneva', December 1984, p. 11.

69 Hussein, *Ra'i*, 29 September 1978, 4 February 1980 (interview to the *Observer*), 18 April 1980 (interview to the *Washington Post*); Hussein, *Dustur*, 8 July 1981 (Interview to the BBC), 20 March 1982 (interview to the *Los Angeles Times*), Hussein (at the UN), 25 September 1979, *Hussein's Speeches 1977–1987*, pp. 131–42; Hussein, *Mustaqbal* (Paris) 5 September 1981.

70 Hussein, *Dustur*, 15 September 1982 (interview to the BBC); Hassan, 'Jordan: the Quest for a Centrist Position', p. 4; Hussein's speech in Washington (to the NAAA), 4 May 1985, *JPS*, Vol. 14, No. 4 (summer, 1985), pp. 16–17.

71 Minister of Information Adnan Abu Odeh, *Dustur*, 17 April 1983; Hussein, *Ra'i*, 15 May 1983, 18 June 1984; Hussein, *Jordan Times*, 19 August 1984.

72 See for example, Hassan, *Ra'i*, 27 November 1986; Director General of Jordan's Ministry of Foreign Affairs, Taysir Tuqan, *Ra'i*, 10 March 1987, Hussein, *Ra'i*, 15 September 1987. Information Minister Hani al-Hasawna, *Ra'i*, 30 January 1988.

73 Hassan, *Ra'i*, 22 October 1986; Prime Minister Zayd al-Rifa'i, *Ra'i*, 9 April 1987.

74 Hussein, Speech of 19 February 1986 (termination of his agreement with Arafat), *JPS*, Vol. 15, No. 4 (summer, 1986), p. 224; Foreign Minister Tahir al-Masri, *Ra'i*, 2 May 1987.

75 Foreign Minister Tahir al-Masri, *Ra'i*, 1 March 1988.

76 Hussein, *Ra'i*, 29 January 1988 (interview to the *Washington Post*); Foreign Minister Tahir al-Masri, *Ra'i*, 16 August 1987.

77 For decisive criticism of the communist ideology of the Soviet Union, see King Hussein's autobiography, *Uneasy Lies the Head*, pp. 84–5, 88, 93, 95–6.

78 Prime Minister Bahjat al-Talhuni, *Anwar*, 8 October 1968; Hussein, *Dustur*, 12 April 1969 (in the US), 22 April 1969 (in the UK); Hussein in Washington, 13 December 1970, in *Shu'un Filastiniya*, 1 March 1971, p. 165. See also *The Middle East Record*, Vol. V, 1969–1970, pp. 104–5.

79 Hussein, *Dustur*, 14 June 1979 (in France), 27 May 1981 (in the USSR); Joint Soviet-Jordanian Statement at the end of Hussein's visit to Moscow, 29 May 1981, *JPS*, Vol. 11, No. 1 (autumn, 1981), p. 236; Hussein, *Mustaqbal*, 5 September 1981; Hussein, *Ra'i*, 18 June 1984 (to British TV); Abu Odeh, 'Bridging the Peace Gap', pp. 64–5; Foreign Minister Tahir al-Masri, *Ra'i*, 2 May 1987; Hassan, *Palestinian Self-Determination*, p. 126.

80 *Middle East Contemporary Survey* (MECS), Vol. 3, 1978–1979, p. 637.

81 Hussein in Moscow, 3 December 1982, *JPS*, Vol. 12, No. 3 (spring, 1983), p. 243.

82 Hussein, *Ra'i*, 15 September 1987, 8 February 1988; Foreign Minister Tahir al Masri, *Ra'i*, 2 May 1987, 1 March 1988 (to a Soviet newspaper).

83 *MECS*, Vol. 1, 1976–1977, p. 52.

84 *MECS*, Vol. 1, 1976–1977, pp. 49–52; Hussein's speech at the UN, 25 September 1979, *King Hussein's Speeches 1977–1987*, pp. 134, 157–8; Hussein, *Ra'i*, 3 July 1980.

85 Moshe Gabai (ed.), *Hatzharot VeHachlatot BaNose HaPalstine* [Hebrew: Declarations and Resolutions on the Palestine Issue 1950–1989] Yad Tabenkin, Efal, 1990, pp.138–9; *MECS*, Vol. 4, 1979–1980, pp. 72–3.

86 Hussein's speech in Washington, 20 June 1980, *King Hussein's Speeches 1977–1987*, p. 184; Hussein, *Ra'i*, 26 June 1980 (Interview to British TV); *MECS*, Vol. 6, 1981–1982, pp. 679–80; Vol. 9, 1984–1985, p. 522.

87 Hassan, *Palestinian Self-Determination*, pp. 125–6; *MECS*, Vol. 9, 1984–1985, p. 522.

88 Foreign Minister Tahir al-Masri, *Ra'i*, 24 February 1987; Minister of Information Hani al-Hasawna, *Ra'i*, 30 January 1988; *MECS*, Vol. 10, 1986, p. 459.

Conclusion

1 Jordanian spokespersons confirmed this stance in various speeches and pronouncements. In practice, however, King Hussein met secretly several times with Israeli officials between 1963 and 1967, and resumed such meetings shortly after the war .

2 Hussein made it clear to his clandestine Israeli interlocutors that even if Israel met all his demands to the letter, he still could not make a formal peace unless other Arab states joined in.

BIBLIOGRAPHY

Documents

'Asharat 'Aawam min al-Kifah w'al-Bina [Arabic: Ten Years of Struggle and Building: King Hussein's Speeches 1977–1987], Markaz al-Kitab al-Urduni, 1988.

Central Zionist Archives, Files of the Political Department of the Jewish Agency (S25) 4004

Israel Ministry of Education, Peace Treaty Between the State of Israel and the Hashemite Kingdom of Jordan, 26 October, 1994, Government Printing House, Jerusalem, 1994.

Israel's Statistical Yearbook, No. 39, Jerusalem, 1988.

John P. Glennon (ed.), *Foreign Relations of the United States 1958–1960*, Vol. XI: *Lebanon and Jordan*, US Government Printing Office, Washington, 1992.

Al-Mamlaka al-Urduniya al-Hashemiya, Wizarat al-Kharijiya, *Al-Urdun w'al-Qadiya al-Filastiniya w'al-'Alaqat al-'Arabiya* [Arabic: Jordan, Ministry of Foreign Affairs, Jordan and the Palestine Problem and the inter-Arab Relations], Amman, July 1962.

Dov Zakin (ed.), *HaSichsuch HaAravi-Israeli* [Hebrew: The Arab-Israeli Conflict, A Collection of Documents 1973–1984], Arab Studies Institute, Giva'at Haviva, 1985.

Moshe Gabai (ed.), *Hatzharot VeHachlatot BaNose HaPalstine* [Hebrew: Declarations and Resolutions on the Palestine Issue 1950–1989] Yad Tabenkin, Efal, 1990.

Books

Adnan Abu Odeh, *Jordanians, Palestinians and the Hashemite Kingdom in the Middle East Peace Process*, United States Institute of Peace, Washington 1999.

Geoffrey Aronson, *Creating Facts: Israel, Palestinians and the West Bank*, Institute of Palestine Studies, Washington, 1987.

Joseph Alpher, *Settlements and Borders*, Study No. 3, Final Status Issues: Israel–Palestinians, Jaffee Center for Strategic Studies, Tel Aviv University, 1994.

Dan Bavly, *Halomot VeHizdamnoyot SheHuchmetzu* [Hebrew: Dreams and Missed Opportunities 1967–1973], Karmel, Jerusalem, 2002.

Meron Benveniste, *Lexicon Yahuda VeShomron* [Hebrew: West Bank Handbook], Kana, Jerusalem, 1987.

Alexander Bligh, *The Political Legacy of King Hussein*, Sussex Academic Press, Brighton & Portland, 2002.

Neil Caplan, *Palestine Jewry and the Arab Question 1917–1925*, Frank Cass, London, 1978.

——, *Futile Diplomacy*, Vol. 1, Frank Cass, London, 1983.

Uriel Dann, *Studies in the History of Transjordan 1920–1949: The Making of a State*, Westview Press, Boulder, 1984.

——, *King Hussein and the Challenge of Arab Radicalism: Jordan 1955–1967*, Oxford University Press, New York and Oxford, 1989.

Moshe Dayan, *Avnei Derech* [Hebrew: Story of My Life], Idanim, Jerusalem, Dvir, Tel Aviv, 1976.

Rony E. Gabbay, *A Political Study of the Arab–Jewish Conflict: The Arab Refugee Problem (A Case Study)*, Librairie E. Droz, Geneva, 1959.

Adam Garfinkle, *Israel and Jordan in the Shadow of War*, St. Martin's Press, New York, 1992.

Yoav Gelber, *Jewish Transjordan Relations 1921–1948*, Frank Cass, London, 1997.

Yehoshafat Harkabi, *Emdat Ha'Aravim BeSichsuch Israel-Arav* [Hebrew: The Arab Position in the Arab-Israeli Conflict], Dvir Publishing House, Tel Aviv, 1968.

Hassan Bin Talal, *The Palestine Question*, Department of Press and Publication, Ministry of Culture, Amman, 1968.

——, *A Study on Jerusalem*, Longman, London and New York, 1979.

——, *Palestinian Self-Determination: A Study of the West Bank and Gaza Strip*, Quartet Books, London, 1981.

——, *Search for Peace: The Politics of the Middle Ground in the Arab East*, St. Martin's Press, New York, 1984.

Cecil Hourani, *An Unfinished Odyssey*, Weidenfeld and Nicolson, London, 1984.

Hussein A. Hassouna, The League of the Arab States and Regional Disputes: A Study of Middle East Conflicts, Oceania Publication, New York, 1975.

Hussein Bin Talal, *Uneasy Lies the Head*, Bernard Geis Associates, New York, 1962.

——, *Mihnati KaMalik, Ahadith Malikiyya* [Arabic: My Profesion as a King] Muassasat Masri LilTawzi', [n.p.], 1987.

——, *Harbuna ma' Israil*, [Arabic: Our War with Israel] Dar al-Jalil Li'Tabaat Wa'lnashr, Acre, n.d.

Ephraim Kam (ed.), *Hussein Pote'ach BeMilhama* [Hebrew: Hussein Starts a War: The Six Day War in Jordanian eyes], Ma'arachot, Tel Aviv, 1974.

Henry Kissinger, *Years of Upheaval*, Little Brown, Boston, 1982.

James Lunt, *Hussein of Jordan, Searching for a Just and Lasting Peace, A Political Biography*, Macmillan, London, 1989.

Madiha Rashid al Madfa'i, *Jordan and the United States and the Middle East Peace Process 1974–1991*, Cambridge University Press, Cambridge, 1993.

Yossi Melman, *Shutafut Oyenet* [Hebrew: Hostile Partnership: The Secret Ties between Israel and Jordan], Meitam, Tel Aviv, 1987.

Benny Morris, *The Birth of the Palestinian Refugee Problem, 1947–1949*, Cambridge University Press, Cambridge, 1989.

Samir A. Mutawi, *Jordan in the 1967 War*, Cambridge University Press, Cambridge, 1987.

Joseph Nevo, *King Abdallah and Palestine: A Territorial Ambition*, Macmillan, in association with St. Antony's College, Oxford, Basingstoke and New York, 1996.

Avi Plascov, *The Palestinian Refugees in Jordan 1948–1957*, Frank Cass, London, 1981.

Kamal Salibi, *The Modern History of Jordan*, I.B. Tauris, London and New York, 1993.

Robert Satloff, *From Abdullah to Hussein: Jordan in Transition*, Oxford University Press, New York and Oxford, 1994.

Dan Schueftan, *Optzia Yardenit* [Hebrew: A Jordanian Option] Yad Tabenkin, Ramat Efal, 1986.

——, *Korach HaHafrada* [Hebrew: Disengagement: Israel and the Palestinian Entity], Zmora-Bitan and University of Haifa Press, Haifa, 1999.

Avraham Sela, *Ahdut BeToch Perod* [Hebrew: Unity within Conflict in the Inter-Arab System], Magnes, Jerusalem, 1982.

——, *Mimaga'im LeMasa U'Matan* [Hebrew: From Contacts to Negotiation: Relations of the Jewish Agency and the State of Israel with King Abdullah, 1946–1950], Tel Aviv University, Tel Aviv, 1985.

Eli Shaltiel, *Pinhas Rotenberg* [Hebrew: Pinhas Rotenberg 1879–1942: Life and Times], Am Oved, Tel Aviv, 1990.

Moshe Shemesh, *The Palestinian Entity 1959–1974: Arab Politics and the PLO*, Frank Cass, London, 1988.

——, *Me Ha Nakba La Naksa* [Hebrew: From the Nakba to the Naksa, the Arab–Israeli Conflict and the Palestinian National Problem 1957–1967: Nasir's Road to the Six Day War], Ben-Gurion University Press, Beer Sheva, 2004.

Avi Shlaim, *Collusion Across the Jordan: King Abdullah, the Zionist Movement and the Partition of Palestine*, Oxford University Press, New York, 1988.

Peter Snow, *Hussein, A Biography*, Barrie and Jenkins, London, 1972.

Kenneth W. Stein, *Heroic Diplomacy: Sadat, Kissinger, Carter, Begin and the Quest for Arab-Israeli Peace*, Routledge, New York and London, 1999.

Asher Susser, *On Both Banks of the Jordan, A Political Biography of Wasfi al-Tall*, Frank Cass, London, 1994.

Said al-Tall, *Al-Urdun wa Filastin* [Arabic: Jordan and Palestine]. Dar al-Liwa Lil-Sahafat Wa'l-Nashir Wa'l-Tawzi' Amman, 1986.

Mary C. Wilson, *King Abdullah, Britain and the Making of Jordan*, Cambridge University Press, Cambridge, 1987.

Moshe Zak, *Hussein Ose Shalom* [Hebrew: Hussein Makes Peace, Thirty Years of Secret Talks], Bar-Ilan University Press, Ramat Gan, 1996.

Laura Zittrain Eisenberg and Neil Caplan, *Negotiating Arab Israeli Peace: Patterns, Problems, Possibilities*, Indiana University Press, Bloomington and Indianapolis, 1998.

Unpublished Dissertations

Clinton Bailey, The Participation of the Palestinians in the Politics of Jordan, PhD thesis, Columbia University, New York, 1966.

Abd al-Majid Ali al-Ersan, *The Making of Jordan Foreign Policy under King Hussein*, PhD thesis, Claremont Graduate School, 1983

Iris Fruchter-Ronen, *Yarden Ve'HaEtgar HaFalstini: Hitmodedota Shel Yarden Im HaSugiya HaFalastinit KeHelek MeTahlich Gibush Zehuta HaLeumit VeKefi SheHaNose Mishtakef BeSifrei Limud Yardenim 1964–1994* [Hebrew: Jordan and the Palestinian Challenge: Jordan's Handling of the Palestinian Issue as Part of the Coalescence of its Own National Identity and as Reflected in Jordanian Text Books 1964–1994], PhD thesis, University of Haifa, 2003.

Ra'ad Al-Kadiri, *Strategy and Tactics in Jordanian Foreign Policy 1967–1988*, DPhil thesis, Oxford, 1995.

Abdelfattah A. Rashdan, *Foreign Policy Making In Jordan, The Role of King Hussein's Leadership in Policy Making*, PhD thesis, University of North Texas, 1989

Nasser Tahabub, *Jordanian Foreign Policy: A Case Study Analysis of the February 11th Agreement*, PhD thesis, Duke University, 1991

Articless

Adnan Abu Odeh, 'Bridging the Peace Gap in the Middle East,' *Jornal of Palestine Studies*, Vol. 6, No. 2 (winter, 1977), pp. 53–65.

Hassan Bin Talal, 'Jordan's Quest for Peace,' *Foreign Affairs*, Vol. 60, Spring 1982, pp. 802–813.

——, 'Jordan: The Quest for a Centrist Position', *Journal of Palestine Studies*, Vol. 13, No. 2, (winter 1984), pp. 3–12.

——, 'Return to Geneva,' *Foreign Affairs*, Vol. 62, Winter 1984, pp. 8–13.

Hava Lazarus-Yafeh, 'An Inquiry into Arab Textbooks', *Asian and African Studies*, Vol. 8, No. 1, 1972, pp. 1–19.

Joseph Nevo, 'Tqufat Wasfi al-Tall BeYarden: 1970–1971' [Hebrew: Wasfi al-Tall's Era in Jordan 1970–1971: Endeavours to Create a Jordanian Entity], *Studies*, No. 18, Jewish–Arab Center, University of Haifa, Haifa, February 1979, pp. 1–11.

——, 'The Political Context of the Triangle: An Overview,' in Joseph Ginat and Onn Winckler (eds.), *The Jordanian–Palestinian–Israeli Triangle: Smoothing the Path to Peace*, Sussex Academic Press, Brighton and Portland, 1998, pp. 11–27.

Reuven Padehzur, 'The History of Gaza since 1967' [Hebrew], *Haaretz*, 7 November 2003, p. B-7.

Elyakim Rubinstein, "Chapters in the Quest for Peace with Jordan" in *Yahasei Israel-Yarden* [Hebrew: Israel-Jordan Relations], Bar Ilan University Press, Ramat Gan, 1997, pp. 3–16.

Anita Shapira, 'The Option of the Ghur al-Kibd: Contacts between Amir Abdullah and the Zionist Executive 1932–1934', *Studies in Zionism*, No. 2 (August 1980), pp. 239–283.

Moshe Shemesh, 'The IDF Raid on Samu': The Turning Point in Jordan's Relations with Israel and the West Bank Palestinians' *Israel Studies*, Vol. 7, No. 1, Spring 2002, pp. 139–67.

Newspapers and Periodicals
Dailies

Al-Ahram
Al-Amal
Al-Anwar
The Daily Telegraph
Al-Difa'
Al-Dustur
Le Figaro
Filastin
Ha'aretz
The International Herald Tribune
Al-Jarida
The Jerusalem Post
Al-Jihad
The Jordan Times
Al-Jumhuriya
Al-Kifah
Maariv
Al-Manar
Le Monde
Al-Mustaqbal
Al-Nahar
The New York Times
Al-Ra'i

Weeklies, Periodicals and Annuals

HaMizrah HeHadash
The Journal of Palestine Studies
The Middle East Contemporary Survey
The Middle East Record
The New Outlook
Newsweek
Le Nouvel Observateur
The Observer
Al-Risala
Al-Watan al-Arabi
Shuun Filastiniya

Broadcast Summaries

Foreign Broadcast Information Service, Daily Report (DR).
BBC World Service

Internet Sites

<http://www.un.org/documents/sc/res/1967/scres67.htm>
<http://www.un.org/documents/ga/res/3/ares3.htm>

INDEX

Abd al-Aziz ('Ibn Saud'), 83
Abd al-Nasser, Jamal, 14, 15, 16, 24, 25,
    26, 27, 28, 29, 31, 32, 37, 38, 42, 80,
    129, 130, 133, 141, 147, 159, 166,
    169
Abdullah (Amir and later King of Jordan),
    5, 9–15, 18, 20, 26, 81, 83, 115, 129,
    132, 139
Abu Odeh, Adnan, 60, 133
Abu-Zayd, Salah, 158
Afghanistan, 154
Algeria, 50, 52
Algiers, 39, 45, 55, 60, 87, 107, 113
Allon Plan, 38, 44, 75, 80, 95, 130, 135,
    142
Allon, Yigal, 95
American *see* United States
Amman, 19, 24, 36, 39, 40, 41, 42, 43, 44,
    46, 57, 81, 83, 92, 104, 112, 126,
    152, 161, 163
Aqaba, Gulf of, 24, 32, 133
Al-Aqsa mosque, 13, 82, 83, 86, 93
Arab League, 11, 39, 50, 51, 69, 164
Arab world, 13, 15, 18, 20, 24, 25, 26, 41,
    45, 47, 49, 54, 89, 99, 100, 107, 123,
    133, 134, 141, 142, 143, 144, 150,
    156, 157, 169, 170
Arafat, Yassir, 1, 39, 45, 46, 55, 56, 57, 58,
    59, 114, 118, 131, 133, 144, 145,
    149, 155, 156
Al-Asad, Hafiz, 43, 45, 47, 56, 133

Badran, Mudir, 74
Baghdad, 18, 19, 47, 50
Bailey, Clinton, 9
Balfour Declaration, 9
Baqa' Valley, 52
Bavly, Dan, 27
Begin, Menachem, 48, 49, 50, 53, 73, 95,
    96, 102, 103, 127
Beirut, 36, 52, 53, 56, 130

Ben-Gurion, David, 20
Black September *see* September 1970
Brezhnev, Leonid, 154, 155, 164
Britain (and British), 9–12, 14, 18, 19, 30,
    31, 33, 100, 124, 155, 162, 163, 164,
    165
Bourguiba, Habib, 16, 21, 31

Cairo, 18, 24, 25, 36, 39, 41, 43, 44, 47,
    69, 80, 147, 148
Camp David, 47, 49, 50, 51, 53, 56, 71,
    73, 74, 96, 117, 142, 143, 144, 154,
    160, 161, 164
Carter, Jimmy, 48, 49, 157, 160, 164
Casablanca, 58
Cato the Elder, 68
Chamber of Deputies (Jordan), 47, 57, 60
China, 30, 155
Christianity (and Christians), 82, 86, 90,
    92, 93, 130, 132, 136
Church of the Holy Sepulchre, 82
Churchill, Winston, 9
Cyprus, 19

Damascus, 23, 36, 44, 56
Dann, Uriel, 15
Dayan, Moshe, 75, 112, 147
Dead Sea, 60
Dome of the Rock, 82
Al-Dustur (newspaper), 100

Egypt, 5, 14, 15, 18, 20, 22, 24, 25, 26, 27,
    28, 31,37, 38, 42, 43, 44, 45, 48, 49,
    50, 51, 52, 67, 68, 69, 71, 72, 73, 74,
    75, 76, 78, 79, 80, 81, 96, 105, 107,
    108, 110, 112, 114, 117, 123, 126,
    129, 130 133, 139, 140, 141, 142,
    143, 144, 145, 147, 148, 151, 154,
    158, 159, 160, 162, 164, 166, 168,
    170
Elon Moree, 95

Eshkol, Levi, 20, 146
Etzion Bloc, 94–5
Europe, 4, 124, 137, 157, 162, 164, 165
European Economic Community (EEC), 51, 74, 164–5

Fahd (Saudi Crown Prince and later King), 54, 133
Fahmi, Isma'il, 45
Faruq (king of Egypt), 15
Al-Fatah, 23, 39, 46, 56, 59, 69, 110, 118
Fez, 54, 131, 132, 136, 144, 149, 155, 161, 164
Fida'iyun (and Fida'i), 39–41, 46, 52, 69, 70, 105, 106, 110, 111, 123, 124, 125
France (and French), 9, 30, 155, 164, 165

Gaza, 17, 22, 37, 42, 50, 53, 59, 60, 67, 68, 73, 74, 78, 79, 80, 81, 84, 88, 89, 106, 108, 109, 112, 113, 114, 115, 116, 117, 118, 132, 143
Geneva, 44, 48, 87, 96, 114, 141, 142, 151, 152, 153, 155, 157, 159, 160, 161, 163, 164, 169
Georgetown University, 30, 72, 99
Germany, 18, 30, 164
Golan Heights, 26, 27, 44, 67, 68, 69, 71, 74, 75, 78, 79, 94, 143, 153
Green Line, 94, 95, 97
Gromyko, Andrei, 48
Gush Emunim, 97

Hague Convention, 96
Haifa, 17
Al-Hammah, 22, 106
Hashemite (and Hashim), 1, 2, 5, 12, 13, 15, 17, 19, 21, 22, 23, 24, 26, 41, 42, 45, 53, 56, 61, 71, 78, 80, 82, 83, 89, 99, 101, 102, 103, 105, 106, 113, 114, 115, 135, 137, 140, 141, 142, 144, 145, 146, 162, 163, 169
Hassan (Crown Prince of Jordan), 1, 2, 3, 17, 18, 23, 30, 67, 74, 85, 88, 90–2, 95, 96, 102, 103, 105, 106, 114, 116, 129, 132–5, 138, 143, 161, 165
Hassan (King of Morocco), 49
Hebron, 17, 23, 95
Herzog, Haim, 20
Herzog, Jacob, 20, 29
Hitler, Adolf, 18
Al-Husayni, al-Hajj Amin, 10
Hussein bin Ali (King of Hijaz), 31, 83, 114
Hussein bin Talal (King of Jordan) see also Palestinians; Palestine Liberation Organization; West Bank; Palestine;
Intifada; September 1970; Jerusalem; and Camp David
autobiography, 15
attitude towards Israel, 3, 4, 13, 14, 15, 16, 17, 18, 20, 22, 23, 29, 36, 38, 39, 43, 44, 45, 55, 58, 60, 70, 71, 75, 96, 99–103, 116, 117, 119, 125, 126, 127, 129, 130, 132–7, 142, 148, 149, 166, 168, 169, 170
meeting with Israeli officials, 1, 3, 20, 29, 43, 58, 75, 76, 80, 148
relations with Arab world, 2, 3–4, 15, 19, 20, 21, 24, 25, 29, 30–3, 38, 43, 47, 49, 70, 84, 113, 129, 130, 139, 140, 141, 143, 147, 148, 166, 167
federal plan (and United Arab Kingdom) of, 41–3, 51, 54, 55, 59, 70, 80, 81, 87, 88, 90, 106, 111, 112, 113
attitude towards the West and UN, 17, 28, 31, 32, 33, 34, 51, 53, 60, 72, 73, 74, 76, 105, 110, 115, 129, 138, 143, 150–65

Ibn Saud see Abd al-Aziz
Intifada, 27, 59, 78, 79, 93, 118, 128, 157
Iraq, 12, 15, 18, 19, 20, 48, 50, 52, 72, 143, 162
Islam (and Muslims), 10, 16, 68, 81, 82, 85, 86, 89, 90, 92, 93, 100, 136, 150, 163, 170
Israel see also Hussein; Jordan; Palestine; Palestine Liberation Organization; Palestinians; West Bank
Jordanian Recognition of, 4, 16, 21, 30, 43, 53, 55, 56, 92, 99, 107, 130, 132, 145, 146, 149, 156, 158
Israel Defence Force (IDF), 15, 26, 27, 44, 52, 68, 75, 76, 94

Jaffa, 17
Jarring, Gunnar, 36, 37, 38, 43, 72, 126, 140, 141, 148, 150, 151, 158, 159
Jenin, 17
Jericho, 16, 39, 44, 75, 109, 114, 130
Jerusalem, 4, 10, 13, 19, 20, 24, 27, 30, 36, 37, 42, 44, 54, 65, 66, 67, 68, 70, 71, 75, 78, 79, 81, 82–93, 95, 96, 105, 107, 115, 116, 117, 135, 136, 141, 143, 148, 149, 167, 168, 169
Jews (and Judaism), 9–13, 16, 18, 25, 30, 31, 82, 90, 91, 92, 93, 99, 100, 136, 138
Jewish Agency, 10, 11
Johnson, Lyndon, 28, 29, 129
Johnston, Eric, proposal, of, 15

Jordan *see also* Palestinians; Palestine
    Liberation Organization; West Bank;
    Palestine
  army of (and Arab Legion), 11, 38, 39,
    40, 76, 94, 111, 141
  'Jordan is Palestine', 53, 102, 103, 137
Jordan river, 15, 41, 44, 46, 61, 75, 126,
    135, 138, 153, 160
Jordan Valley, 10, 12, 21, 39, 40, 44, 46,
    94, 117, 135, 153
Judea, 67, 94
June 1967 war, 1, 2, 3, 13, 20, 21, 23,
    25–7, 31, 32, 34, 36, 39, 67, 69, 79,
    83, 84, 85, 88, 92, 94, 123, 124, 126,
    127, 129, 130, 131, 133, 135, 166

Al-Kadiri, Ra'ad, 36
Karama, 39, 76, 124
Kefar Etzion, 94
Khaddam, Abd al-Halim, 45
Khartoum, 29, 30, 31, 32, 73, 107, 110,
    130, 135, 140, 147, 148, 150, 167
Kiryat Arba, 95
Kissinger, Henry, 43, 44, 75, 137, 160
Knesset, 84, 92, 146
Kuwait, 157

Labour party (Israel), 48, 94, 95, 97, 135
Latrun, 95
Al-Lawzi, Ahmad, 70
Lebanon, 19, 48, 52, 53, 54, 56, 102, 103,
    108, 117, 144, 149, 154, 161, 164
Libya, 50
Likud party, 48, 58, 95, 97, 102, 103, 127
Litani, Operation, 52
London, 19, 20, 29, 52, 58, 60, 157

Al-Madfa'I, Madiha Rashid, 136, 149
Madrid, 145, 149, 157, 169
Al-Majali, Haza', 20
Mandelbaum gate, 20
Maryland, 49
Al-Masri, Tahir, 149, 156, 161
Mecca, 31, 82, 83
Medina, 83
Meyerson (Meir), Golda, 11, 12, 20, 43,
    44, 75, 76
Middle East, 1, 12, 14, 17, 18, 27, 30, 32,
    33, 34, 36, 37, 39, 44, 45, 48, 49, 51,
    53, 54, 56, 60, 66, 70, 76, 79, 88, 93,
    99, 100, 102, 116, 127, 129, 131,
    132, 133, 134, 137, 138, 139, 141,
    150, 152, 153, 154, 156, 158, 159,
    160, 163, 164, 165, 169
Morocco, 49, 54
Moscow, 36, 154, 163

Muhammad (The Prophet), 83, 163

Nablus, 17, 44, 81
Nahal *see* Israel Defence Force
Naharayim, 60
Naif (Prince), 14
Nazareth, 17
New York, 36
Newsweek, 113

October 1973 war (or: Yom Kippur war),
    38, 43–4, 45, 49, 73, 75, 76, 87,
    112–13, 126, 127, 130, 141, 147, 151,
    152, 153, 159, 163
Oman, 50

Palestine, 2, 9–13, 16, 20, 21, 22, 23, 30,
    31, 42, 53, 57, 65, 70, 74, 79, 83, 87,
    89, 99, 103, 108, 167
  under British Mandate, 9, 13, 17, 20, 67,
    79, 84, 106
  Jewish Community during British
    Mandate (and Yishuv), 2, 9, 18
  partition of, 11, 13, 16, 20, 82
  people of *see* Palestinian people;
    Palestinians
  question (problem) of *see* Palestinian
    problem (question)
Palestine Liberation Army (PLA), 53
Palestine Liberation Organization (PLO),
    see also Palestine, Palestinians;
    September 1970; *Intifada*
  and Israel, 1, 5, 29, 52, 58, 66, 71, 78,
    106, 117, 145, 149, 157, 168, 169
  and Jordan, 24, 34, 41, 42, 47, 50, 51,
    52, 53, 57, 60, 69, 78, 106, 107, 117,
    118, 136, 152, 155, 156, 161, 163,
    165–6, 167, 168
  foundation of, 22–4, 107
  affiliated organizations, 39, 46 *see also*
    Al-Fatah; PDFLP *and* PLFP *below*
  debate over right to be Palestinian repre-
    sentative *see* Palestinians, debate over
    representation
  question of American recognition, 48, 55
Palestine, the Popular Democratic Front
    for the Liberation of (PDFLP), 40, 58
Palestine, the Popular Front for the
    Liberation of (PLFP), 40, 58
Palestinians *see also* Palestine; Palestine
    Liberation Organization; West Bank;
    Refugees
  Jordanian proposals for confederal ties
    with, 55, 57, 58, 59, 81, 112, 114
  rights of, 16, 17, 18, 47, 48, 56, 57, 58,
    59, 65, 70, 71, 72, 74, 87, 89, 101,

Palestinians, rights of *(continued)*
106, 108–19, 131, 152, 155, 168
debate over representation, 21, 43, 45,
47, 49, 51, 54, 56, 66, 70, 89, 90,
107, 108–19, 153, 157, 160, 161, 162,
168
Palestinians, people, 10, 11, 16, 17, 108
and Israel, 1, 4, 5 *see also Intifada*;
Palestine Liberation Organization
Palestinian National Council (PNC), 39,
55, 57, 80
Palestinian National Covenant, 22, 39
Palestinian problem (question), 3, 4, 5, 17,
21, 22, 23, 26, 27, 29, 31, 34, 45, 47,
48, 51, 54, 57, 60, 65, 68, 69, 70, 72,
89, 101, 102, 104, 105, 106, 107,
108, 119, 132, 145, 147, 149, 150,
165, 167, 168
Palestinian state (or entity), 4, 19, 21, 22,
41, 47, 52, 53, 54, 55, 80, 88, 102,
103, 105, 106, 111, 112, 115, 161
Peace for the Galilee, Operation, 52–3
Peel Commission,, 10
Peres, Shimon, 58, 60, 139, 149, 157
Persian Gulf, 19
Pope Paul VI, 87–8

Qaddumi, Faruq, 45

Rabat, 45, 46, 47, 48, 49, 51, 52, 54, 60,
69, 70, 71, 74, 80, 81, 88, 110, 113,
114, 117, 126, 136, 153, 156, 157,
168
Rabin, Yitzhak, 1, 5, 44, 90
Al-Ra'i (newspaper), 93
Ramallah, 44
Reagan, Ronald, 53, 96, 138, 156, 161,
164
Reagan, Plan, 53, 54, 55, 56, 88, 149, 155,
161
Refugees, 4, 16, 17, 23, 30, 32, 33, 34, 37,
40, 52, 53, 57, 65, 68, 70, 74, 79, 80,
100, 102, 104, 105, 106, 108, 109,
110, 111, 115, 116, 118, 119, 131,
150, 167
Rhodes, 12, 37
Rhodesia, 100
Al-Rifa'i, Zayd, 71, 75, 78, 152, 161
Al-Rifa'i, Abd al-Mun'im, 87, 151, 159
Riyadh, 47
Rogers Plan (or: initiative), 38, 72, 140,
158, 159, 160
Rogers, William, 37, 158

Al-Sadat, Anwar, 38, 42, 43, 45, 47, 48,
49, 50, 51, 96, 110, 116, 117, 126,
133, 139, 141, 142, 143, 147, 149,
153, 154, 159, 169
Salih, Abdullah, 132
Samaria, 67, 94, 95, 96
Samu', 23, 25
Saudi Arabia, 19
Security Council Resolution 242, 25, 28,
31–4, 36, 37, 38, 43, 44, 49, 50, 51,
53, 56, 57, 58, 59, 72, 73, 74, 76, 78,
105, 109, 117, 118, 119, 130, 132,
133, 136, 140, 141, 147, 148, 150
Security Council Resolution, 338, 43, 44,
51, 73, 78, 119, 136, 164
Settlements, Jewish, 4, 53, 55, 65, 66, 68,
94–8, 143, 167, 168
September 1970 ('Black September'), 38,
40–1, 46, 111, 125, 141
Six Day war *see* June 1967 war
Shamir, Yitzhak, 53
Sharon, Ariel, 53, 96, 103
Shemesh, Moshe, 23
Shukayri, Ahmad, 22, 23, 24, 29
Shultz, George, 60, 157, 161
Shuna, 12
Sinai (peninsula), 24, 25, 26, 27, 42, 43,
44, 49, 50, 51, 67, 68, 69, 71, 73, 74,
75, 78, 79, 130, 141, 142, 143, 153
Soviet Union *see* Union of Soviet Socialist
Republics
Spain, 30
Sudan, 52
Suez Canal, 27, 30, 31, 32, 37, 38, 42, 131,
133, 141, 147, 159
Syria, 9, 15, 18, 19, 20, 23, 24, 26, 27, 31,
36, 40, 43, 44, 45, 48, 50, 52, 56, 58,
67, 68, 69, 72, 75, 76, 79, 107, 108,
123, 126, 147, 148, 159, 160, 162,
170

Talal (king of Jordan), 14
Al-Talhuni, Bahjat, 86, 100, 109, 151, 158
Al-Tall, Wasfi, 41
Tel Aviv, 19, 52
Temple Mount, 82, 83
Thalmann, Ernesto, 85
Thant, U, 36
Tho, Le Duc, 137
Tiran, Straits of, 25, 27, 30, 37
Transjordan, 2, 9–12, 31, 41, 83
Tripoli, 52, 56
Tunisia, 52

Union of Soviet Socialist Republics (and
USSR and Soviet Union), 4, 23, 31,
37, 44, 48, 51, 56, 58, 152, 153, 154,
157, 161, 162–4

United Arab Republic (UAR), 18, 19
United Kingdom (UK) *see* Britain
United Nations (or: UN), 4, 11, 12, 15, 16, 24, 28, 30, 31, 32, 34, 36, 37, 38, 43, 44, 45, 48–54, 56, 57, 58, 59, 72, 73, 74, 78, 82, 84, 85, 92, 96, 100, 105, 108, 109, 110, 115, 117, 118, 125, 126, 134, 141, 143, 145, 147, 148, 150–3, 154, 157, 158, 159, 160, 161, 163, 164, 165, 169
United States (or US; and American), 4, 17, 19, 20, 21, 27, 28, 30, 33, 37, 38, 40, 42, 43, 44, 48, 49, 51, 52, 53, 55, 56, 58, 59, 60, 72, 75, 80, 81, 88, 96, 111, 126, 129, 132, 135, 138, 139, 149, 152, 153, 154, 155, 156, 157, 158–62, 163, 164, 165

Vance, Cyrus, 48
Venice, 164, 165

Wailing Wall, 82, 135
West Bank
    demilitarization and deployment of weapons in, 4, 20, 21, 28, 80, 129, 130, 134
    Hussein's attitude toward, 14, 17, 29, 38, 56, 88, 101, 130, 132, 137, 143, 147, 158, 166 *see also* Hussein; federal plan
    Israel's attitude toward, 38, 41, 53, 65, 66, 83–4, 94–8, 102, 111, 135, 160, 167, 168
    Jordan's administration and its disengagement in 1988, 2, 46, 60, 119, 125, 145, 157, 168
    Jordan's claim to, 12, 13, 22, 28, 34, 38, 41, 44, 47, 49, 50, 54, 57, 59, 60, 61, 65, 67–79, 80, 81, 86, 89, 98, 103–5, 112, 115, 124, 136, 146, 168
    loss of, 1, 25–7, 83, 113, 166
    Palestinians' and PLO's claims to, 19, 20, 22, 23, 34, 42, 43, 45, 50, 51, 55, 59, 80, 105, 107, 108, 109, 110, 114, 115, 116, 117, 168 *see also* Intifada
White House, 1

Yalta, 150
Yemen (South), 50
Yom Kippur war *see* October 1973 war

Zarqa, 40
Zionist (and Zionism), 9–10, 15, 16, 18, 30, 99–101, 103, 125